Sailor King

■ ■ ■

The Life of King William IV

Tom Pocock

TO
ELIZABETH AND DAVID WOODWARD

Contents

Illustrations Index

Mrs Jordan on stage at Cheltenham (Photograph, the late Brian Fothergill).

'A True British Tar', a caricature (British Museum).

'Promis'd Horrors of the French Invasion' by Gillray (British Museum).

The Duke of Clarence by James Northcote (National Trust).

The Duchess of Clarence by Franz Winterhalter (National Portrait Gallery).

The Death of Nelson by Gillray (Author's collection).

The Battle of the Nile re-enacted on the Serpentine (National Maritime Museum).

The Lord High Admiral by M. W. Sharpe (National Maritime Museum).

Vice-Admiral Sir George Cockburn by J. J. Halls (National Maritime Museum).

Vice-Admiral Sir Edward Codrington by Sir Thomas Lawrence (National Maritime Museum).

The Battle of Navarino (National Maritime Museum).

Captain Tom Johnstone (Author's collection).

Plans for a submarine by Lieutenant William Pocock, RN (Author's collection).

'The New Preventive Man', a caricature by William Heath (Author's collection).

The King as Admiral of the Fleet by A. Morton (National Maritime Museum).

The Accession, a caricature by William Heath (Author's collection).

'Reform Triumphant', a caricature (Author's collection).

Queen Adelaide on board HMS *Hastings*, after O. Borland (National Maritime Museum).

Acknowledgements

I have to thank Her Majesty the Queen for graciously permitting me to make use of the papers relating to King William IV in the Royal Archives at Windsor Castle.

I am grateful to Lord Digby, Charles Schomberg and Commander Humphrey Jenkins and Major Richard Jenkins (descended from the Winne family) for generously allowing me to make use of their relevant family papers and reproduce portraits. Lady Joan Cator, Miss Mary Birkbeck and Sir Rupert Hart-Davis were most helpful over their delightful ancestor, Dorothy Jordan.

I must thank for advice, practical help, or both, Lady Silvia Combe, Michael Dash, Peter Hopkirk, Lieutenant-Commander Peter Kemp, Admiral of the Fleet Lord Lewin, Richard Ollard, Dr Nicholas Rodger, Sir Anthony Stamer, the Hon. Georgina Stonor, and Philip Ziegler.

Lady de Bellaigue, the Registrar of the Royal Archives, and her staff, and Roger Morgan, the Librarian of the House of Lords, were exceptionally helpful. I am also grateful to Douglas Matthews, Librarian of the London Library, and to the staff of the National Maritime Museum, the British Museum, the Royal Naval Museum and the Public Record Office.

J. T. Brown of the National Physical Laboratory gave me permission to visit Bushy House and Colin Cornwall kindly showed me around.

My special thanks are due to Christopher Hibbert for reading and commenting upon the manuscript. Ian Hessenberg was tireless and skilful in photographing portraits in distant country houses.

Thanks are also due to Andrew Lownie, my agent, and Christopher Sinclair-Stevenson, the most sympathetic of publishers. For help in the production of the book, I am grateful to Biddy Martin, Jackie Gumpert and my wife, Penny, who compiled the index.

I must also recognise the contribution of one or two friends of my youth, whose characters gave me insight into that of the young Prince William and Duke of Clarence. Finally, with the unabashed sentiment he himself might have shown, I am grateful to His Late Majesty King William IV for proving such lively company as a boy, an officer, a man of varied affairs and the monarch, although two centuries away.

Introduction

The names of Prince William Henry, the Duke of Clarence and King William IV – as the subject of this book was successively known – have never appeared in the pantheon of British naval heroes; except, perhaps, his own. He may have come to see himself as King Neptune but to his contemporaries he was, at best, a nautical John Bull.

He was also, of course, Sovereign of the United Kingdom and Northern Ireland, Defender of the Faith, and so on, for the seven years that separated the Georgian from the Victorian worlds. His reign, despite its brevity, was of the greatest importance and most of his few biographers have concentrated upon it. Yet its events and implications are of most interest to students of political history. If his life is taken at a more even pace, a fresh historical character emerges: often comic, sometimes pathetic, alternately contemptible and endearing, selfish and good-hearted; but always fascinating and ultimately significant.

This book takes his life, as he saw it himself, as that of a naval officer who happened to become King rather than of a king who happened to have been a naval officer. The career of what one contemporary saw as 'a thoroughbred seaman' and another as 'a cranky old sailor' shaped the character that had to preside over the great political and social upheavals in the Age of Reform.

He was always a man of contradictions, enthusiasms and appetites and these human traits proved as much a strength as a weakness. While his elder brother, King George IV, was the archetypal drawing-room dilettante and voluptuary of the period, William was the salty Jack-the-Lad. Yet it was William, not George, who exercised the greater influence on their successors to the throne.

King William's youthful character was lively and enquiring but vulnerable and pliable, and it was shaped by strong influences, more often negative than positive. His royalty brought advantages but also the handicap of being seen as a superhuman being and coming to believe this himself. Despite that, and because of a few strong and positive influences, he survived flattery and ridicule to show, as King, what one of his biographers, Roger Fulford, described as 'a gleam of greatness'.

He was the first king to be fully trained and tested by service in the Royal Navy. Other monarchs – notably Alfred, Henry VIII, Elizabeth I, Charles I and Charles II and James II – had shown intense interest in naval power as the first line of national defence, for the promotion and protection of trade and for expanding their domains. Two of King William's uncles – the Dukes of York and Cumberland – had been sent to sea as naval officers but been promoted on grounds of their royalty alone and at such absurd speed that their brief appearances on quarterdecks damaged the reputations of both the Royal Navy and the monarchy.

It was King George III who recognised that the controlled environment of a warship could provide ideal training for a prince, and so decided that his third son should follow a full naval career for the foreseeable future. King William himself sent one of his illegitimate sons into the Navy and his successor, Queen Victoria, decided on a naval career for her second son, Prince Alfred, the first Duke of Edinburgh, who eventually commanded the Mediterranean Fleet.

The only monarch, other than King William IV, to be called a 'Sailor King' was George V, upon whom the experience had a lifelong effect, not least in giving him as near-mystical an attitude to the Navy as to the monarchy itself. As a boy brought up in his reign, I recall regarding the Royal Navy, the Church of England, the British Empire and the monarchy as the four pillars of civilisation. I also remember that my father, who had taught English and history to cadets at the Royal Naval College, Dartmouth, saw the Navy as far more than an armed force, unlike the Army, which he considered wholly concerned with killing and parades.

King George V sent three of his five sons – the Prince of Wales and the Dukes of York and Kent – into the Navy. For the first and last of these it was not a success, neither being temperamentally suited. The Prince of Wales suffered from bullying at first and later had more pressing calls on his time than watch-keeping. The Duke of Kent was charming and popular but ineffective; my father recalled the choruses of, 'Ooh, *George!*' from the touchline at football matches when he missed the ball yet again; later he was remembered for the strength of his eau-de-cologne and was reputed to have had a toe amputated on each foot so as to be able to wear more pointed shoes. The naval careers of both were cut short, the latter's for health reasons, but their promotion through the higher ranks continued.

It was the future Duke of York who benefited most. As a young officer, he was present at the Battle of Jutland in 1916 and the experience of action gave the hitherto timid youth the self-confidence he was to need when he unexpectedly came to the throne as King George VI. His grandson, the present Prince of Wales, an intelligent, sensitive young man, may have become more confident in the Royal Navy in which he eventually commanded a minesweeper. His younger brother, Prince Andrew, became a naval officer, took part in the Falklands campaign of 1982 as a helicopter pilot and continued his career when Duke of York.

Among other members of the royal family and their relations, the Battenbergs (who changed their name to Mountbatten) were preeminent. Prince Louis, a grandson-in-law of Queen Victoria, became First Sea Lord, and two of his sons, George and Louis, became naval officers. As Marquis of Milford Haven, the former showed promise before his untimely death, and the latter achieved the greatest fame of any as Admiral of the Fleet Earl Mountbatten. Following his father as First

Sea Lord, he had served as Chief of the Defence Staff before his assassination by Irish terrorists.

Both first and second Dukes of Edinburgh, living a century apart, became notable naval officers remembered by their contemporaries as efficient but, respectively, as taciturn and abrasive. The latter's period of service covered the transition of the nation from being the keystone of a global empire with a Navy that was the final arbiter of international dispute to a second-rank power poised uneasily between Europe and English-speaking North America.

The life and times of King William inevitably suggest parallels with the attitudes and behaviour of his successors. One of the more obvious is that of the ecstatic welcome he was accorded on returning from his first experience of battle and that of Prince Andrew, two centuries later, on his homecoming from the Falklands.

Indeed, our own times throw back many echoes of his. So perhaps his story can usefully be read as a parable.

Tom Pocock
Chelsea, 1991.

Prologue

At three minutes to six on the morning of Saturday, 2 May 1778, just as London was beginning to stir, a carriage, attended by mounted grooms, jingled through the gates of the Queen's House, the palace at the western end of The Mall. In the clear morning light, not yet clouded by the smoke of the cooking-fires of the capital, its two pairs of horses paced briskly beneath the fresh leaves of the trees in St James's Park and crossed the Thames by Westminster Bridge before taking the road across Surrey and into Hampshire. Its passengers were the King and Queen of England.

Two days before, the first of a succession of court officials and servants – Gold Stick-in-Waiting, an aide-de-camp, two equerries, grooms and footmen – had been sent ahead to prepare refreshments along the road at Godalming, Hindhead and Petersfield, together with a succession of relief horses, the last of them being the four fine black coach-horses which would draw the royal post-chaise into Portsmouth. King George III and Queen Charlotte were to review the principal power of the kingdom: ships of the Royal Navy and their great base on the Channel coast.

Exactly seven hours after their departure, as the King noted, the cavalcade clattered over the cobblestones of Portsmouth and the first royal review for five years began. Much had happened in that time and now the arrival of news from across the Channel and the Atlantic gave an edge of crisis to the well-rehearsed festivities.

The eight admirals, who stood bare-headed in their blue, white and gold uniforms to greet the King, had for the past three years been primarily engaged in the war to hold the American colonies. For the past three months they had been preoccupied with a threat rather than a challenge, for the increasing support given to the American rebels by the French had finally forced the British government to declare war on France. Now there was a major fleet to fight and reports had arrived that a strong French squadron, commanded by the Comte d'Estaing, had sailed from Toulon and might be bound for America, while another waited at Brest on the Atlantic coast.

The signs of crisis were apparent: Spithead, the great anchorage between Portsmouth and the Isle of Wight, was crowded with warships and merchantmen. The warships belonged to the Channel Fleet and to the detached squadron commanded by Admirals Keppel and Parker respectively; the merchantmen were mostly of the huge West India convoy, which should have sailed three weeks before but which had been delayed because of the danger of interception.

Nor was this all. The Earl of Sandwich, the tall imposing First Lord of the Admiralty – and fashionable rake; a former member of the Hellfire Club – was responsible for a Navy which seemed to have lost the self-confidence and professionalism it had gained in the seven years of war which had won and held India and Canada. Now, at this time of crisis, there was such uncertainty that the King, who knew more about royal protocol than maritime strategy, was asked to preside over an urgent meeting to decide on a counter to the reported French move. What should already have been ordered – that Admiral Parker should take his ships from Portsmouth, join Admiral Byron's at Plymouth and sail in hot pursuit of d'Estaing – was decided upon before dinner was served at three. Only then could the inspections, receptions and jollifications begin.

The royal couple were popular among the officers who welcomed them. Approaching his fortieth birthday, the King was a big, florid man, whose bulging blue eyes gave his face a fishlike cast; affable but punctilious in protocol, he radiated an aura of stolid resolution. The Queen, also amiable, had wide-mouthed, motherly looks and a formidable air of decorum. Together they seem to symbolise the stability and continuity of the monarchy.

That evening the King was conducted around the slipways, where several ships of the line and frigates were on the stocks. But there was no noise of hammers and saws because all the shipwrights were busy preparing Admiral Parker's ships for sea. The royal party then returned to the Commissioner's House in the dockyard, where they were to stay as guests of Commodore Samuel Hood. A handsome man of fifty-three with a magnificently patrician high-bridged nose, he was a natural courtier, although the sharp-tongued Admiral Rodney – the most effective fighting admiral afloat – had described him as 'an old apple-woman'[1] and it seemed that his active career might be over. Indeed his present employment suggested as much, for the joint appointment of Commissioner of the Dockyard and Governor of the Naval Academy was civilian, well-paid and, although a naval officer to whom it was given also drew half-pay, it was regarded as a path to graceful retirement. But the King liked Hood and the way he steered his guests through the social engagements which now began.

After church on Sunday there was a levée, followed by a first visit to a ship of the line. The following morning, the King and Queen visited the squadron anchored off the harbour mouth at Spithead – the broad sound between the flat shores and chalk downs of Hampshire and the low hills of the Isle of Wight – and, while the Queen was spared the indignity of clambering up and down ladders and viewed the ships from the seemly comfort of the royal yacht *Princess Augusta*, the King was rowed in his barge out to the *Prince George*, the ninety-gun ship in which Admiral Keppel flew his flag.

Gun-smoke spouted from the sides of the squadrons at anchor and their royal salutes of twenty-one guns echoed from the ramparts of Portsmouth. As the King's barge swept alongside and her crew tossed their oars to the vertical, the admiral and his officers, waiting on the quarterdeck, removed their tricorn hats, and boatswains' silver calls squealed a salute. On board the flagship all was scrubbed, holystoned, polished and painted; the canvas sails and awnings washed white, new ropes coiled into neat cheeses on decks across which the caulking of pitch and oakum had been trimmed straight as ruled lines. The officers wore their best unfaded uniforms, the marines' cross-belts were freshly whitened with pipeclay and, although the sailors wore no uniform, their short jackets and loose trousers were scrubbed free of paint and tar.

Host and guests were party to an illusion. No effort of the imagination could have connected this ship and her company with the realities that concerned her and them. No trace was visible of the horrors of fighting at sea, ship to ship; of tropical heat and freezing gales; or of the epidemics which could carry away more men than a raking broadside. But the King 'visited the three Decks to see the Men exercise as in Action', as he put it in his journal, 'then saw the whole economy of the Ship'.[2] On the quarterdeck the admirals and the captains of all the vessels at Spithead were presented to him and he invited the admirals to follow him in their barges for dinner on board the *Princess Augusta*.

Next day it was the turn of the dockyard and the King watched the sheathing of a ship's bottom with copper to protect it from the tropical wood-boring teredo worm; he visited the rope and hemp stores and finally the Naval Academy, where Hood told him that there were at present only fourteen boys training for careers as naval officers.

It was those boys and the others whom he had seen in the flagship and commanding ships' boats who had particularly caught his eye. They were bright-eyed and brown-skinned, fit and alert; quick to obey and to command. They were future officers of the Royal Navy, first sent to sea as able seamen, or 'captains' servants', and then as midshipmen, before taking the exam for promotion to lieutenant; mostly sons of the middle and upper social classes, they were aged between twelve and eighteen. By the look of them – commanding ships' boats, attending on their captains and, on deck or aloft, preparing a ship for sea – their self-confidence and air of responsibility were the qualities the King had been trying to instil into his own sons of the same age. It was obvious that the Royal Navy was having more success than he and his sons' tutors in producing boys like those he had once imagined would be princes of the blood and heirs to the throne.

1

The Young Sailor

The sons of King George III were not, as he himself realised, turning out well. The eldest, George, Prince of Wales, was now seventeen; a tall, plump boy with a soft, pretty face and wavy hair, he was already a worry to his parents. His manners could appear polished – perhaps too polished – and he was showing a quick wit and signs of sophisticated taste. Yet there was something dissolute about him, apparent in the way he looked at young women, and he had already been seduced by the wife of a palace servant. The second son, Prince Frederick was a year younger and a big, beefy boy with some of the same tendencies. Both, as first and second in succession to the throne, would have to be kept close to the seat of the monarchy, although they would soon command their own households. George would have to be groomed for his destiny as sovereign, but Frederick might be allowed to occupy himself with the Army.

The third son, William Henry, was only twelve and yet to encounter the temptations of adolescence to which his brothers had succumbed. He was a vigorous boy with the distinctive, Germanic looks which the House of Brunswick had brought to the British royal family: fair hair, a high colour and protuberant blue eyes. As a small child he had shown himself wilful and aggressive. Once, after persuading a nursemaid to be hauled around the nursery standing in a broken drum, the girl fell and angrily pushed the child so that he fell too; whereupon the three little princes lodged a joint complaint to the controller of the children's establishment accusing the nurse of violence towards them. Wearily, the King remarked of such tantrums, 'William has ever been violent when controlled.'[1]

Aware that his grandfather and great-grandfather, the first and second Georges, had been unpopular among their British subjects, the King took pains to model himself on his idea of the English country gentleman. Family life based upon rather puritan Christian principles was at the heart of his ideals, and advancement was to be achieved through industrious endeavour; his manner and preferences earned him the nickname 'Farmer George'. Discipline was to be firm but fair and a visitor to the princes' schoolroom recalled seeing them being 'thrashed like dogs' by their tutors.

The Queen, meanwhile, was anxious that her children – the three elder princes and the succession of six princes and six princesses who were to follow them – should become familiar with titles, protocol and the ceremonial of the court. At an early age, the Prince of Wales had been awarded the Order of the Garter and Prince Frederick not only the Order of the Bath but a German ecclesiastical title and was created Prince-Bishop of Osnaburgh. His mother also adopted a custom of German princely courts by instituting what became known as 'infantine drawing-rooms'.

To accustom the children to the more elaborate courtly pomp, she decided that they, rather than their parents, should preside over a levée. Accordingly in October, 1769, when the Prince of Wales was seven, he, his two younger brothers and his sister, the three-year-old Princess Royal, were dressed according to their rank. George wore scarlet and gold with the robes of the Order of the Garter; Frederick, blue and gold with the sash of the Order of the Bath; William, a miniature Roman toga; and Charlotte, a stiffly-starched muslin dress. Thus attired, they received their parents' courtiers at St James's Palace with 'the utmost grace and affability'.

When the bowing and kissing of hands was over, the Queen was gratified by its apparent success. As one report put it: 'to allay the popular frenzy and turn the current of public opinion into the peaceful channel from which it had been diverted by faction, the Queen adopted an ingenious expedient, which was both pleasing in itself and beneficial to trade'.[2] It was not, however, pleasing to public opinion, which was often sympathetic towards the rebellious republicans in America. In the windows of London print-shops appeared caricatures of the scene, showing the Prince of Wales wearing an enormous wig, a large sword trailing at his side and holding the string of a kite; the Duke of York riding a hobbyhorse; Prince William spinning a top; and Princess Charlotte's sanitary needs being attended to by a nurse behind a screen. But this did not prevent their mother from arranging another (albeit slightly modified) public occasion a few months later when a 'juvenile ball' was held at Buckingham House.

The royal children had spent most of their early years in the idyllic surroundings of the Queen's House – also known as the Dutch House, because of its architectural style – in the gardens of Kew. But, in 1772, it was decided that the education of the two elder princes had to be taken more seriously. While their parents and their growing family moved into the larger White House nearby, the boys remained at the Dutch House with a team of tutors for rigorous lessons in the Classics, German, French and Italian, mathematics, writing, drawing, music, dancing and the manly accomplishments of fencing and riding.

Meanwhile William and his younger brother Edward were moved to a house on Kew Green with two principal tutors of their own. One of these, who also supervised Prince Frederick, was a General Jacob Budé – pronounced 'Bewdie' by the English – one of those continental courtiers with whom the King felt more at ease than with the native English he tried to imitate. A tall Swiss, he had once been a page to the Prince of Orange; his military experience had been confined to a commission in 'the Sardinian service' and the honorary rank of Hanoverian major-general. When the sharp-eyed Fanny Burney – daughter of the musician Charles Burney – was introduced to him, an imposing figure 'dressed in the King's Windsor uniform, which is blue and gold turned up with red', she noted that 'his person is tall and showy and his manner and appearance are fashionable. But he has a sneer in his smile that looks sarcastic and a distance in his manner that seems haughty.'[3]

The other was an ageing clergyman of Huguenot descent from Exeter, Dr Henry Majendie. A classicist, he had also instructed the Queen in English when she had first arrived in the country, but he now considered himself too old to handle the boisterous princes and nominated his son, also named Henry, to come down from Christ's College, Cambridge, to replace him.

Under the eye of such masters, William had filled his copy-book with improving texts in handwriting fit for an apprentice engraver. 'Vicious habits are so great a stain to human nature and so odious in themselves that every person, acted by right reason, would avoid them,' he wrote, and, 'Content is a precious Jewel of human life, the way to attain it is surmounting difficulties and unruly Passions in overcoming temptations....'[4]

The temptations to which the child was surely about to be introduced by his elder brothers, despite their segregation in a separate establishment, were a constant worry to the King. But here at Portsmouth was an illustration of what was possible. Seaports were notorious for loose-living, yet these lively, clean-cut boys showed no signs of dissipation. Perhaps William could emulate them? So he discussed with Commodore Hood, who as Governor of the Naval Academy was responsible for their initial education, the possibility that William be entered for the Royal Navy.

There was ample time for such talk because the King's visit to Portsmouth had been extended. Instead of leaving, as planned, after five days, following a finale in which the dockyard workers, wearing blue ribbons in their hats and waving fronds of laurel, bid him farewell, his presence was required for operational reasons. Both Admiral Keppel and his second-in-command Admiral Palliser had complained to him that inefficiency and muddles over victualling for foreign service were delaying the departure of Admiral Parker's fleet for American waters. So, at their suggestion, the King decided to remain in Portsmouth until the ships were ready for sea and refuse to receive their captains until that time. 'This has put a great alacrity into all of them,' he wrote to his Prime Minister, Lord North, in London, 'Sir Hugh Palliser has since told me privately that my taking that step would make them sail many days sooner than they would else.'[5]

While he waited, there were opportunities to question Hood and Captain Robert Digby, who commanded the *Ramillies*, about the advantages of a naval career for William. There were precedents for this. A number of British monarchs had shown keen interest in naval affairs. His own brothers, Prince Edward and Prince Henry – later the Dukes of York and Cumberland – had both served in the Royal Navy. But he was aware that this had not enhanced the popularity of the royal family since their promotion had been so accelerated that both had flown their flags as admirals and commanders-in-chief while still in their twenties.

Young William was unlikely to succeed to the throne but he might eventually become a positive influence on his two elder brothers if he developed as hoped. Although the life of a naval officer combined social standing with training for command and responsibility, the King was aware in vague terms of the risks: the dangers of disease, shipwreck and battle; but he saw in this masculine society an ideal preparation for the life of a royal prince. Commodore Hood was encouraging and Captain Digby, who, unlike Hood, was expected to continue his career afloat, was delighted when the King asked whether he would be prepared to take his son to sea in his ship. A tough, handsome officer of thirty-nine, Digby was well-connected socially and seen as an efficient, ambitious officer, suited to this responsibility.

Even when the provisioning of the squadron at Spithead was complete, high and contrary winds prevented it sailing down-Channel to join Admiral Byron's ships for the Atlantic passage. Then, on the evening of 7 May, the winds moderated and the King sent a message to Admiral Parker that he himself would sail from Portsmouth harbour in the royal yacht early the next morning to watch him weigh anchor and make sail. 'This I am certain will redouble his ardour to sail as soon as it is possible,'[6] he wrote tartly to Lord North.

But, despite the accusing stare of those protuberant Hanoverian eyes from the quarterdeck of the royal yacht, Parker insisted that the weather was unsuitable. Two days later he was still at anchor and the King realised that his stay at Portsmouth had been extended without effect and that he had to return to London.

Yet the visit had been worthwhile in formulating the plan for embarking his third son on a different course from that being followed by the first and second. Delighted by this, the King set the seal on his new and intimate involvement with the Royal Navy by creating his principal confidant of the past days, Commodore Hood, a baronet. Gratified as much as his brother-officers were surprised, Hood responded to this sudden patronage with professional advice. While at his house in the dockyard, the King had complained about his admirals' tardiness in getting to sea and after the enemy. Once they had done so and crossed the Atlantic in pursuit of the Comte d'Estaing, the plan was that they should make their landfall off the Canadian port of Halifax and then sweep south to New York. Now, on the day that the King left for London, Hood wrote to him suggesting that this be reversed and that they should steer for New York, then, taking advantage of the south-westerly winds prevailing in summer, head north to Halifax. This confirmed the royal belief that the commodore – although apparently at the end of his active career-was the most impressive as well as the most sympathetic senior officer he had met during his stay at Portsmouth.

The King's enthusiasm was unabated by his return to London, the cares of war and the court. Although William would not be going to sea for another year, he had asked Captain Digby to send a list of clothing that the boy should bring with him. This arrived but was in such general terms that he wrote to his new friend, Sir Samuel Hood, asking for the detail his practical mind demanded.

'When at Portsmouth I opened unto you my intention of placing my third son William into the Naval Profession,' he wrote, 'Since that time I have received a short memorandum from Captain Digby of the things that might be necessary for the Young Sailor, but it was so much in general that I cannot well act without further explanation. I therefore shall be particularly obliged to you, Sir Samuel, if you will write down what cloaths, necessaries and books he ought to take.

'This will enable me to be ready when called upon by the Captain for this Young One; he has begun Geometry and I shall have an attention to forward him in whatever you may hint of as proper to be done before he enters into that glorious Profession.'

In his imagination, the King was already on board ship with his son, aware both of the special requirements of rank and that there should appear to be none. He continued his letter, 'I trust you will, whenever my intentions come to be publickly known, throw out to your friend the propriety of his allowing a small place to be made with light sufficient for William's following his studies as I should rather wish this appear'd politeness of the Captain than an application from me.'[7]

Hood replied promptly with a long letter, the first page of which was a paean of patriotic prose: 'It ever has been, Sire, and ever will be, my greatest pride and glory to put forth on all occasions my utmost exertions for the honour and dignity of Your Majesty's Crown and Government and I want words to express the happiness I feel at your Majesty's most gracious approbation of my humble services....'

He suggested subjects for Prince William's preliminary study, continuing, 'His Royal Highness is undoubtedly in the best train possible for becoming in love with the profession your Majesty has done the Navy the very great honor of pointing out to him and I am of the opinion he cannot do better than attend to navigation....'

He invited the prince and his tutor to stay with him at 'your Majesty's House, which I have the honor to possess' in the dockyard and 'with the purest sentiments of gratitude and obedience' enclosed a list of clothes and books the boy should bring with him the following year. The list began with '2 uniforms, a short blue coat of the jacket make, with uniform buttons and waistcoat and breeches ... 3 dozen of shirts ... 3 dozen pairs of stockings ... 2 Hatts and 2 round ones – Hatts are liable to be lost overboard! Pocket handkerchiefs, night caps and netts ... Basons, washballs, brushes, combs, etc.'[8] He was to bring navigational instruments, various relevant text-books, *The Mariner's New Calendar*, mathematical tables, the latest *Nautical Almanac*, slate and pencils, pens, ink powder and paper and books in which to keep his log and journal.

It was not until the fifth of June that confirmation reached London from a patrolling frigate that d'Estaing had indeed left the Mediterranean and was presumably bound for America. Four days later the combined squadrons of Byron and Parker sailed from Plymouth in pursuit and three days after that Keppel left Spithead with twenty-one sail of the line to cruise off Brest, where the other main French fleet was thought to be preparing for sea. In fact, the Comte d'Orvilliers had sailed from there with thirty-two of the line the day before Keppel's departure. The two fleets sighted each other on 23 July and, after four days of manoeuvre, joined action a hundred miles west of Ushant.

The battle was indecisive. Confusion in the British fleet's orders and signalling, combined with lack of initiative, produced nothing more than a large-scale skirmish from which both fleets withdrew. There was rancour among the British, sharpened by the fact that Keppel and his second-in-command, Vice-Admiral Sir Hugh Palliser, were political enemies, respectively an ardent Whig and a Tory; so strongly did Keppel disapprove of the American war that he declined to serve on the western side of the Atlantic. The dispute between the two admirals over the conduct of the action off Ushant became so heated that both were tried by court martial. Both were acquitted but Palliser's reputation suffered more than Keppel's and the morale and reputation of the Navy suffered most of all.

If the British Army could be worsted by rebel colonists in America and the Royal Navy could not decisively command the seas there were no grounds for optimism.

The Earl of Sandwich was so close an associate of the Prime Minister, Lord North, that he was unassailable, but admirals could be sent ashore. The failure off Ushant meant the end of their sea-going careers for both Keppel and Palliser but it was the making of Commodore Hood. Royal influence on naval promotion was usually oblique but a word to the senior admiral or politician, who might have a favour to ask of the King, could have decisive effect. So the consequence of the favourable impression the King had formed of Sir Samuel at Portsmouth and in subsequent correspondence, was that in September, two months after Keppel's action, Hood was promoted rear-admiral.

He was not immediately given a sea appointment. One reason for this was the King's anxiety that he should be at Portsmouth to greet Prince William and see him safe on board Captain Digby's ship. It was not until 27 May 1779 that he heard that this duty was about to be required of him. On that day the King wrote from Kew to say, 'By the Portsmouth waggon, which will arrive on Saturday, I have sent a trunk, two chests and two cots done up in one mat to be delivered to you for the use of my Young Sailor ... I flatter myself you will be pleased with the appearance of the boy, who neither wants resolution nor cheerfulness, which seem necessary ingredients for those who enter into that noble Profession.'[9]

Prince William himself would arrive during the following month accompanied by General Budé, who would see him safely aboard ship and spend a short spell with him at sea before returning to report to his father. The boy would join as a midshipman, dispensing with the usual preliminary euphemism of 'captain's servant'. Also going to sea with him but staying on board with the courtesy rank of midshipman would be the Reverend Henry Majendie. For Majendie, this would be a startling change not only from the Dutch House at Kew but from the Fellows' rooms at Cambridge, from which he had been summoned, but the probability that his present task would lead to future preferment made the sacrifice worthwhile.

A clergyman and classicist like his father, Majendie was a heavily-built, rather pompous young man of twenty-four with an imperious Roman nose, full, pursed lips and a sonorous voice, well-tuned for preaching. He was well aware of the King's expectations and these were confirmed again in a letter written to General Budé early in June so that he could pass on the King's wishes as occasion arose on the way to Portsmouth. 'Mr. Majendie from his natural Modesty must feel anxious on entering into so new a Scene of Life,' began the King, and then set out his particular wishes.

The first was that Majendie 'should take every proper opportunity of instructing my Dearly Beloved Son Prince William in the Christian Religion, to inculcate the habitual reading of the Holy Scriptures and to accompany these with Moral Reflections that may counteract the evil he may have but too many Opportunities of hearing'.[10] This the tutor had already been punctilious in doing, with the boy transcribing sentiments such as 'Prudence without Courage is useless; and Courage without Prudence is madness', and 'The vicious avoid the company of the Virtuous in the same manner as the Owl does the rays of the Sun.'[11]

The second subject was to be Latin so that 'he should not only read it with ease but taste its beauties'. The third was English composition and writing, the King stressing that while Majendie might well correct the style and spelling of the boy's letters home, 'the sentiments should not on any account be altered'. Then there was history and he was told to 'merely teach him the Facts and omit much Political Reasoning'. There was to be conversation in French, as well as translation, with the recommendation that 'all Books of Recreation ought to be in that language as that will be one of the most pleasing means of learning the language and, at the same time, there are more Books of that kind void of evil than in his native tongue.'[12]

It was decided that the Prince would embark on the fifteenth of June, when Digby, who, like Hood, had been promoted rear-admiral, would be at Spithead, flying his flag in the *Prince George* of ninety

guns. Three days previously, the King wrote from Kew to both admirals. To Hood, he introduced the two tutors and said that 'the young
midshipman' should be expected between one and two o'clock on the
following Monday. 'I desire he may be received without the smallest
marks of parade,' he asked. 'The young man goes as a sailor and, as
such, I add again, no marks of distinction are to be shown unto him;
they would destroy my whole plan.'[13]

He repeated these instructions to Digby: 'You will direct him to be
treated with civility but no visible marks of respect.'[14] The boy should
be 'obliged to perform most rigidly every duty of the station in which
he is placed on board the Admiral's ship'. Nevertheless, he insisted
'a Lieutenant be always on the Watch when it is his turn of Duty, who
must report very exactly how he has behaved' and 'a proper Officer to
go with him at such times as the Admiral may think it right to send him
to sail in small vessels and also when he goes to swim'. Otherwise,
wrote his father, he was to be 'thoroughly instructed in every branch
of Nautical knowledge' and 'early taught obedience and to conduct
himself with politeness'.[15]

Having done all he could to ensure that the further education of his
son was punctilious yet without apparent favouritism, the King turned
his attention to the boy himself. He decided against giving advice at
a farewell meeting because, as he put it, 'had I taken the common
method of doing it in Conversation, it would soon have been forgot.'
So he took time and trouble with the letter, writing a draft and sharp-
ening the language; for example, changing 'the All-wise Disposer of
Creation' to that of 'the Universe'. It remained an Olympian testimony
of English bourgeois ideals phrased with Germanic stateliness.

'You are now launching into a Scene of Life, where you may either
prove an Honour, or a Disgrace, to your Family,' he began, hoping
that the boy would 'frequently peruse this, as it is dictated from no
other motive than the anxious feelings of a Parent that his Child may
be happy and deserve the approbation of Men of Worth and Integrity.'
After urging him to rely upon 'the All-wise Disposer of the Universe',

adding that such pious reflections were 'still more necessary to be foremost in the minds of those at Sea', he became more specific. 'Remember you are now quitting Home, where it has been the object of those who were placed about you to correct your faults, yet keep them out of sight of the World; now you are entering into a Society of above seven hundred Persons, who will watch every step You take, will freely make their remarks and communicate them to the whole Fleet; thus what would, I hope, have been cured must now be instantly avoided, or will be forever remembered to Your disadvantage.

'Though when at home a Prince, on board the *Prince George* You are only a Boy learning the Naval Profession; but the Prince so far accompanies You that what other Boys might do, You must not.

'It must never be out of your thoughts that more Obedience is necessary from You to Your Superiors in the Navy, more politeness to Your Equals and more good nature to Your Inferiors, than from those who have not been told that these are essential to a Gentleman.'[16]

Final farewells were made. As the sun rose over Kew on 15 June 1779, the fast post-chaise carrying Prince William, General Budé and Mr Majendie took the road to Portsmouth.

2

The Intrepid Boy

At midday on that day His Royal Highness Midshipman Prince William Henry arrived at Portsmouth. At the age of thirteen, wearing his new blue uniform jacket with bright brass buttons, his fair hair tied with a black ribbon at the nape of his neck, he looked like any other boy about to embark on a naval career. He was stocky and strong, lively and talkative; his wide mouth and the alert blue eyes, prominent in his ruddy face, did not impart good looks but gave him an air of restless vigour. He seemed accustomed to both the deference and authority of others.

At the Commissioner's House he was greeted by Admiral and Lady Hood, members of the Hood family and Vice-Admiral George Darby, the second-in-command of the Channel Fleet. As the King had asked, there was no delay ashore and at one o'clock Admiral Digby escorted the boy and his two tutors to his barge and they departed for Spithead and the *Prince George*.

'I went away to every part of the ship, where I was received with universal joy,' wrote Prince William in the first entry in his new logbook, adding the more customary details, 'Moored at Spithead. Variable winds. Light airs and fair.'

The admiral showed the Prince and Majendie to their quarters, which were, as the King had discreetly asked, roomy and light enough to be used for study. General Budé was conducted to the cabin he would use for the few days he would spend on board.

After his first night sleeping in a canvas cot slung from a beam, William was woken early and told to look across the anchorage to the flagship, the great *Victory*, with her one hundred guns the most powerful ship in the Navy. Admiral Keppel's successor as Commander-in-Chief, Admiral Sir Charles Hardy, was flying his flag in her and the boy was told that one duty of midshipmen was to watch her signal halyards for orders. Sure enough a hoist of signal flags ran up to her yardarm and William recorded in his log, 'At sun rise the *Victory* made the signal to unmoor.' At this the captain of the *Prince George* ordered that the ship be moored only by a single anchor so as to be ready for sea. The midshipman then recorded that a tender came alongside to deliver 1,137 pounds of beef and, later, that a convoy of merchant ships had arrived and anchored in St Helen's Bay at the eastern tip of the Isle of Wight.

The sixteenth of June, which seemed so exciting to him and so ordinary to the rest of the ship's company, saw the rise of the curtain on a new act of war. On that day, Spain, which was already supporting France and the American rebels, declared war on Great Britain. The most immediate consequence of this was that the fleets and squadrons of the Royal Navy would have to face double the number of enemy ships at sea. One of the possibilities that would exercise Admiral Hardy was an invasion of the British Isles.

At first light next morning, telescopes were again trained on the *Victory* and William noted in his log, 'Fresh breezes and cloudy. At 4 a.m. the *Victory* made the signal to weigh ... I went on the forecastle and saw the anchor catted and fished.'[1] He was picking up such nautical terminology, whether to do with the stowing of the anchor, or the slang of his messmates. It was clear that William would be a natural member of the midshipmen's mess in the gunroom, the dark space, or 'flat', at the after end of the lower gun-deck, where the boys lived, ate, slept and brawled.

His messmates found him lively and direct. Inevitably there were problems of address, which he clarified on the first day, saying, 'My father's name is Guelph [one of the family names of the Hanoverian monarchs] and you are welcome to call me William Guelph.'[2] He was lucky that a number of other midshipmen were from the upper social strata – like Legge, Stopford and Oliver – and so were less likely to bully him because of his royal rank. Also several of the lieutenants – notably Richard Keats and Thomas Foley[*] – were officers of high professional quality, friendly and instinctive teachers.

It was not so easy for the more senior officers. The King might insist that he be treated like any other midshipman but they could not forget the reality of his standing and that his father was the ultimate fount of patronage, although seldom directly so. In the case of the passed-over Commodore Hood, the King had marked his favour with a baronetcy and that, together with appropriate words of royal praise, had led to promotion; now Hood was to command a squadron bound for the West Indies. To more junior officers it was clear that while their superiors hoped for royal patronage, they might find advantage in whatever services they could perform for royalty for which their seniors could claim credit.

Admiral Digby was acutely conscious that the third in succession to the throne was in his care. He might not be able to ensure the Prince's immunity in battle, storm, shipwreck or epidemic, but he could offer some relief from the squalor of the gunroom and food that was often cooked by the boys themselves. Certainly General Budé had to be a guest at his table and, almost at once, he decided that Majendie and Prince William should also dine with him whenever possible.

The arrangement served to strengthen the contrary aspects of William's life. If he ate with his fellows at the rough table in the gun-room by candlelight faintly glimmering from horn lanterns, the talk was as rough as the food. There he would be told that 'the son of a whore is as good a fellow as the son of a king'[3] and take it in good part. Or he and his tutor would climb the ladders to the admiral's quarters, where the deck was covered with canvas painted with large black and white

---

[*] Both became lifelong friends; both serving Lord Nelson as captains and subsequently becoming admirals and knights.

squares to simulate marble paving and the mahogany table reflected silver. There they would join the other guests for a substantial meal, which the admiral's cook would record in his menu book with confidently phonetic English. Starting, perhaps, with 'turtil' or 'solt fish', they might move to 'boild foul', 'stued guse' or 'boild mutton smuthered with inyons' served with 'frinch beans', 'turnips and grins' and 'pickils' and they might finish with 'apil pye' or 'gusbery torts'.[4]

The first experience of the sea was stimulating. There was the remarkable sight of the fleet of thirty sail sweeping down-Channel under a full press of canvas and of the ship herself as an organism of wood, canvas and hemp. There was the constant rush of bare-footed sailors along decks, up and down ladders and into the rigging and out along the yards to loosen or take in sail. He was already getting accustomed to the smells of tar, paint, hemp, canvas, wet wood and unwashed bodies; but now there was the salt breeze and there were sights and sounds which soon became the background to all else: the swing of the lattice of the shadows of masts, yards and rigging across the deck and the constant creak and groan of the ship as she pushed her blunt bows through the heaving seas. Then there was another familiar routine: on the second day at sea William noted, 'punished Jn. Wright with 12 lashes for being absent without leave'.[5]

The short voyage ended with the fleet anchoring in Torbay to await any move by the thirty French sail of the line from Brest, or an attempt by the Spanish fleet to join them. While there, General Budé went ashore and William, having learned the value of flattery and ingratiating words from the old courtier, wrote to his father, 'I have been formerly very much displeased with General de Budé. But now I am as much attached to him; and I wish that if ever I return (for I may be killed) I may give your Majesty and him as much satisfaction as possible.'

He was now to be in more robust hands, as well as those of the ubiquitous Majendie, and he continued, 'I have been three times on shore with Admiral Digby. He has allowed me to begin to swim and I have been twice in the water with which I am very much delighted.' He then sent a message to his mother with the formality he knew would please his tutor when he read the letter before its dispatch: 'Will your Majesty be graciously pleased to thank the Queen in my name for her good wishes and assure her that, as I know how she wishes me to behave, I will keep as strictly as I can to her desire.'[6]

The Channel Fleet had not lingered long in Torbay and Admiral Hardy had taken his ships to cruise south-west of the Scilly Isles, ready to intercept an approaching enemy. There was not only alarm at the prospect of the British being outnumbered two-to-one by enemy ships in the Channel but of an invasion of the English coast. It was reported that fifty thousand French troops had been assembled at Le Havre and St Malo, together with four hundred ships to transport them. Booms had already been towed across the mouth of Plymouth harbour and there were plans to sink blockships there, while the coastal defences were mobilised and those who could moved inland from seaside towns and villages.

At the end of August, Hardy was ordered into the Channel to intercept any attempted landing, the Isle of Wight being thought particularly vulnerable. At sea, the admiral finally received confirmation from a British warship that the combined French and Spanish fleets were within striking distance of the English coast but he was not to know that an easterly gale had driven them back down-Channel and that their intended landing-place was now to be on the coast of Cornwall.

In the British flagship, Prince William was well aware of the danger and, for the first time, saw a ship of the line begin clearing for action; the partitions and furniture of the admiral's quarters were removed so that they became part of the main gun-deck, stretching clear from stem to stern, its two curving, convex lines of guns at their open ports; rolled hammocks were packed in netting along the gunwales of the upper deck as some protection against musketfire and netting was spread taut above it to deter boarders and as a shield from falling splinters and rigging; the decks were strewn with sand to prevent the gun-crews' bare feet slipping in blood.

'We received information from the *Southampton* of the French and Spanish fleets being in the Channel,' he told his father in a letter on 3 September. 'We were, as Your Majesty may suppose, very much surprised and alarmed, being apprehensive of their invading England....

'In the evening of the 30th, we saw some cutters making signals, as was supposed, to the combined fleets. Next morning we saw from the masthead upwards of sixty sail. We were in a very disagreeable situation all day....

'I wish that the Queen's health may not have been impaired by the anxiety of the mind occasioned by the sudden news of the combined fleets appearing in the Channel.'[7]

There had been no battle. Hardy, outnumbered two to one, avoided action while the Comte d'Orvilliers, the senior allied admiral, although ready to fight, was short of supplies and the health of his men was poor; he was recalled to Brest on 3 September.

Despite their admiral's understandable prudence, there was some shame amongst his ships' companies. In the *Royal George*, an officer was surprised to see a boatswain's mate lashing a hammock round the face of the figurehead – a brightly painted effigy of King George III – like a blindfold, and asked what he was doing. 'Only securing his peepers', replied the sailor. 'Peepers? What do you mean?' 'Why, we aren't ordered to break the old boy's heart, are we? I'm sure if the King once gets a sight of this here day's work and knows that we have run away like cowardly lubbers it will be the death of him, poor soul.'[8]

Relieved as the British were, there was renewed criticism of the naval command. Hardy with his thirty ships of the line should have been sent to blockade the French in Brest and fight the Spanish at sea, it was being said, for he would have been evenly matched with both.

Now a new danger arose. As soon as Spain had declared war, the British stronghold of Gibraltar, commanding the entrance to the Mediterranean, was blockaded by land and sea and what promised to be a long siege began. The objectives of France and Spain were now seen to go beyond the support of the American rebels and the discomfiture of their British rival for dominance in worldwide trade. The French planned to secure and extend their possessions in the West Indies while the Spanish hoped to wrest Gibraltar and Minorca from the British.

In the Channel, the immediate danger was past but a new worry had arisen for the King. His son had behaved well, but now that the initial awe of naval discipline had been lessened by familiarity and he had acquired self-confidence after the prospect of action, he was becoming cheeky to his tutor. This had been reported to his father, to whom he had had to write a letter of apology. William added to this an account of pheasant-shooting ashore with Admiral Digby and a minor accident, which he hoped might arouse his parents' sympathy. 'We had to deal with brambles and thorns and at last got into a swamp,' he wrote. 'When we returned on board the cutter, we had a fire lighted and I pulled off my shoes and stockings to dry. As I was sitting by the fire, a cinder fell out and burnt my foot. This has turned into a sore, which is troublesome and makes me limp a little.'

Discipline was tightened for the ship's company in the *Prince George*, including Prince William. On several occasions he was mustered with the rest to watch men being tied to wooden gratings, rigged vertically in the waist of the ship, and flogged until their backs streamed with blood. 'There have been several Courts Martial upon deserters and mutinous people, most of whom have been condemned to be flogged,'[9] he wrote to his father during the autumn, adding with some satisfaction in a further letter, 'I have seen martial discipline kept up and the severity arising from it executed: the manner Courts Martial are held: the justice that is done in a free country.'

His own freedom was being somewhat curtailed by study and to reassure his parents he wrote, 'I have gone three times through the six first books of Euclid, once through part of Logarithms and some more Algebra and Trigonometry. With Mr Majendie I have written a short account of the History of England from the Reformation till the

Revolution and am now reading Sully's M*emoires*. I have translated French, Latin and English.... The drawing has not gone on quite so well; I am sensible I have been negligent about it.'

Prompted by Majendie, he wrote of his own failings and hopes of secular redemption with smug self-righteousness: 'I hope that ... by the accounts your Majesty will receive from the Admiral it may be known that I am in the way of proving an honour to my country and a comfort to my parents; that my moral conduct is not infected by the great deal of vice I have seen; nor my manners more impolite by the roughness peculiar to most seamen....'[10]

This was leading up to a request that he return home for Christmas. The ship was preparing for another cruise but, with the cunning he was beginning to show in his dealings with his parents, he wrote a pleading letter to his mother and she persuaded the King to sanction his return to Windsor. It was only to be a short holiday. William was required to rejoin his ship before the end of the year because she was to sail with a strong force of the Channel Fleet, which was to escort a large convoy of supplies bound for Gibraltar, Minorca and the West Indies. The whole was to be under the command of Admiral Sir George Rodney who, at the age of sixty-one, would sail on with several ships of the line to the West Indies, where he was to become Commander-in-Chief.

The armada was finally assembled and on 29 December sailed from Plymouth, the merchantmen under the guns of twenty-two ships of the line and fourteen frigates. Nine days later the ships for the West Indies parted company and steered westward, although Rodney remained with the main force, to follow once the two other divisions of the convoy had been escorted through French and Spanish waters. Then, early on the morning of 8 January 1780 as they sailed before a light wind, sails were sighted through the haze.

Drums beat and there was the thudding of bare feet on decks and ladders as the British ships prepared for action. Again furniture was folded and stowed below, partitions swung up to be made fast to the deckheads; gunports were opened and the guns run out, while ammunition was brought up from the magazine. When all was ready, with the guns' crews closed up and lieutenants with drawn swords standing in command on each of the gun-decks, William took his place on the quarterdeck of the *Prince George* close to Admiral Digby. The convoy was ordered to take in sail and wait while the fleet sailed ahead in line of battle.

The following hours were recorded by the midshipman; first in his log and later in a letter to his father. 'Saw a strange fleet to wind'd: after which the whole fleet chaced by signal,' he noted in the log. 'At 8 tack'd after the strangers, who had tacked before. At 10, the *Edgar* and *Dublin* brought to several of the chace. Rep'd the signal for the convoy to make sail and for the ships astern to board the Prizes.'

That afternoon success was complete. 'Rep'd the signal for the Prizes to be carr'd to the Adl.: at 2 our ships ret'd having taken all the convoy, which proved to be a Spanish fleet from St Sebastian bound to Cadiz, 23 in number and belonging to the Caracas merchants.'[11]

Then he wrote home with the loyal flourish of which his tutor approved, 'I am very happy to congratulate your Majesty upon the success of Sir George Rodney and give you an account of what I myself saw. Yesterday morning we fell in with a fleet, which proved to be a Spanish fleet of merchantmen bound from S. Sebastian to Cadiz under the convoy of a 64-gun ship, 4 frigates and 2 sloops, laden with corn and naval stores....

'I have been present at the taking of the first line of battle ship this war and I hope to see such a number of them taken before the end of it that our enemies, who have undertaken the war upon such unfair grounds, may suffer for their temerity.'[12]

The Spanish ship of the line, which had surrendered after a brief encounter with the *Bienfaisant*, herself taken from the French, proved to be the *Guipuscuano*. She was a new, well-fitted ship so Rodney manned her with a British crew and sent her to escort the prizes back to a British port having, as he told the Admiralty in his despatch, 'named her the *Prince William*, in respect to his Royal Highness, in whose presence she had the honour to be taken.' The British captain, to whom the Spanish ship had surrendered, paid another graceful compliment to the King's son, who entered in his log, 'Rec'd from Cpt. MacBride the Colours and Pendant of the Spanish 64-gun ship named the *Prince William Henry*.'[13]

As Rodney's fleet continued to make its way south, news was heard from ships which were passed and stopped that a strong Spanish squadron was cruising off Cape St Vincent between them and Gibraltar. Soon after midday on the sixteenth of January, masthead look-outs sighted sails and the fleet again cleared for action.

'Fresh gales and hazy,' Prince William wrote in his log that morning. 'The *Bedford* made the signal for a fleet to the so'ward. At 1, re'd the signal for a line of Battle abreast and at 2 to prepare for action. Made all clear. At 6 or 7 minutes past 2, re'd the signal for a general chace and made sail. At 12 minutes past 2 re'd the signal to engage to Leeward. Made the chace to be a Spanish Fleet of the Line.'[14]

By four o'clock, the leading British ships were closing with the enemy, which now looked as if they might be another convoy under heavy escort. On the quarterdeck of the *Sandwich*, the British flagship, Rodney told the master of the ship, who was responsible for navigation, 'Master, take notice that this ship is not to pay any attention to the merchantmen, or small ships of war. Lay me alongside the largest ship you can see, or the admiral's, if there be one.'[15] Nearby, Midshipman Prince Williams said to another boy, 'Won't we give these Dons a sound thrashing!'[16]

But it was not a convoy. Rodney had come up with a fleet of eleven Spanish ships of the line and two frigates under the command of Don Juan de Langara. Although the need to provide an escort for the West Indies convoy had reduced his own force to twenty-one sail of the line and eleven frigates, it was still twice the enemy's strength. The Spanish did not immediately run for safety but formed a line of battle steering towards Cadiz, a hundred miles to the south-east. Rodney ordered his ships to crowd canvas in pursuit.

A few minutes later, the four leading British ships, which had had their bottoms sheathed with copper and so were the fastest, opened fire. As smoke, shot with flashes, burst from their sides, hiding their view of the enemy ships, the Spanish broadsides were heard rolling like distant thunder; action had been joined. A few minutes later the smoke cleared and William looked over the barricade of rolled hammocks stowed in nets above the gunwales and saw a ship of the line on fire. A moment later she blew up. 'A most shocking and dreadful sight,' he told his father in a letter, 'Being not certain whether it was an enemy or a friend, I felt a horror all over me.'[17]

But it was an enemy, the *Santo Domingo*, of seventy guns, which had blown up and been lost with some six hundred lives in the Prince's first experience of the horrors of war.

Then the *Prince George* herself was in close action. 'At 10 mins past 4 came up with a Spanish ship without top mast, who had been engaged by the *Invincible* and was making off,' recorded William. 'We fired 4 broadsides. At 10 mins before 6, she struck and proved to be a Spanish line of battle ship of 70 guns named St *Julian*. Sent Mr Williams, an offr. of Marines, 2 Petty Offrs. and 30 men on board of her and took possession of her. Took out of her the 2 Captains (the 1st being wounded), 4 Lieuts. and 14 men. It blew too hard for to ship any more. The Adl. and some of our ships in sight. Had 4 men wounded and one mortally. During the action (the first I was ever in) I was quartered near Adl. Digby and the Captain to receive their orders. 4 shot went through our main and maintop sails. Another wounded our F[ore] mast. Fresh gales and very hard squalls.'[18]

It was now dark and in the wild night the battle broke up into a series of actions between two or three ships. Five more Spanish ships of the line surrendered, four escaped towards Cadiz and, at two o'clock in the morning, when the leading ship in the enemy line surrendered, the fighting ended in victory for the British. Not only their weight of numbers but Rodney's skill in keeping his ships under tight control and his resolution in continuing the action at night and in bad weather off a lee shore, had given the Royal Navy a triumph to redeem Keppel's failure off Ushant the year before.

Daylight on 17 January showed scattered ships tossing on a spume-streaked sea, with the cliffs of Spain dangerously near. The big British ships – Rodney's flagship, the 100-gun *Royal George* and Digby's *Prince George* – could not lie with their heads to the wind under storm sails for fear of being blown ashore so they had to take the slightly lesser risk of making sail to drive farther out to sea and relative safety. 'Ditto weather,' wrote William in his log, later having to add, 'Departed this life Jn. Smily Seaman wounded in the action.'[19]

Next day the storm still blew. 'Strong gales and very hard squalls with thunder, lightning and rain,' the Prince's log recorded. Then through the driving rain loomed the enormous shape of 'Gibraltar hill' and the shelter of the bay below. Yet such was the current pouring through the straits between Europe and Africa combined with the gale, that the *Prince George* and other ships, unable to reach the anchorage, were swept past Europa Point and found themselves 'plying at the back of the Rock'.[20] Only on the twentieth was William able to report that the ship was safely at anchor in the lee of Gibraltar.

In the storm, two Spanish prizes, including the ship which had struck to the *Prince George*, had been driven ashore in Spain but four had been brought into Gibraltar, including the 80-gun *Fénix*, the flagship of Admiral de Langara. These now lay at anchor among their captors, but the danger was not yet over for several lay within range of the Spanish batteries sited on the isthmus between the mainland and the Rock for the siege of Gibraltar. Boats from the fleet were sent across to tow two British ships of the line and a Spanish prize out of their range, but only did so after they had suffered damage from shot.

So scattered had Rodney's ships been by the storm that the admiral himself reached Gibraltar only on 20 January. He was accorded a triumphant welcome for not only had he almost destroyed a Spanish fleet, which had been under orders to join the French in an offensive against British islands in the Caribbean, but he had brought relief –

both in material and to morale – for the beleaguered garrison. When Rodney and Digby were invited to dine with General Eliott, the governor, they took Prince William with them and the boy wrote to his father, 'The last time the General invited us, Don Juan de Langara, the Spanish commodore and the Captains of the Spanish ships were of the party.'[21] Later Digby invited Langara on board the *Prince George* and when the Spanish admiral left the ship he was amazed to see that the midshipman commanding the barge which was to take him ashore was Prince William. Since the mood was one of mutual courtesy, he exclaimed to his host, 'Well does Great Britain merit the empire of the sea, when the humblest stations in her Navy are filled by princes of the blood!'[22]

Ashore, William visited one of his ship's wounded, an old seaman named John Adams and nicknamed 'the old commodore', who had been keeping a kindly eye on him. Having first been to sea as a cabin-boy in a ship named the *Royal William* and having an aversion to swearing, his customary oath was to swear 'by the Royal William'. Since he and the Prince had been shipmates, he had taken to calling the midshipman 'my Royal William' and had volunteered small services for him. In the action he had lost a leg and when the Prince visited him, he said, 'Well, my Royal William, I am now a sheer hulk for life, my starboard timber's gone and I shall go no more aloft.'[23] The Prince shook his hand and told him not to worry. Later he made an application for the old sailor's entry to Greenwich Hospital for naval veterans and made out an order for him to be paid a small annuity from his own funds.

The boy was allowed to explore the Rock, scrambling over its peaks and ridges and being conducted with more formality around its defences. He was growing strong and, being aggressive, had taken to using his fists in gunroom brawls and quarrels on board ship. Once he had cut the slings at the head of a sleeping companion's hammock – a dangerous, yet familiar, practical joke on board warships – and his victim had taken revenge with his fists. On another occasion, he squabbled with a Lieutenant George Moodie of the Royal Marines, who had said, 'If it was not for your coat, I would give you a basting.' 'My coat shall not stain my honour,' replied the Prince, pulling it off. Fisticuffs were stopped by a passing officer and the two ordered to shake hands. 'You are a brave fellow,' said William to Moodie, 'though you are a marine.'[24]

Such traditional gunroom belligerence was now extended to Main Street in Gibraltar, where tavern brawls between soldiers and sailors, sailors from different ships, and soldiers from different battalions, had long been part of daily life. On this occasion William and another well-born midshipman, Lord Amelius Beauclerk, fought some soldiers he thought were insulting the Navy. Arrested by a military patrol and consigned to the town lock-up, the intervention of Admiral Digby was needed to arrange his release before his appearance in the magistrate's court. So the embarrassment of the governor learning that his royal guest had been arrested during a drunken brawl was avoided by his return to sea.

On 13 February, Rodney sailed again with his fleet, leaving one ship of the line at Gibraltar. The admiral was bound for the West Indies and after three days he parted company with the main force, which sailed for England with its prizes under the command of Admiral Digby. Then, after ten days at sea, on a clear, windy day, action again seemed imminent. 'Fresh gales and fair,' recorded William. 'The *Triton* made the signal for a sail to the NE. At 2, the *Resolution* made a signal for a sail to the NW. Saw a fleet from the masthead consisting of 16 sail. Made the signal for a general chace. The strange fleet made sail from us. At 4 made the signal to prepare for action and at ½ past 4 to engage to Leeward. Made the chace to be French.'

The leading British ships were soon in action and the enemy ships began to strike their colours. 'Hailed a French snow taken by the *Marlborough*, who gave us an account,' noted William, 'that it was a French fleet of merchantmen bound from Port l'Orient to the Mauritius under convoy of 3 64-gun ships, 1 Frigate, 1 Corvette and 2 armed Brigs, laden with warlike stores.'[25] This time success was less complete, but Digby was able to hoist British colours in one French warship, the *Prothée*, and three merchantmen.

It was a fitting climax to a successful cruise in which William had faced dangers by battle and by storm. It was also a gratifying reversal of the failure of the previous year and, off the Scilly Isles, as the fleet prepared for its homecoming, the boy wrote to his father, 'Thus far in the year '80 everything has been successful on our side as if Providence was resolved to punish our enemies for having begun the war so unjustly. When I return home I will be happy to present your Majesty with the Ensigns taken from on board the *Prince William* formerly the Santo *Domingo*, [in fact, the *Guipuscuano*] the *St Julian* and *La Prothée* as trophies of our success.'[26]

Word had already reached London of Rodney's action off Cape St Vincent and the Earl of Sandwich had written to him from the Admiralty, 'You have taken more line-of-battleships than had been captured in any one action in either of the last preceding wars';[27] their captor himself had called these 'as fine ships as ever swam'. His fellow-professionals realised that not only had he succeeded where Keppel had failed but that only bad weather and nightfall had prevented even greater success, for he had hoped to try out revolutionary tactics he had in mind of breaking through the enemy's line, contrary to the accepted principles of fighting at sea. When Keppel – a rich man from prize money after the capture of Havana in the Seven Years' War – had returned to London, he had been presented with the Freedom of the City in a handsome oaken box; but Rodney's scroll was now to be presented in a gold casket and a balladeer wrote,

> For Rodney brave, but low in cash,
> You golden gifts bespoke;
> To Keppel, rich but not so rash,
> You gave a heart of oak.

It was known, too, that the victory had been won 'in the presence of his Royal Highness Prince William' and this had enhanced the patriotic zest of the celebrations. It was also the first dividend of the King's decision to send his third son to sea for his part in the battle – exaggerated as it was by the popular newspapers – did something to offset public awareness of the infatuation of the Prince of Wales, now aged seventeen, with Mary Robinson, a married but fast-living actress at the Drury Lane theatre. So the King ordered that General Budé should go to Portsmouth to meet the fleet and bring William directly to him in London, where he could be acclaimed by his father's subjects.

With Budé arrived a letter of welcome from his father, written in the ringing phrases of a proclamation. 'You may easily guess the joy I felt at the Bravery, Skill and Humanity shown on this glorious occasion,' he wrote, 'and that from the Admiral down to the lowest man in the Fleet that conduct has appeared which makes them an honour to their Country and Profession. I am sincerely happy that your conduct has been such as to deserve the approbation of your Admiral. Dear William, you cannot doubt that if on your returning to Spithead, and Rear-Admiral Digby thinks it proper, you may come to us, that the Queen and I shall feel great joy at seeing you again.'[28]

On 6 March, the fleet anchored at Spithead and William recorded, 'At 9 am left the *Prince George* with Rear-Admiral Digby in his barge. Shortly after I arrived at Sir Samuel Hood's, the Commissioner's House, where I set off soon after with Genl. de Budé for London and I arrived at the Queen's House at 6 in the evening. Had the great happiness of presenting to the King the Colours taken from the *Prince William*, St *Julian* and *Prothée*, the first Spanish and French ships taken this war and of which I was a Spectator. His Majesty received them from me with great pleasure.'[29]

He also gave the King the flag of Don Juan de Langara, whose flagship, beautifully built of mahogany and cedar in Havana, had been renamed the *Gibraltar*. The presentation was made the occasion for a full court reception and Prince William was formally introduced by the

First Lord of the Admiralty. Later, Admiral Digby told the King that the boy would, in his view, become 'a very great sea officer'.[30]

Meanwhile the Poet Laureate, Henry Pye, had written celebratory verse in praise of the royal midshipman rather than the admiral's victory. This began,

> Now last, not 'least in love', the Muse
> Her WILLIAM'S name would fondly chuse
> The British youth among ...

Another of the many laudatory ballads written on the same theme ran,

> Still on the deep does Britain reign,
> Her Monarch still the trident bears;
> Vain-glorious France, deluded Spain,
> Have found their hostile efforts vain.
> As the young eagle to the blaze of day,
> Undazzled and undaunted, turns his eyes;
> So, unappall'd, when glory led the way,
> 'Midst storms of war, midst mingling seas and skies
> The genuine offspring of the Brunswick name
> Prov'd his high birth's hereditary claim;
> And the applauding nation hail'd with joy
> Their future hero in the intrepid boy.

Not surprisingly William became an immediate national hero. Any victory would have been popular after so many defeats and so much failure, but one over the traditional enemies, France and Spain – rather than the Americans, against whom so unpopular and humiliating a war was being fought – and one in which a member of the royal family proved himself a hero, was fuel for loyal hysteria.

When Prince William attended a performance at the Theatre Royal, Drury Lane on 13 March, such crowds forced their way in to catch a glimpse of him that the management had to lay a bridge of planks from the pit to the stage to prevent anyone being crushed.

Broadsheets of sailors' songs glorifying him were being sold on the streets, one of them, 'The Royal Sailor', declared,

> When Neptune arose from his wat'ry throne
> In a coral-red suit he most beautifully shone;
> He call'd for his Tritons and bade them repair
> To the Court of Great George, for young William was there.
> 'He's Royal, he's Noble, he's chosen by me
> This Isle to protect and reign Prince of the Sea.'
> O'erjoy'd at the message, the youth rear'd his head,
> 'I'll fight like a Prince', were the words that he said …
> The Dons they have felt the effects of his rage;
> No more with Blood Royal they'll dare to engage …
> Humanity touch'd him, tho' not with base fear,
> When one noble ship was blown into the air.
> His courage gave rapture to each jolly Tar,
> Who look on Prince William their bulwark in war.

The self-confidence which experience of war would have given the boy turned to conceit. This was aggravated by the flattery of his two elder brothers, who were delighted to find public attention distracted from their escapades. William, in turn, was excited to be invited to join them as an equal on nocturnal forays into the pleasure gardens of Vauxhall and Ranelagh, where revellers sometimes wore masks and fancy dress as at a Venetian carnival, which offered useful anonymity. Indeed, a current rumour was that one dressed as a Spanish grandee quarrelled violently over a girl with another dressed as a sailor, only to discover, when unmasked by constables, that they were the Prince of Wales and Prince William respectively.

The King's initial delight in welcoming his son home gave way to dismay as he saw the boy swept up in more dissipation than he would be likely to find among the taverns of Portsmouth Point, and he urged the Admiralty to hasten his recall to duty. In May, Admiral Hardy died and was replaced by Admiral Sir Francis Geary, who flew his flag in the *Victory*. Admiral Digby again commanded one of the Channel Fleet squadrons and Prince William returned to join him in the *Prince George* on 24 May, 1780.

Admiral Geary took his fleet to sea in June and a few weeks later surprised and captured twelve French merchantmen from a convoy homeward-bound from the West Indies. Then, in August, the Channel Fleet returned to Portsmouth, where Geary resigned his command because of failing health and was succeeded by his third-in-command, Vice-Admiral George Darby. Geary's farewell dinner was held in the *Victory* and, for the occasion, William was asked to make his first formal speech in response to the loyal toast. All were agreed that he spoke well even if for too long. Speaking of his father, he said, 'There are few monarchs, who have swayed the sceptre of these realms, to whom the title of the father of his people is more justly due. Involved as the nation is at present in a most unnatural war, for it cannot be considered in any other character than that of a child fighting against its parent; it becomes everyone to join heart and hand to bring the rebellion to a speedy and fortunate issue ... I am proud to say that the safety, the glory and honour of this country depend upon its Navy and when I see myself surrounded by such men as are here present, I have no fear for the stability of my father's crown....

'For myself individually, I shall consider those days the proudest and noblest in my life, in which I may be called upon to shed my blood in the defence of my father's flag, and should I ever be called upon to lead his fleet against his enemies, my first study shall be to imitate the example of that brave and noble officer, who has done me the honour this day to invite me to his table....'[31]

Then, after another succession of pleasantries, he proposed the health of Admiral Geary. However much this composition owed to Mr Majendie, it was thought creditable that a midshipman could deliver so stately an oration to an assembly of admirals and captains and a fine example of the way a naval career could mature the most callow. Nor were they empty words, for William admired his demanding father and held him in awe, as he did his mother, who was again pregnant. Prompted perhaps by his tutor he wrote a letter hoping that she was well and that she had not been worried by the London mob, rioting in protest over Catholic emancipation in what were named the Gordon Riots after their instigator, Lord George Gordon.

'By the late unfortunate riot of a deluded multitude, I am sensible that the Queen must have been alarmed,' he wrote. 'I thank God it is at an end and hope that the punishment of the Rioters will prove an example for the future.'[32] He was becoming a disciplinarian: writing from Torbay at the end of September to congratulate his mother on the birth of a son, Alfred, he told her, 'We have had Courts Martial held every day on board the *Prince George*. A man belonging to the *Foudroyant* was sentenced to receive 300 lashes for having struck his Officers; and four deserters from the *Valiant* were condemned to death, not only for their desertion but for High Treason in appearing in open arms against their King and Country, having been taken on board a French privateer.'[33]

Throughout the autumn, the Channel Fleet cruised in search of enemy squadrons or convoys but without success. Instead, while they were at sea, a huge British convoy escorted by a ship of the line, the *Ramillies*, and two frigates, had been intercepted by a Franco-Spanish fleet and, while the warships escaped, more than fifty merchantmen were taken. Meanwhile, fourteen ships of another convoy, outward-bound from Quebec, were captured off Newfoundland by American privateers. But Admiral Digby's squadron, during three months at sea, only once managed to 'catch a glimpse' of an enemy fleet, arousing the mockery that a more determined admiral would have 'obtained a full view of them, conducting them afterwards into a British port'.[34]

Now that the euphoria over Rodney's victory had faded, the view was again widely held that the Admiralty was supine, corrupt or both, and that its admirals spent too much time at anchor or cruising without effect. Symptomatic of this, it was being said, was Prince William's new-found hankering after his brothers' company in London, now expressed in another request for leave to see Frederick before he left for a spell of military training in Hanover and to spend Christmas at Windsor. His tactful enquiries after his mother's health had been provident in these aims, for she supported his application and turned away even the First Lord of the Admiralty's protest that the midshipman was now spending too much time away from his ship. As Lord Sandwich left her presence, he was heard to mutter, 'If the Queen does not know her duty, I know mine.'[35]

This time the distractions of London were not so much debauchery with his brothers but the consequences of attending a ball at St James's Palace to celebrate the Queen's birthday on 18 January. There the Prince danced with a girl called Julia Fortescue, a 'truly angelic girl',[36] who lived with her rich parents in a house overlooking St James's Park. She would have been the perfect sweetheart for any other midshipman well-advanced in adolescence. But the King was so obsessed by the need to ensure the legitimacy of the succession and to prevent his two eldest sons from marrying women he considered unsuitable that, in 1772, he had drawn up and had ratified by Parliament the Royal Marriage Act, which severely limited their choice, virtually confining it to Protestant royalty and making it subject to the King's permission. So, although flirtation led to assignations and the Prince was said to have proposed marriage, his declarations of love were fruitless and the girl was quickly banished to Scotland by her parents, with the approval of the boy's.

After their final meeting, the couple corresponded for a while and the King felt it necessary to lecture his son on his future matrimonial duty. In explaining the need for the Royal Marriage Act he stressed the responsibility of the Privy Council (rather than his own) for its strictures. Prince William was not impressed and remarked tartly, 'I should think it a great act of presumption in Admiral Digby telling me what

I shall eat and I deem it equally an act of presumption in the Privy Council, dictating to me whom I shall love, or whom I shall not love.'[37]

In January 1781, he returned to the *Prince George* at Spithead, giving a dinner party for his messmates in the gunroom on his first evening on board. Admiral Digby's squadron sailed a month later on another fruitless cruise but joined the rest of the Channel Fleet early in March, for an important operation. This was to be another convoy for the relief of Gibraltar, which had received none since Rodney's arrival there a year before. Since then, the siege had become intense and the needs of the garrison acute.

On 13 March, Admiral Darby sailed with twenty-eight sail of the line and about a hundred and seventy merchantmen; they were joined by smaller convoys bound for more distant destinations, taking advantage of the powerful escort. Although Darby's fleet outnumbered the French lying in Brest and was a more effective force than the larger Spanish fleet at Cadiz, there was a risk. Westerly gales were blowing and it was difficult to prevent the vast convoy being scattered and attacked by the French privateers which hung about their flanks. The passage was unopposed and a month after sailing the supply ships reached Gibraltar, while their escorts cruised off-shore to deter interference. But they could do nothing to prevent the long-range bombardment of the jetties by the Spanish batteries or the more effective attacks by their gunboats, powered by both sails and oars and mounting 24-pounder guns. Yet this did not greatly hinder the unloading, and in a week it was complete and Darby sailed for England, reaching Spithead a month later.

Before shore leave could be given, Darby's squadron sailed on yet another unsuccessful search for French ships reported to be in the Channel. When they returned, much of the Channel Fleet had entered Portsmouth to refit. Now there was leave for the *Prince George's* officers and William returned to London. At first all went happily but again he was spending more of his time with the Prince of Wales, whose philandering, gambling and carousing had reached such a pitch that his younger brother Frederick had written from Hanover to warn, 'You cannot stand this kind of life'.[38]

The King and his eldest son were estranged not only because the Prince of Wales – now aged eighteen – was wilful and dissolute but because he had fallen into what his father regarded as bad political company. In London, the politicians of the Whig faction were not high-minded, land-owning aristrocrats, as they tended to be in the country, but sophisticated, fast-living intellectuals whose company the heir to the throne found congenial. Now that Prince Frederick was abroad, William would inevitably fall into their company in the capital, as well as that of other hard-drinkers, gamblers and voluptuaries.

George III was again alarmed for the morals of his third son, who was increasingly absent from his parents' side. When his leave ended, the King wrote a letter of rebuke which General de Budé was to give him on his return to Portsmouth in July. He told him that he had behaved well for the first fortnight at home but then had too often left the room, where he had joined his parents, for what the King implied were immoral purposes. 'I can assure you, Sir,' replied his son, 'that I never did anything wrong when I left your Majesty.'[39]

At Portsmouth, he and General Budé first called at Commissioner's House, where Admiral Hood – now commanding a squadron in the West Indies – had been replaced by Captain Sir Henry Martin. A veteran of the Seven Year's War, he had been recalled from retirement at Bath with his wife and eight children to succeed Hood, and, like him, play host to visiting royalty.

The Commissioner lined up his family in the hall to be presented to Prince William. One of his sons, the eight-year-old Byam, was also destined for a naval career and observed the royal midshipman with a sharp eye and retentive memory. He recalled him wearing the star of the Order of the Garter with his midshipman's uniform and as being 'a fine-looking youth with a florid complexion, light hair and of pleasing countenance but of squat form'. He was also 'very animated in his matter and conversation', adding 'in a humbler individual it might have passed under another name', presumably as being excitable and garrulous.

Byam Martin's lack of reverence for their visitor produced in him a sense of wonder. As he later remembered, the 'respect, ceremony and submission shown to a boy of the Prince's age by my father and the other official elders quite astonished my young mind and made me think it could scarcely be a human being to whom such adulation was due ... I cannot help thinking that royal infants are set up too much like idols, and that consequently pride and presumption ... are early implanted and cherished with rival zeal by the many sycophants who find their way about a court, often to its great discredit ... I declare I have shuddered at times when I have seen the approach to royalty putting on so much the form of adoration.... The great respect shown to the young Prince by my father and others we looked on with amazement, almost doubting if the youth could be of the same flesh and blood as ourselves.'[40]

Byam Martin and his ten-year-old brother Joe put their scepticism into practice when Prince William had stayed a few days at Commissioner's House. A squabble between the three of them in the garden was being settled with fists and was stopped only by the Commissioner rushing from the house, waving his gold-headed cane, closely followed by an agitated General Budé. For the Prince it had been much like the continual horseplay in the gunroom; for the Martin boys, it was an act of rebellion.

When William returned on board the *Prince George*, he found the ship alive with activity. He was told that they were ordered on foreign service across the Atlantic. On arrival at New York, Admiral Digby was to succeed Rear-Admiral Marriot Arbuthnot in command of the squadron based there. Before they sailed, Digby sent for William and told him that henceforth he would keep day and night watches as a qualified midshipman. Writing to his father to tell him of this he added excitedly that he now felt that he had 'an advantage over all others in my situation of life, both in seeing the characters of different nations and at making myself acquainted with the service in active scenes.'[41] That was the first reason, he wrote, for his present sense of satisfaction, but he continued with the sycophancy young Martin had noticed with such distaste. 'The second reason,' he wrote, 'is because very unfortunately the Prince of Wales has taken a terrible course of life, which he might perhaps (had I been at home) have induced me to lead, which would have been very much to my own detriment and very much to yours, Sir, and the Queen's mortification and grief.'

So the *Prince George*, two other ships of the line and a frigate sailed from Spithead to St Helen's Bay at the easterly tip of the Isle of Wight to anchor and await a favourable wind to carry them down-Channel. It came early on Tuesday, 15 July 1781, and at nine o'clock that morning the ships weighed anchor. As their sails filled, the flagship's company was mustered in the waist of the ship to witness a seaman being punished with thirty-six lashes for theft and three marines with twenty-four lashes each for 'neglect of duty'. Then they steered west, past the Needles and Portland Bill for the Atlantic and America, where their own duty lay.

3

Welcome to this Western Shore!

For a boy brought up on stories of exploration, war and rebellion in America, the landfall would have been an anti-climax when a long, low shore was sighted from the deck of the *Prince George*. The ship's chart showed a complex of large islands and lagoons which formed an enormous natural habour at the heart of which lay the city of New York, the headquarters of the British administration and command attempting to hold the North American colonies for the Crown.

The great anchorage below New York was, Prince William was told, secure yet under threat. It stretched some fifteen miles from The Battery at the southern tip of New York Island to Sandy Hook, where it opened into the Atlantic, and could safely shelter the largest fleets and convoys. Although the seaward mouth appeared wide, it was barred by sandbanks except for a narrow channel running close to the spit of Sandy Hook from which it could be commanded by guns. Within the lagoon there were several good anchorages and landing-places in Sandy Hook Bay and Rariton Bay, off Staten Island, where there was a reliable source of fresh water, and in the East River, which ran northward up the eastern side of New York Island. To the west of the city flowed the wide Hudson (or North) River and its far shore was the province of New Jersey, which was held by the rebels. Indeed the winter camp of their army, commanded by General George Washington, was just beyond the river bank and their sentries could see the rooftops and spires of New York.

The *Prince George* arrived off the point of Sandy Hook on 24 September but could not get over the sand-bar because of the strongly-running tide; the next day, a contrary wind held her back. It still blew on the third day so, hearing of this in New York, the Commander-in-Chief, General Sir Henry Clinton, sent his own cutter to the harbour mouth to collect Prince William and Admiral Digby. As they sailed across the great expanse of water bounded by low, wooded shores, they could see the anchorages crowded with warships and merchantmen, in all thirty-two sail of the line, twenty-four frigates and twenty sloops and fireships. From mastheads flew the flags of four admirals for this was the heart of British power in the western hemisphere.

At six o'clock on the evening of the twenty-sixth, the first member of the royal family to land in North America stepped ashore at New York. Jetties, quays, walls and windows were crowded with cheering citizens while a line of senior Army and Navy officers were presented to the Prince on the dockside. Then all walked in procession around the parade-ground, past the statue of King George III, to the senior naval officer's house, where they were greeted by a Captain's Guard with Colours. For the first time, William was being treated as his father's representative and, as he told the King in a letter written next day, 'I was received by an immense concourse of people, who appeared very loyal, continually crying out, "God Bless King George".'[1]

There followed a succession of inspections, receptions and dinners. After the commanding officers, those who had distinguished themselves in the fighting were presented to the Prince and they included Brigadier-General Benedict Arnold, the American turncoat, who had tried but failed to betray the rebels' position at West Point on the Hudson River a year before, when his British contact, Major John André, had been captured and hanged as a spy. William was shown the city and visited British and Hessian regiments manning the defences at Hell Gates and Bunker's Hill. He dined with the senior officers and the mayor and assured them that he would tell his father of their expressions of loyalty to the crown.

The rector of the Episcopal church, Dr Inglis, preached at a service of thanksgiving, taking as his text the ninth verse of the Book of Deuteronomy: 'When the host goeth forth against thine enemies, then keep thee from every wicked thing.' He spoke of the Prince as a paragon of the virtues and of their own inexpressible gratitude to the King for sending one of his sons to join them, but such was the flattery, ran one account, that 'he became nauseated with it'.[2]

The euphoria was fed by the newspapers, which printed long accounts of the celebrations and fulsome ballads of welcome:

> Rising o'er the Atlantic main,
> William the Star of Morn appears;
> Night with all her grisly train
> Of dangers and fears
> Is flying fast away!
> Soon shall the Royal Sun arise,
> To speed his glories through the skies,
> And give the long-expected day!

The object of this adoration was to live ashore at Admiral Digby's official residence in Hanover Square, where he would be expected to study with Mr Majendie for several hours each morning. Now that they could see him at close quarters, the New Yorkers were delighted with the 'fine, bluff boy of sixteen; frank, cheery and affable'.[3] He himself was not particularly struck with the city which, he told his father in a letter, was 'built in the Dutch way with trees before the houses. The streets are in general narrow and very ill-paved. There is but one Church, all the others being converted into magazines or Barracks.... The inhabitants of the town are in number 25,000. They have 3,000 Militia, besides which there are about 1,000 men raised at their own expense and clothed and armed.'[4]

Despite the common language, he was struck by the differences in manners as much as by the looks of the city. Once a Quaker approached him, blessed the King's name but excused himself for failing to doff his hat: 'It is not for want of respect ... but because my Religion requires it.'[5]

Crowds gathered around his house to cheer when he appeared and a balladeer put their enthusiasm into fulsome verse:

> See rapture beam from every eye,
> While round the Royal Youth they pour!
> And, hark! the universal cry,
> 'Welcome to this Western shore!'
> Hail, lovely Prince, in whom we trace
> The virtues of thy Royal race;
> Thy mother's softer charms in thee we find,
> Thy father's steady truth and firm undaunted mind.

Dining in the *Prince George* with Prince William and Admiral Digby, Chief Justice Smyth was delighted by the boy. 'Paying our compliments on departure,' he recounted, 'the Admiral observed the boat was not yet manned. The Prince instantly started up and took his hat. "I, Gentlemen, will see your boat manned." I told the Admiral that I little expected ... to have the honour of such assistance from a Prince. "The Prince", said the Admiral, "is a Midshipman on board this ship and never stops at any part of the duty of his station." '[6]

The beleaguered city's elders wanted to see his presence as an omen of success:

> Most gracious Prince, compassion wounds thy heart,
> At all the wrong which loyalty sustains,
> For public good, with private joys you part,
> To share our dangers and to soothe our pains.
> See Royal William's genius rise!
> Each ardent youth exciting cries,
> We conquer or we die!

During the autumn, as the leaves of the woods along the shores of the rivers and the great lagoon turned red and gold, Prince William stayed ashore in Hanover Square, where his studies with Mr Majendie included those 'relative to the present state of affairs in this country',[7] as he put it. So he was well aware of the dangers to the tenuous British hold on their American colonies. Both their main armies were under pressure: Clinton had early in the year expected to be besieged in New York, and, on the shores of Chesapeake Bay, General Cornwallis was already besieged within the defences of Yorktown. His force reduced from some 7000 to less than 3500 men by casualties and sickness, he was faced not only by the rebels but by 3000 fresh French soldiers, escorted across the Atlantic by the Comte de Grasse, and bringing the besiegers' strength to about 16,000. Early in September, Admiral Graves had tried to break through the blockade of nearly forty French ships of the line to relieve Yorktown but had failed and returned to New York.

On arrival there, William had been appalled by the state of the British ships. 'The Fleet are lying some at New York and others at Staten Island in a most wretched condition,' he told the King in a letter on 28 September. 'They expect to be ready about the 7 or 8 of next month. However I believe they will not be ready so soon as that time, for many ships are lying without lower masts and there is a great scarcity of lower masts and, in short, of all stores here.'[8]

Even after Admiral Digby had arrived with his three ships, the British were seriously outnumbered by the French, and Admiral Graves flatly declared on his return that the enemy had 'so great a naval force in the Chesapeake that they were absolute masters of its navigation'.[9] His second-in-command, the courtly Admiral Hood, was appalled by the lack of initiative that had brought about Graves's failure to relieve Cornwallis. He reported in a private letter to the Admiralty that 'Mr Graves proposed … the following question, "Whether it was practicable to relieve Lord Cornwallis in the Chesapeake?" This astonished me exceedingly, as it seemed plainly to indicate a design of having difficulties started against attempting what the generals and admirals had *most unanimously* agreed to ... and occasioned my replying immediately that it appeared to me a very unnecessary and improper question.' Officially, he only disassociated himself from his superior, declining to given any opinion and only writing that he 'really knows not what to say in the truly lamentable state we have brought ourselves'.[10] For his part, General Clinton surveyed the strategic situation and said hopelessly, 'I see this in so serious a light that I dare not look at it.'[11]

It seemed that the British command in New York were trying to forget the crisis in Virginia in the patriotic ecstasy of welcoming the King's son. But another attempt to relieve Yorktown had to be made and, on 17 October, Admiral Graves again sailed from New York with General Clinton and seven thousand British, Hessian and loyalist troops. The *Prince George* accompanied them and ten days later arrived off the Virginia capes. On the twenty-eighth, William wrote in his log, 'At 12 saw the French Fleet of 37 sail with their topsails loose at anchor.' But, ashore there was no smoke on the horizon and no distant rumble of gunfire. Then a small boat was sighted and stopped and her crew gave the news. On the day that the British had sailed from New York, Cornwallis had finally given up hope of relief and had surrendered Yorktown to General Washington. William added to his log, 'Bore away with the whole Fleet for New York, where we arrived on Nov. 1.'[12]

There the bigger ships were unable to get over the bar and anchored off Sandy Hook to await a wind. They were joined by the sloop *Bonetta*, which had been lying off Yorktown when it fell and which Washington had allowed to sail for New York with Cornwallis's aide-de-camp and whoever else the defeated general wished to evacuate before the final surrender. He chose to send four hundred and eighty survivors of the British Legion, the ferocious cavalry regiment raised in America and commanded by the dashing but ruthless Colonel Banastre Tarleton. Such was their reputation for giving no quarter in battle and the consequent risk of reprisals if captured, that they were crowded into the sloop and saved. Captain Dundas, who commanded the *Bonetta*, dined with Admiral Digby and the Prince and told them the story of the siege and surrender.

This William relayed to his father in a long letter, laying stress on the gallantry of the defenders. He also apologised for the Navy's failure: 'I wish it had been in our power to have given a good account of the French Fleet: but unfortunately they were so positioned to such advantage that we could not attack them without much loss, particularly after having heard of Lord Cornwallis's surrender.'

He described how Captain Dundas had been invited on board the French flagship, the *Ville de Paris* and been received by the Comte de Grasse ('a very tall old man, a very good Officer and a man of the greatest honour',) before being allowed to sail. There was tension between the rebels and their French allies who, he wrote, 'treat the Americans with a great deal of hauteur'.[13] He illustrated this with a story of an American officer who had ignored a French sentry's order to halt, was thereupon arrested, tied to a gun and given twenty-four strokes with the flat of a sabre.

When William finally returned to New York he again took up residence at the admiral's house in Hanover Square. The mood of the city was subdued and that of the headquarters depressed by the disaster at Yorktown, but those who were now deeply pessimistic tended to keep their forebodings to themselves. The British still fielded thirty thousand troops in America, and Canada remained loyal. As for the Prince himself, the onset of winter was in itself enjoyable. Before the snow fell, he had taken to exploring the environs of New York on foot and had seen the lakes which were now frozen hard.

'The Prince manifested, when on shore, a decided fondness for manly pastimes,' ran a contemporary American account, 'One of his favourite resorts was a small freshwater lake in the vicinity of the city, which presented a frozen sheet of many acres; and was thronged by the younger part of the population for the amusement of skating. As the Prince was unskilled in that exercise, he would sit in a chair fixed on runners, a crowd of officers environed him and the youthful multitude made the air ring with their shouts for Prince William Henry. It was an animated scene in the bright, sunny winter days.'[14]

Not all the spectators were so friendly. Since his arrival in New York, he had been watched by rebel spies and reports of his activities and daily routine sent back across the Hudson, where they had been read with mounting interest by a Colonel Ogden, who commanded the 1st Jersey Regiment. He noted that the house in Hanover Square where the Prince and Admiral Digby were staying, was only lightly guarded, and his knowledge of guerrilla warfare suggested that it would be simple to overpower the sentries at night, seize the Prince and the admiral and hustle them down to boats which would ferry them across the Hudson into captivity. Once in rebel hands, they would prove useful hostages to bargain against a British evacuation and the establishment of an independent American nation.

So Ogden drew up a detailed plan and sent it to General Washington for his approval. The raid would be mounted from his regiment's winter quarters in an encampment of wooden huts not far from the west bank of the river and should be accomplished overnight, 'between sun and sun'. Colonel Ogden wrote: 'It will be necessary to have four whale-boats (which can be procured without cause for suspicion); they must be well manned by their respective crews, including guides, etc; besides these, one captain, one subaltern, three sergeants and thirty-six men, with whom the boats' crews can row at ease ...

'The time of embarkation must be the first wet night after we are prepared. The place is not yet agreed on, as it will be necessary to consult those skilled in the tides, which must be put off until we are as nearly prepared as possible for fear of inferences being drawn from our inquiries. We must, however, set off from such part of the Jersey shore as will give us time to be in the city by half-past nine. The men must be embarked in order of debarkation.

'The Prince's quarters in Hanover Square has two sentinels from the 40th British regiment that are quartered in Lord Stirling's old quarters in Broad Street, 200 yards from the scene of action. The main guard, consisting of a captain and forty men, is posted at the City Hall – a sergeant and twelve at the head of the old slip – a sergeant and twelve opposite the coffee-house: these troops we may be in danger from and must be guarded against. The place of landing, at Coenties Market, between the two sergeants' guards, at the head of the old slip and opposite the coffee-house.

'The order of debarkation to agree with the mode of attack, as follows:

'First – Two men with a guide, seconded by two others, for the purpose of seizing the sentinels, these men to be armed with naked bayonets and dressed in sailors' habits: they are not to wait for anything, but immediately execute their orders.

'Second – Eight men, including guides, with myself, preceded by two men with each a crow-bar, and two with each an axe – these for the purpose of forcing the doors, should they be fast – and followed by four men entering the house and seizing the young Prince, the Admiral, the young noblemen, aides, etc.

'Third – a captain and eighteen to follow briskly, form and defend the house until the business is finished and retreat half a gunshot in our rear.

'Fourth – a subaltern and fourteen, with half the remaining of the boat's crew, to form to the right and the left of the boats and defend them until we return: the remainder of the crews to hold the boats in the best possible position for embarking.

'Necessary – two crow-bars, two axes, four dark lanterns and four large oil-clothes.

'The manner of returning as follows:

'Six men with guns and bayonets with those employed in carrying off the prisoners to precede those engaged in that business, followed by the captain (joined by the four men from the sentry) at a half-gunshot distance, who are to halt and give a front to the enemy until the whole are embarked in the following order:

'First – the prisoners, with those preceding them.

'Second – the guides and boatmen.

'Third – the subalterns and fourteen.

'Fourth – the rear.'

This was sent to Washington at his headquarters at Morris Town in March 1782, and the general replied, giving his approval, on the twenty-eighth of that month:

The spirit of enterprise so conspicuous in your plan for surprising in their quarters, and bringing off, the Prince William Henry and Admiral Digby, merits applause; and you have my authority to make the attempt in any manner, and at such a time, as your judgement shall direct.

I am fully persuaded that it is unnecessary to caution you against offering insult or indignity to the persons of the Prince or Admiral, should you be so fortunate as to capture them; but it may not be amiss to press the propriety of a proper line of conduct upon the party you command.

In case of success, you will, as soon as you get them to a place of safety, treat them with all possible respect; but you are to delay no time in conveying them to Congress and reporting your proceedings, with a copy of these orders.

G. Washington

But the British were on their guard and were aware of actual and probable rebel forays across the river. Espionage, covert military operations, sabotage and kidnapping had already been employed by both sides in the war, and the affair of Benedict Arnold and Major André had made everybody wary. Indeed, General Clinton quickly became aware that some form of dramatic *coup de main* was planned against New York. On 23 March, a message was sent by a rebel spy in the city, warning Colonel Ogden: 'Great seems their apprehension here. About a fortnight ago a great number of flat boats were discovered by a sentinel from the bank of the river, which are said to have been intended to fire the suburbs and, in the height of the conflagration, to make a descent on the lower part of the city and wrest from our embraces his Excellency Sir H. Clinton, Prince William Henry and several other illustrious personages, since which great precautions have been taken for the security of these gentlemen by augmenting the guards and to render their persons as little exposed as possible.'

Then on 2 April, Washington wrote to Ogden from Newburgh,

After I wrote to you from Morris Town, I received information that the sentries at the door of Sir Henry Clinton were doubled at eight o'clock every night, from an apprehension of an attempt to surprise him in them. If this be true, it is more than probable the same precaution extends to other personages in the city of New York, a circumstance I thought it proper for you to be advised upon.[15]

So the plan to kidnap Prince William was abandoned.

But his prolonged stay in New York was not only a concern to General Clinton on grounds of his security. At Windsor, his father had been increasingly worried by the risk to his son's morals while living ashore in a seaport, particularly as there had been little recent news from him because the ship carrying mail from New York had been captured by a French privateer in the English Channel. But he did receive a letter written on Christmas Day and immediately replied with a word of caution: 'I trust your stay this Winter at New York will prove as little detrimental as such a place can be; but certainly it is not advantageous to your profession and you must in a winter quarter see a great deal of bad; but I trust you have too much Religion, good sense, love for my felicity and feeling of what is to be expected of a Prince to be a sufferer by it.'[16]

This homily was reinforced by another from his brother Frederick, doubtless prompted by their father or General Budé, in which he gave a warning illustrated by the cases of their two unemployable uncles. Writing from Hanover, where he was undergoing military training, he told his younger brother, 'Let me, my Dearest William, give you the advice of now applying yourself strenuously to your Profession. Consider that as both of us must rise faster in our different lines than others, we have less time left us to learn, for only think a moment of the situation of our two uncles the Dukes of Gloucester and Cumberland, who at this alarming moment are at home unemployed because it is impossible to give them any commands as they are so totally ignorant of the Professions into which they have entered.

'I suppose during the winter you will be obliged to remain quiet in New York but, as soon as that is over, you will probably have a very busy campaign.'[17]

Prince William had, at first, performed well as the representative of the royal family in America and had enjoyed being the object of adulation. But the winter ashore had been dull and frustrating and he had hankered after – and sometimes been able to indulge in – the amusements of his contemporaries, which included some heavy drinking, gambling and sex. He became difficult to manage, his studies slackened and he fell below standard in mathematics. Confidential reports of this were duly sent to the King, worded as tactfully as possible. William was told that his behaviour and slackness had been reported to his father and advised that a letter of confession and a promise of reform from him might lessen the wrath that would inevitably strike from Windsor.

It was clear to Admiral Digby that the boy would be far better off at sea under the eye of a brisk captain and that, after the abortive plan to kidnap him, it would be safer too. However, in the spring of 1782, there were no major naval operations planned since Admiral Hood had returned to his station in the West Indies, while Admiral Digby concentrated on organising patrols against the privateers which preyed on commerce bound to or from New York. So the admiral shifted his flag to a smaller ship, while the *Prince George* sailed to join Hood under the command of Captain James Williams, her former first lieutenant, a fine seaman who had been promoted from the lower deck and had been among Prince William's instructors.

The boy's restlessness increased when news arrived that at the end of January Hood had already fought the Comte de Grasse. A two-day action off the island of St Kitts had not resulted in the relief of the British garrison besieged in the fortress of Brimstone Hill, but it had been a limited success. Finding the enemy at anchor in an unassailable roadstead, Hood had lured them to sea and then occupied the anchorage himself, so achieving strategic dominance. French attacks on the anchored British line were beaten off and Hood remained in position for another fortnight before slipping away to join Admiral Rodney, who had just arrived at Barbados from England with twelve sail of the line. Brimstone Hill had fallen to the French and de Grasse could again lie in the anchorage, but Hood's initiative had given the British the self-confidence they had lacked.

Then at the end of April came news that the combined British fleets of thirty-six sail of the line under Rodney's command had met and defeated de Grasse near the islands of Les Saintes between Guadeloupe and Dominica. He had achieved victory by flouting the tactics specified in the Admiralty's *Fighting Instructions* to break through the thirty sail of the line and bring his overwhelming firepower to bear on individual ships. The French, their formation broken, had tried to escape but five were captured including the flagship, the *Ville de Paris*. But the victory could have been more complete and Hood blamed Rodney for halting the pursuit of the Comte de Grasse.

Only in a ship of the line could such a battle be experienced and Prince William asked Digby if he could spend the summer in another even though this would not be a flagship. The admiral agreed and he joined the *Warwick*, a small ship mounting only fifty guns but commanded by the redoubtable Captain the Honourable George Elphinstone. A fine seaman and tactician but also a disciplinarian, he was a tough, haughty Scot from whom the royal midshipman would probably not be accorded undue privileges. However, with Elphinstone, the Prince would doubtless see some particularly active service.

That summer, the *Warwick* was to patrol off the Chesapeake, which was now fully under rebel and French control, with another ship of the line and two sloops under Elphinstone's command. Their task was to harry whatever traffic was passing in and out of the great bay. After some dull weeks at sea, their patience was rewarded on 11 September, when sails were sighted on the horizon and the British gave chase. As the *Warwick* gained on her quarry, this was seen to be three ships: two frigates and what seemed to be an armed merchant ship. Next day, the latter was overhauled and struck her colours. She proved to be the *Sophie*, a new, well-armed brig, bound from Bayonne to Philadelphia. She was an important prize, but more important was the result of interrogating her crew. Elphinstone learned that the two frigates he had also chased were *L'Aigle* and *La Gloire*, which were carrying important passengers and large sums of money to America. So he continued the pursuit and followed them into an estuary, where he boarded and captured the larger, although her passengers and bullion had been got ashore.

The Prince had taken no active part in this because of a 'terrible accident' – probably a fall on board ship – which had injured, and possibly broken, his arm. But this first taste of the brisk, inshore action in which the Royal Navy excelled had given him new enthusiasm for his profession. Moreover he was seen to be a success, as Captain Elphinstone was to tell the Prince of Wales, who wrote to his father – albeit with exaggeration – that he had said that 'there cannot be a more gallant or a better officer than our dear William is already and promised to be ... he is now a remarkable good Officer, and in all probability will be one of the best in the whole Navy.'

But when the *Warwick* anchored off Sandy Hook this was dashed by letters from England. The frank reports of his behaviour during the winter in New York had brought parental rebukes couched in Olympian language. While he had been cruising off the Chesapeake, his father had written to acknowledge the receipt of his apologies and 'your confessing how improper your conduct has been and your intention thoroughly to reform. At your age it is to be hoped you are apprized of the weight that attends a promise and consequently of the real aggravation if not attended by scrupulous compliance....

'I flatter myself that Mr Majendie will be enabled to send me such accounts as will set my mind at ease that your Religious principles have not suffered by the idle discourse of some of the young persons you may have met with; indeed, dear William, the older you grow the more you will meet with trials that nothing can support but a real trust in the Assistance of Divine Providence and how can that be expected unless by due obedience to the Will of the Almighty?'[18]

His mother had written from Kew on the same day to accept his promise to reform. 'You are drawing nearer towards Manhood and the former excuses of mere vivacity will no longer befriend you,' she warned. 'Therefore I beseech you to set earnestly about mending your behaviour.... Openness of character is natural to you but you frequently mistake *roughness* for *sincerity* and *openness* which leads you to be inattentive to those that are to direct you and this is owing to the *great* and *favourable* opinion you entertain of your own *dear self*. When this is checked by proper representation you indulge your passion for talking and arguing of which the consequence is *indecency*....'[19]

It now seemed almost as important to his parents that William be kept away from the temptations of New York as of London and again the means to achieve this would be banishment to sea. While with Admiral Digby he would inevitably spend much time within reach of the city, so the King decided that a spell with Admiral Hood – his favourite admiral, who had been elevated to the peerage in recognition of his action with de Grasse – in his flagship, the *Barfleur*, would be good for the boy. So he wrote to Hood, saying what a 'misfortune it would be for my third son to remain on shore the next winter when most probably there will be an active scene in the West Indies ... I shall be happy if William can be witness to as brilliant actions as have attended the *Barfleur* ever since she has left this Island.'[20] He also wrote to Admiral Digby with instructions to hand over his charge to Hood and told William of the move, which would be for the 'improvement of Nautical knowledge which can alone be acquired by Service'.[21] Digby replied to the King, acknowledging his instructions, pointing out sharply that detailed orders for the Prince's future should reach Lord Hood from the King rather than himself since the two admirals had 'differed in opinion about a matter too common to differ about (I mean prize-money)'.

Although the King had told William that Mr Majendie would accompany him to the West Indies if his health permitted, Admiral Digby suggested otherwise, concluding his letter, 'As I have written very fully to General Budé, it remains only to inform your Majesty that upon considering Mr Majendie's situation with Prince William in every respect I think it well that he should separate from his Royal Highness....'[22]

The boy and the tutor had been together too long, the former finding his tutor too sanctimonious and his continual presence inhibiting. It had already been agreed that, whether Majendie accompanied him to the West Indies or not, he would be attended by a young and accomplished naval officer, who would act as instructor, aide-de-camp and companion. Admiral Digby had already chosen for this duty Captain the Honourable Patrick Napier, who, he told the King, 'is out of employ, having lately been taken by a French frigate'. He was, he continued, 'a man of Family, a steady, firm man and a man of honour, has lived much in my family and is the fittest person I know at present to attend Prince William'. Lord Hood had, however, thought otherwise. Digby wrote, 'I have positively insisted, tho' much contrary to Lord Hood's inclination, upon Captain Napier's attending his Royal Highness' although 'I flatter myself when Captain Napier is a little better known to him, he will be of my opinion.'[23]

The Prince, happy to be rid of his tutor, approved of Napier as 'a very deserving and very amiable young man'.[24] As for the captain himself, there were hopes of promotion and Digby had already asked the King that he should be given a place on the post-captain's list to ensure his automatic rise through the senior ranks. But his instructions were vague, Digby having told him only that he would be employed 'not as his Tutor, nor as an attendant upon him, but as his Companion and as an Officer under whose direction he should be'. He had warned him that 'the task is delicate' and suggested that 'it would be right to check that great tendency to violent laughter, and ridiculing and to keep bad example from him'. The admiral warned that 'His Royal Highness wants application ... and will soon forget what he has learnt. His log should never be omitted above one day and if it could be made an entertainment by inserting little drawings of the land, tho' done by another hand, and plans of the Fleet in different positions, such as the different changes of Lines of Battle, it would be worth any trouble. For, you must have observ'd, his Royal Highness wants amusement from Education.'[25]

This was a task to challenge the most experienced teacher and Captain Napier had no experience, let alone training, for such a role. Yet, like all naval officers who came into close contact with royalty, he had high if unspecific hopes of favours to come.

So, at the end of the year Henry Majendie parted company with his difficult pupil, who, he said, had 'treated him handsomely and, at the same time, delicately', and Digby had presented him with 'a very elegant piece of Plate'. The Prince also gave him a miniature of himself, which, declared the tutor, was 'a picture that will be dear to me as long as I live'.[26] Finally he gave Majendie a letter to hand to his father, reminding him that the tutor had been with him 'between 7 and 8 years and particularly for the last three years on board a ship' and asked the King to 'provide for him'.[27] He sailed for home in the *Warwick*, which was escorting a convoy, which was struck by 'such a high wind and dangerous seas as I had never before seen.... The poor *Warwick* was pooped; the deadlights stove in and I found myself afloat with about 2 feet of water in the cabin about 2 o'clock in the morning ... above a fortnight we were almost constantly wet and never once sat at table.'[28]

Admiral Digby and the Prince were parting too, and Digby told the King that Majendie would give him an account of his son when he arrived at Windsor. 'As your Majesty will soon see him,' he wrote, 'I shall leave it to him to represent his Royal Highness's little foibles and dangers and indulge myself with assuring you, Sir, that he is at present a very fine young man, fond of his profession to a degree ... and of a temper to make an excellent officer and spirits to go through anything yet perfectly ready to comply with any rules or advice I have ever given him. Tho' in many instances not so prudent as I could wish, but I should be ungrateful if I did not feel great obligations and affections.'[29]

Then Digby wrote to Hood with details of the Prince's routine. He began by stressing that the King insisted that the boy be treated 'as much like the sons of Gentlemen as his situation would allow without court or without any parade or your usual attendance upon Princes. This has been constantly attended to tho' in some instances broken thro' since I have been in this country.' He listed his own rules, 'most of which I recommend strongly to your Lordship to adhere to. I made it my rule never to dine or lay out of the ship without his Royal Highness – and it was a rule that his Royal Highness should not go out of the ship without me, that he should receive no visits and never be sent for but to the Commander-in-Chief, nor dine with anybody but the officers of the Fleet and the Commissioned officers on shore, that when any officer his Royal Highness had not seen was in the Fleet, I always invited him to dinner and introduced him before we sat down. It was a rule that he employ his morning in studying mathematics till noon when his Royal Highness with all the young people in the ship went to their exercise. That he should every day write his log-book, that he should wear the same dress as the midshipmen and that he should not on any account go off the deck in his watch and should not frequent the wardroom. These were the chief rules I recollect.'[30]

Both Hood and the Prince were delighted by the prospect: Hood because he could resume and strengthen his royal connections; William because he expected less discipline from Hood and was glad to see the last of Majendie. At the end of October, the admiral wrote a flowery letter to the King declaring that, 'My eye shall be constantly kept upon his Royal Highness and to the utmost of my power will be watchful not only to encourage every laudable pursuit but to check and restrain whatever I may see amiss.'[31] The boy wrote a scarcely less elaborate letter to his father, saying, 'As for promises, I shall make none but will endeavour to behave as an Officer and as a Prince, keeping always before my eyes the prospect of being, one day or other, a Glory to the Nation and a comfort to my Parents.'[32]

Now it was Admiral Digby's turn to proffer advice. In a long, flattering and guarded letter he tried to warn the boy against his increasing tendency to mock others behind their backs, using his royal status as protection against mockery in return. 'In your high station of life with the eyes of all the world upon you, a few imprudences would soon lose you all you have acquir'd,' he wrote, 'Your Royal Highness must, I am sure, feel what I chiefly allude to … I mean the talking unguardedly of people when absent and the joining in turning them into ridicule.… The very people who may be the most forward in encouraging such discourse will some time or other suspect it may be their turn … I need not point out the consequences; one however I will mention, that you will have no true friend and that your enemies will daily increase. This I have particularly charged Captain Napier to keep in your mind and as it is not the most pleasing task to be observing the Foibles of others, I beg you to consider that his present happiness is in your hands.'[33]

On the fourth of November, Prince William, accompanied by Admiral Digby and Captain Napier, sailed from New York by schooner to join the *Barfleur*, which was lying off Staten Island. The flagship, together with more than twenty sail of the line, from both Hood's squadrons in the West Indies and Digby's in American waters, was awaiting orders for sea. They were to attempt the interception of the French fleet now lying at Boston, under the command of the Marquis de Vaudreuil, to prevent it reaching the West Indies and attacking Jamaica. The *Barfleur* was, like the *Prince George*, a big ship of ninety-eight guns with spacious and elegantly-furnished quarters for the admiral which the royal midshipman would continue to frequent.

After the formalities, Hood and Digby discussed William with forced friendliness, the former telling his wife in a letter of his strained relations with the other admiral, who was 'all condescending' and that they showed 'the appearance of good friends but I can never hold him in the future in the respected light I have hitherto done'.[34] Relations between the two now deteriorated further. Hood had heard that twelve French sail of the line were about to leave Boston for the West Indies and he wanted to sail. But his ships' companies were under strength from sickness – his flagship had suffered particularly from scurvy – and he did not consider his squadron battle-worthy. Even after collecting the less incapacitated patients from the naval hospital, he was seriously short-handed and asked Digby to lay up some of his smaller ships when they came in from sea and send him their crews. But Digby was reluctant to comply, ostensibly on compassionate grounds, and because of his need for men to guard American prisoners of war.

To this Hood replied, 'With respect to cruelty, as you are pleased to call it, of taking men just come from sea to proceed instantly again, you surely cannot be serious, upon the present emergency, when they are so much wanted in His Majesty's Ships.' As for the prisoners, he urged Digby not to house them in ships 'as great evils are not unlikely to happen to the King's service from prisoners of such rancorous and dangerous principles, as the Americans have in so many instances shown themselves, beyond those of any other nation.'[35] The angry exchange continued and on 13 November alone Hood sent eight letters to Digby, one of them declaring, 'Your great want of candour in imputing words to me I never uttered astonishes me beyond measure ... and it is all I shall further say except that I neither wish nor mean to engage in any Paper War, as you are pleased to express yourself.'

So it was with relief that Hood turned his attention to the welfare of the Prince, writing to his wife after the boy had been on board for a few days, 'Prince William ... seems perfectly happy, very observant of all I say, is studious even to guess at my wishes and to do everything that is proper.'[36] On the same day, he wrote to the King, 'His Royal Highness is in high health and fine spirits and to my very great satisfaction and delight appears most perfectly happy.

'By the last accounts from Boston, the French fleet is getting forward and I imagine will push to get to sea ... I flatter myself much, in that case, your Majesty's squadron under my command will stop his voyage ... I am now at single anchor and only wait wind and tide to put to sea. His Royal Highness's impatience is great.'[37]

He was impatient but he was not perfectly happy. Although Hood seemed less demanding than Digby had been, Captain Napier was not the deferential aide-de-camp he had expected. Assuming that as the Prince's director of studies and instructor in seamanship, his manner should be friendly but brisk and, when necessary, brusque, the young captain followed the King's orders in treating him much like any other midshipman. But William, now accustomed to dining with admirals who treated him with a studied courtliness, and being fawned upon by civic dignitaries ashore, assumed that Captain Napier should attend upon him and act as an adviser. His resentment at being treated like the seventeen-year-old youth he was, soon began to show.

Another captain now came into Prince William's life. On 13 November, when the *Barfleur* was lying off Staten Island where Lord Hood, accompanied by Prince William, was inspecting the defences and the naval hospital, the midshipman noted in his log, 'Passed by for New York H.M. Ships *Albemarle* and *Pandora*'.[38] They briefly hove to while the captain of the former frigate was pulled across to the flagship in his barge to pay his respects to Lord Hood.

Although his frigate, the *Albemarle*, had arrived from Quebec, Captain Horatio Nelson had seen much service in the Caribbean and Hood was anxious to consult him about the likely course of the French fleet should he fail to intercept it. So the captain came aboard and was presented by Lord Hood to Prince William, who never forgot him. He was already well-known to those who had served in the West Indies as the commander of the naval escort of the disastrous expedition to Nicaragua two years before, when he insisted on accompanying the soldiers up the Rio San Juan. He had successfully led them more than a hundred miles up the river in the hope of crossing the isthmus, cutting the Americas in two and beginning to annex the Spanish colonies. The British, already infected with malaria, were almost wiped out by fever and dysentery, the expedition collapsed in chaos and this intrepid naval officer was one of the few to survive.

Captain Nelson was still pale, thin from topical sicknesses and looking more than his twenty-four years. But his ardour was as fervent as ever. When he reported to Digby at New York, the admiral had remarked to him, 'You are come on a fine station for making prize-money,' and he had replied, 'Yes sir, but the West Indies is the station for honour.'[39] That, in fact, was where he expected to go, having written to his father in England, 'I think it very likely we shall go to the *grand theatre* of Actions, the West Indies.'[40]

'He appeared the merest boy of a Captain I ever beheld,' William was to remember. 'He had on a full-lace uniform, his lank unpowdered hair was tied in a stiff Hessian tail of an extraordinary length; the old-fashioned flaps of his waistcoat added to the general quaintness of his figure, produced an appearance which particularly attracted my notice for I had never seen anything like it, nor could I imagine who he was, or what he came about. My doubts were, however, removed when Lord Hood introduced me to him. There was something irresistibly pleasing in his address and conversation; and an enthusiasm when speaking on professional subjects that showed he was no common being.'[41]

The liking was returned and on that day, 13 November 1782, Captain Nelson wrote to one of his lieutenants ashore in New York, 'I had the honour of an introduction to the Prince on board the *Barfleur* by my Lord Hood, was very much pleased with him, he will make a good sailor, or I am much mistaken. We shall be proud of him.'[42]

4

An Ornament to our Service

When captain Nelson sailed up to New York and anchored in the East River, he remained in the minds of Prince William and Lord Hood. The former remembered him as an unconventional officer of high repute, eccentric appearance and original outlook. The latter was anxious that he accompany the squadron to sea on what might prove to be a long chase of the French through the maze of the Caribbean islands.

In readiness for sea, the *Barfleur* anchored in Sandy Hook Bay on 16 November and two days later Hood was again angered by what he saw as Admiral Digby's obstruction; he protested, 'I am this moment informed by a letter from Captain Nelson that His Majesty's Ship under his command was under sail to come to me on the 16th and stop'd by your order, which is a matter of the greatest surprize to me as you have *twice* assured me from under your hand that the *Albemarle* should certainly join me the moment she was ready. I beg, Sir, you will be pleased to consider of what great importance that frigate may be to the King's service ... I will have thirty merchant ships under convoy.'[1]

Digby relented and the *Albemarle* joined the *Barfleur* at Sandy Hook. On the twenty-first, William wrote in his log, 'Fresh gales, cloudy, strong gales and sleet, later strong breezes and clear. P. M. furled sails. Came down and anchored here, H.M. Ship *Albemarle....* Sent on board the *Albemarle* the repeating colours. Recd. from her,

205 boxes of Essence of Spruce.'[2] At last Hood was ready for sea but now there were delays caused by wind, tide and weather: two days because of a calm and fog; two more because of a strong headwind followed by a heavy swell over the bar; then a high tide too late in the evening to negotiate the channel before dark. Finally they got to sea on the twenty-seventh and, realising that he was now his own master, Hood sent a farewell note to Digby saying, 'It is with much pleasure that I tell you Prince William is perfectly well.'[3]

The French had, so Hood believed, embarked at Boston all their available troops in America, and planned to send them to the West Indies under the escort of the Marquis de Vaudreuil, whose twelve sail of the line matched the strength of his own squadron. The particular danger was that they would elude him in the Atlantic, join with the Spanish squadron based at Havana and fall upon Jamaica. So, instead of attempting to intercept in the foggy, stormy expanses of the Atlantic, Hood steered for the Caribbean where he could give closer protection to the likely targets of the enemy.

The British were off Cuba early in December and the sloop Blood *Hound*, sent to reconnoitre Havana, reported that thirteen Spanish ships of the line and five frigates were still lying in the harbour. Continuing to Jamaica, Hood was able to assure the Governor in Spanish Town that there had been no junction between the enemy squadrons, that he was cruising off Kingston and Fort Royal and that consequently they were out of danger. Moreover, there was encouraging news from Europe: although the French and Spanish fleets, based on Brest and Cadiz respectively, had managed to join forces, Admiral Howe had outmanoeuvred them and run another convoy of supplies into Gibraltar.

Indeed there were rumours of peace which did not please Lord Hood, who wrote to another admiral on 22 January 1783, 'We have accounts of Peace from various Neutrals, which I give credit to and

---

[*] 'Repeating colours' were signal flags for repeating signals from ships out of sight of the flagship; essence of spruce was for brewing.

am therefore the more anxious of getting hold of Vaudreuil before we know it for certain as it would make a good finish.'[4] He was not alone in his disappointment for, as he wrote to General Budé, 'Prince William is in the dumps about peace as his heart was set upon seeing service ... and probably does not feel for himself alone but thinks a little longer continuance of the war would have been advantageous to Great Britain; I dare say his Royal Highness is not singular in that idea but I have most strongly recommended to him that whatever his thoughts are to keep them to himself except in our private conversations. With respect to myself, peace is an event I ought to rejoice at, not having the constitution left for much further service, particularly in this climate, but whether I shall have good reason to rejoice at it on the score of my country, I am not without my doubts.'[5]

So Hood urgently sought his enemy before an official announcement that hostilities had ended could pre-empt the victory he expected. Nelson was scouting off Puerto Rico and Curacao and, to the Prince's gratification, one of the ships of the line engaged in the hunt was the *Prince William*, the Spanish prize which Rodney had named after him. But there was no sign of the French and, to await developments, Hood made for Jamaica and anchored his squadron in Kingston Bay in February, landed at Port Royal and took Prince William with him to the capital, Spanish Town. There was a rapturous welcome from the prosperous sugar-planters who had once again been relieved from fear of a French invasion by the Royal Navy. 'I am now at the King's House in Spanish Town with a view to shewing Prince William a little of Jamaica,'[6] noted Hood in a letter. He toured the fortifications and the nearer plantation houses, escorted by a troop of cavalry raised by the planters and named Prince William's Regiment. Apart from spraining an ankle – possibly while dancing – he was in his element, talking, dining, drinking and making speeches to prolonged applause.

Among the officers ashore was Captain Nelson, who wrote of the Prince to a naval friend, 'a vast deal of notice has been taken of him at Jamaica; he has been addressed by the Council and the House of

Assembly…. He has his levées at Spanish Town; they are all highly delighted with him; with the best temper and great good sense, he cannot fail to be pleasing to everyone.'[7]

Then, on 4 April, came news that the preliminaries of a peace agreement between the British government and the American Congress had been signed in Paris and that the war could be assumed to have ended. Mourning his failure to bring the French to battle, Lord Hood wrote to the Secretary of the Admiralty, 'I was in hopes Fortune would have been so far favourable to the Arms of Great Britain as to have enabled the King's Squadron under my command to have made a glorious finish to the war.'[8]

Prince William had other reasons for worry. Since his grovelling apology to his parents for lapses in his behaviour during the winter before last in New York, there had been an ominous silence from that quarter. As Hood wrote to Budé just before they arrived in Jamaica, 'Prince William feels uneasy at not hearing from home. He has received no letter of a later date than September.'[9] In April, a letter reached the Prince from his father. It had been written soon after he had received Mr Majendie on his arrival at Windsor late in January and been given a favourable letter from Lord Hood and the tutor's optimistic account of the boy's progress, which might enhance his own chances of preferment. In this he was successful (soon afterwards he was appointed a canon of Windsor) and his eulogy prompted the King to write the first letter to his son that neither preached nor reprimanded.

'You was pleased to express your approbation of my conduct,' replied William, 'This is the first time I have had the pleasure of receiving a letter from your Majesty as from a tender parent to his son grown up. You was likewise pleased to say I should not return immediately, which is another mark of your great affection, because it is my good fortune to have already served so much of my six years abroad [to qualify him to take the exam for promotion to lieutenant] that it was my wish to stay out till my apprenticeship was completed.'[10]

This happy state did not continue. Not long after Majendie's audience, word reached the King that William had fallen out with his replacement, Captain Napier. Indeed the two had never established a practicable relationship: the Prince thought the captain was primarily a courtier and the captain imagined he was the Prince's instructor. Napier was a believer in firm but friendly discipline; the sharp rebuke followed by the pleasantry. But the Prince, now accustomed to reverent, sometimes obsequious treatment from his superiors in naval rank, complained to Hood and, as the admiral wrote in his report to the King, 'the Prince came to me full of sorrows to say he could no longer put up with Captain Napier's treatment.... His Royal Highness said his language and manner of behaviour was so disgusting and very different from what he had been accustomed to receive that he was made very unhappy.'

Hood had interviewed Napier, who had been unable to give him any precise reason for the friction. He continued, 'When I told him I conceived his being here as a companion to, and an attendant on, His Royal Highness's leisure hours, his answer was he should not have come upon such a footing.'[11] The admiral supported the Prince's complaint, telling Napier that as he was so 'volatile, it was necessary He should be *reasoned* into what was right and not treated with an austerity and harshness of language'; that he himself had 'neither seen in nor heard anything of the Prince but what was truly amiable and proper' and that 'there was a manner and language to be made of to His Royal Highness very different from what a dogmatical country Pedant would use to one of his scholars.'[12]

The admiral criticised the captain in his report on the matter to the King, who had also received a much more strongly worded complaint from William. But he was not convinced by their versions of the trouble and replied to Hood, 'I cannot admire the warmth he has shown in the disputes with Captain Napier, of which his own account to me bears the strongest marks.

'William has ever been violent when controlled ... I totally leave it to your judgement whether he shall remain till you and my son return to Europe, which cannot be many months, or whether he shall sooner quit your ship.' In any case, the King continued, he would be asking Admiral Keppel, now the First Lord of the Admiralty, to make Napier a post-captain on the list for automatic promotion. When Hood and the Prince returned, the admiral was to ensure that the boy was always accompanied by a reliable officer of appropriate seniority 'as it would not be proper he should be left to the sole guidance of his volatile imagination'.[13] General Budé was told of the trouble and he wrote to Hood, 'It concerns me that Prince William has been carried away by his vivacity ... the wrong is never on one side. I observed the King is displeased at Prince William's letters, the contents of which I am ignorant of.'[14]

Captain Napier was at once sent home and, although he was made post-captain, he never went to sea again and his naval career was finished. But the King blamed the boy himself and the Navy for failing to force him into a more princely mould and reprimanded his son in another stern letter, 'Your judgement does not ripen as fast as I could wish. To be fit to command, the knowledge of obedience must first have been obtained, without which self-control cannot be gained.' He realised, he continued, that William was trying to model himself on his elder brother Frederick, whose education was continuing in Hanover but he, 'although two years older, is perfectly compliant to every advice the Officers about him give him'.

The King had already made an important decision, reinforced by a conversation with Lord Howe, who had just replaced Admiral Keppel as First Lord of the Admiralty. If William wished to emulate Frederick, he should be enabled to do so and he wrote to his third son, 'I shall certainly send you to the Continent as soon as you return from sea, that your manners and behaviour may be formed fit for shore and that you may be in time an Officer. Lord Howe, who certainly is a scientific Officer, assures me that he thinks in our Service the attention is carried so long alone to seamanship that few Officers are formed, and that a knowledge of the military is necessary to open the ideas to the directing large Fleets.' Moreover, a spell of military training in Hanover would give him 'that politeness and decorum which is but little met with on service in the Navy and in headquarters on shore, though essential in a Prince, a gentleman and an Officer'.[15]

As one captain disappeared, another re-appeared. The *Albemarle* rejoined the squadron after an aggressive patrol, during which Captain Nelson had attacked a French-held island (albeit without success), taken an enemy supply ship laden with valuable topmasts destined for the French fleet and captured a launch carrying senior French officers – one of whom had been present at the fall of Yorktown – returning from a survey expedition among the islands.

The preliminary peace agreement had indeed been signed at Versailles on 20 January 1783 and, when news of it reached the Caribbean, the war ended. Lord Hood was frustrated both at missing the French and failing to catch the Spanish at sea, remarking, 'I flattered myself with a chance of getting hold of the Spanish squadron before the time was elapsed for the ceasing of hostilities in these seas. But my hopes are now at an end.'[16]

Under orders to return to England in May, together with most of his ships, Hood realised that there was time to make diplomatic capital out of Prince William's presence. He would try to arrange royal visits to both the enemy's main naval bases in the Caribbean, Cap François [now Cap Haitien] on the north coast of Hispaniola, and Havana.

The visit to Cap François was quickly arranged and Hood accompanied the Prince ashore to a royal salute of twenty-one guns. An inspection of French troops was followed by dinner with the governor, then a performance at the opera house, followed by what Hood described as 'a very magnificent supper at the Governor's house, where there was a brilliant shew of ladies'. Finally a ball began at eleven o'clock and the Prince danced until one and was 'charmed with what he had seen'. A few hours later the admiral and the Prince were escorted back to the quay through streets lined by five thousand soldiers. Reporting on the visit, Hood wrote that 'the dignity and propriety of his Royal Highness was such as to gain him the esteem and admiration of all who saw him.'[17]

The proposed visit to Havana would be a much more serious affair. For the city was the cornerstone of the Spanish empire in the Caribbean and the Americas, the terminus of its trade and traffic in bullion, and was said to be the most powerfully defended fortress in the world. Even so, it had been captured by the British in 1762 in an extraordinary campaign attended by both triumph and disaster. The naval commander, Vice-Admiral Sir George Pocock, had surprised the defenders by approaching the city through dangerous shoals, and had put the troops ashore against little opposition. But the army commander, Lord Albemarle, had thrown away this advantage by settling down to a long, formal siege of the fortifications which, although ultimately successful, lasted throughout the summer, during which his force was almost destroyed by yellow fever. The Spanish had been adding even stronger defences to the city in the past two decades and, although Havana had been handed back to Spain under the settlement of 1763, the whole affair was fresh in the memory. Indeed, many of the older men in Hood's ships had taken part in the campaign.

A graceful pretext for a royal visit had been offered by the governor of Havana, who had written to Prince William at Port Royal to make a gesture of goodwill. He told him that some British prisoners of war held in Louisiana had broken their parole and had consequently been condemned to death. 'Will you be pleased, Sir, to accept their pardon and their lives in the name of the Spanish army and of my King? It is, I trust, the greatest present that can be offered to one Prince in the name of another. Mine is generous and will approve of my conduct.'[18]

Prince William accepted the offer with an equally courtly letter, saying that the gesture was 'thoroughly characteristic of the bravery and gallantry of the Spanish nation'.[19] The governor's offer had a precedent in action Prince William had taken not long before, which had greatly enhanced his standing amongst his contemporaries. While at Port Royal, a court martial had condemned a midshipman, Benjamin Lee, to death for an act of insubordination, which had been construed as mutiny. There had been no time to lodge an appeal in London, so the Prince had organised a petition for clemency and been the first to sign it. This had been accepted by Admiral Rowley, who commanded at Jamaica, and the boy had been reprieved.

It was now appropriate for Hood to suggest a royal visit to Havana. So the admiral wrote a tactful letter to the governor requesting permission to make such a visit and adding, 'The King my Master having been pleased to place His Majesty's third son, Prince William, under my care and direction, and as his Royal Highness has a strong desire to see the Havannah, I propose either to attend him or send him with proper Officers to wait upon Your Excellency.'[20] A friendly reply was received from Don Luis de Unzaga and Hood sailed for Havana. The squadron would not enter the harbour and put itself under the guns of its recent enemy, but the admiral would stay at sea, cruising off the harbour mouth instead of lying at anchor, because the current was too strong. Prince William would go ashore with an appropriate suite of officers. Several personable captains were available for this duty but it was important that the young man should be accompanied by one of outstanding quality. Lord Hood's choice was Captain Nelson.

Although Hood had known Nelson only spasmodically for the past few months, he recognised his ability. His career had been given initial impetus by the influence of his uncle, Captain Maurice Suckling, who had become Controller of the Navy at the Admiralty and had exercised his patronage fairly and discreetly, making sure that his nephew earned his promotion. When Suckling died in 1778, the young Nelson was only a lieutenant but had had wide experience at sea, including an expedition to the Arctic.

Although the Suckling family, to which his mother had belonged, were related to the aristocratic, land-owning Walpoles of Norfolk, the

Nelsons were not grand. Like more than a dozen of his relations and immediate forebears, his father was a clergyman and something of a scholar, but there had been tradesmen as well as university graduates in the family. Horatio Nelson was no 'man of family', as Hood would have put it, but his roots were deep in the two pillars of British society: the Church of England and the Royal Navy. This had given him a deep, instinctive reverence for the institution which seemed to embody and depend upon both: the monarchy. This almost religious veneration of those who commanded little respect from many of his intelligent contemporaries had been strengthened by a mystical experience he had when recovering from a serious bout of malaria some years before. A mood of deep depression over what he feared were his bleak professional prospects and lack of patronage had suddenly been overwhelmed by euphoria when (as he recounted) 'a sudden glow of patriotism was kindled within me and presented my King and Country as my patron....'[21] Now he had met and liked one of that King's sons and invested him with the royal aura.

More importantly to his prospects, he was in high favour with the Prince's naval mentor, Lord Hood. As he wrote to his old friend Captain William Locker, 'My situation in Lord Hood's Fleet must be in the highest degree flattering to any young man. He treats me as if I was his son and will, I am convinced, give me anything I ask of him: nor is my situation with Prince William less flattering. Lord Hood was so kind as to tell him ... that if he wished to ask questions relative to Naval Tactics, I could give him as much information as any Officer in the Fleet. He will be, I am certain, an ornament to our Service. He is a *seaman*, which you could hardly suppose. Every other qualification you may expect from him. But he will be a *disciplinarian*, and a strong one: he says he is determined every person shall serve his time before they shall be provided for, as he is obliged to serve his.'[22]

So, on 10 May, the squadron arrived off Havana and the Prince, attended by three captains, embarked in the frigate *Fortunée*, in which he was to enter the harbour escorted by Nelson in the *Albemarle*. Royal salutes were fired from the batteries as the two ships passed the narrow entrance to the harbour beneath the walls of El Moro, the fortress which the British had stormed twenty-one years before, and of Las Cabañas, the even larger fortress subsequently built on higher ground to prevent a repetition. The royal party was received by the Spanish admiral, Don Solano, whose ships of the line crowded the anchorage, and conducted to his house, where the Prince and his suite would stay.

During the two days of the visit, a full programme of inspections, parades and entertainment had been arranged. The Prince was conducted through the dockyard and around the massive fortifications and inspected guards of honour. There were dinners and a levée at which he saw 'some of the Spanish beauties in the fullest grace and voluptuousness which the female form can exhibit'. His host, aware of a robust eighteen-year-old's likely priorities, had arranged that he be accompanied by his own two daughters, one of whom, Maria, was recognised as the belle of Havana.

Several of those attending Prince William claimed that he fell in love with her. He had already shown that he regarded young women either as objects of lust or as goddesses and Donna Maria seemed to be among the latter. Indeed, it was to be said that her Spanish admirers thought 'she averted her looks from them to bestow them upon the more favoured royal youth ... and it is a question whether his Royal Highness would have seen England again, had it not been for Captain Nelson, who plainly saw the danger that impended over his royal friend and urged his immediate departure.'[23]

Such a conflict of emotions and loyalties was much on Nelson's own mind. Only seven months before, while in the St Lawrence river, he had fallen in love with the belle of Quebec, Mary Simpson, the daughter of the garrison's provost-marshal, and had considered resigning his commission to marry her. He had been persuaded to change his mind by her lack of enthusiasm for the match and by the advice of his friend and confidant Alexander Davison, the Admiralty contractor in the port. So he was able to advise the lovelorn Prince with sympathy.

Nelson was now ordered to St Augustine on the east coast of Florida with despatches for the British garrison before crossing the Atlantic independently to Portsmouth, while Lord Hood sailed with his squadron for the same destination. The ocean passage was uneventful until they reached the English Channel and ran into fog and a calm, so that the short run from Land's End to the Isle of Wight took five days. The *Barfleur* anchored at Spithead on 26 June within a few hours of the arrival of the *Albemarle*.

Once at Portsmouth, Prince William was formally removed from the strength of the flagship and, for administrative purposes, transferred to another ship of her class, the *Queen*, which was lying there. While arrangements for his return to London were being made, he lived in the ship and, although he dined with admirals ashore, he berthed with the other midshipmen. One of them, James Grant, would recall him taking his turn in preparing crude meals, joining gunroom squabbles and stealing flour from the mess store to powder his hair before going to a formal dinner party ashore.

In most ways, William had become a typical member of the midshipmen's mess. He was tough, rough and noisy; he enjoyed coarse humour and practical jokes, the more violent the better; he drank more than was good for him and was familiar with seaport trollops; he regularly used sailors' slang and foul language and he was undaunted by storms at sea or the prospect of battle. He was also instinctively generous, humorous and enthusiastic. He was garrulous but had few set opinions on any subject beyond his profession and the qualities of food, drink and women. He delighted in amateur theatricals on board ship, when the more boisterous scenes from Shakespeare – particularly the third scene of the third act of *The Merry Wives of Windsor* – when William liked to play the part of Prince Hal in scenes with Falstaff. As stage manager, supervising the canvas theatre rigged on the orlop deck, he enjoyed introducing gratuitous slapstick. But he had no liking for poetry, excepting the descriptions of battles in *The Iliad*.

When politics were discussed – as they were more often at the admirals' tables than the midshipmen's – he was easily convinced by the most persuasive talker. His one conviction was of the divinely-ordained status of his father and his family. The King was godlike and he and his brothers were young demi-gods, sent to live among mortals at their father's behest. Thus he could mix with his contemporaries and enjoy their company; he could behave as obstreperously as any of them, but when it came to the essentials of his position in the Royal Navy he was not as the others and was not bound by the same natural order of the ruler and the ruled.

Yet he was easygoing and a good listener, so that no one who had got to know him hesitated in airing unconventional, or even radical, opinions in his presence. It was even thought proper to ask for his help in initiating reforms. A Lieutenant Berkeley, who had served with him in the *Prince George*, asked for and received help in presenting a plan for increasing the speed of ships by a new design of hull; in the event the scheme was disregarded by the Board of Admiralty.

Another such proposal – for a new system of signalling – was presented to him for forwarding to the Admiralty, or the King, by a Captain Maxwell [probably Captain George Maxwell], who had commanded a sloop in the Caribbean. This, too, was rejected without consideration and the disappointed captain wrote a verbose letter to the Prince. He began by condemning the naval authorities, who he said, 'despised the improvements offered to them.... It is to be hoped that the eyes of the Lords of Admiralty will be open.' But he then continued, 'The time is not far distant when the voice of the people will be paramount in this country, and that the improvements in the administration of their affairs will depend on other persons, than that of the sovereign, or a junta of men, who preside over the most important branch of the public service....'[24]

A somewhat similar letter was sent to the Prince by an English gentleman who had been a passenger on his return voyage in the *Prince George*, when he had entertained and shocked the wardroom officers with his wit and radical opinions. It arrived with a covering note saying that the letter would be 'more essential value to you than the most splendid jewel in your father's crown'. He continued, 'our very opposite relations in life, it is probable, will never bring us into social communion again' but he was writing in response to 'the kindness and urbanity I have received from your Royal Highness, during our passage home'.

The letter itself began, 'You are about to return to your father's Court, and Courts have always been remarkable for frivolity. I advise you in the first place never to repose the smallest degree of confidence in any man there who professes himself your friend.... Believe no man there a sincere friend to you and do you take care to be a sincere friend to no man ... I would have you every morning, before you go to the Levée, or even that you are to be introduced to your father, which I understand to be the etiquette of the Court to which you belong, to practice in making up your face for the day at your looking-glass in your private apartment, that it may be ready to assume any part in the farce....

'If you attach yourself exclusively to the manners of a Court, your dignity as a human being is sacrificed; on this subject your Royal Highness may take your lesson from the history of France.' After a long, cynical and amusing account of the absurdities of behaviour in royal circles, he continued boldly, 'When you have found out your father's favourite, you have then your cue, remember to keep to the safe side of the vessel; it is only the lubber who goes to windward when he is sick.... If your father's favourite is a downright fool, do not scruple to flatter him.... Consult your own interest in everything, pay more court to enemies than friends ... and you will become one of the most finished courtiers of the times.'[26]

To present such subversive, almost treasonable, sentiments to the third in succession to the throne, even when wrapped in pleasantries, might seem daring in the extreme but such opinions were widespread among educated, liberal Englishmen, particularly those supporting the Whig faction in Parliament, which had opposed the attempted suppression of the American rebels.

This was all the more curious because in most wardrooms naval officers were not supposed to discuss party politics any more than 'speak lightly' of ladies by name. Indeed one the few instructions that Admiral Digby had given Captain Napier, when he was about to attend the Prince, was on this point. 'There is another thing I think very essential for Prince William to attend to,' he had written, 'I mean the keeping clear of all party. He should be belov'd by every party and, with a very little prudence, may. I would wish him always to avoid party conversation and not seem to leap to one side more than the other.'[26]

But when William returned to London, he was to hear loud echoes of such dangerous political talk. He had travelled from Portsmouth to Windsor Castle to be told that his parents were at St James's Palace in London. As soon as they heard of his arrival, a court official was deputed to make an appointment for them to receive their son. His elder brothers were less formal and both George and Frederick gave him an immediate and hearty welcome. The boisterousness of his response surprised them for they had grown into relatively suave and sophisticated young men. Seeing the Duke of York wearing a yellow coat, William was said to have guffawed and said, 'I was not aware that St James's Palace was like Greenwich Hospital.'

'Nor was I,' replied his brother.

'You are,' continued William, 'a decided proof that a great resemblance does exist, but I suppose you have been guilty of drunkenness and they have punished you accordingly.'

'Drunkenness! What do you mean? Explain yourself.'

'Why, do they not punish a pensioner at Greenwich Hospital for drunkenness by obliging him to wear a yellow coat, and he is then known by the name of a 'yellow admiral'? I have been under the command of an admiral of the blue, the red and the white* and now, if you please, I will sail under the command of a yellow admiral into the presence chamber of the King.'[27]

The two royal dukes took particular pleasure in attending their young brother on his formal reunion with their parents in order to demonstrate their unity. For while William had been abroad a rift had opened between them and their father. The reproofs that had been directed at William were nothing to those suffered by the Prince of Wales. Extravagance and fast living had earned him a reputation far outweighing that for his cultivated tastes and his personal charm, and he was deeply in debt. Prince Frederick was a gambler and he shared his elder brother's passion for drink, rich food and loose women. Worse, both had taken up with Whig politicians – the hard-living, intelligent and amusing bohemians who surrounded their leader, Charles James Fox – whose opinions outraged the King. Opposing the Tories, whom the King favoured, and their robust support of British pre-eminence in world trade, the Whig faction had combined many of the aristocratic landowners with the more liberal intellectuals in opposition to the war in America; indeed the colours of their party were the buff and blue of George Washington's rebel volunteers. It was intolerable to the King that his heirs should oppose his government.

This range of conflict had developed into alienation and now, it seemed, young William was on his brothers' side. To them he might be a rough sailor but he was amusing and an entertaining talking-point for their friends and courtiers. Rough though his jokes and swearing might sometimes be, he had charm. A witness of this was Horace Walpole, the literary dilettante and wit, who met him while visiting the King's sister, Princess Amelia, at her summer home, Gunnersbury Park in Middlesex, outside London. 'She presented me to him,' recalled Walpole, 'and I attempted, at the risk of tumbling on my nose, to kiss his hand, but he would not let me. You may trust me ... who

---

* Flag officers of the Royal Navy were allocated to the command of the red, white or blue squadrons, in that order of seniority.

am not apt to be intoxicated with royalty, that he is charming. Lively, cheerful, talkative, manly, well-bred, sensible and exceedingly proper in all his replies. You may judge how good-humoured he is when I tell you that he was in great spirits all day, though with us old women — perhaps he thought it preferable to Windsor!'[28]

On their meeting, the King told William that at the end of July he would be going to Hanover to learn languages, undergo military training and acquire polish. He would be accompanied by his old tutor, General Budé, and Captain William Merrick, an affable officer who had been one of those attending him in the frigate *Fortunée* on his visit to Havana. He invited another naval friend to visit him before he left: Captain Nelson. When the *Albemarle* had been paid off at Portsmouth early in July, her captain came to London, where, on the eleventh, Lord Hood took him to St James's Palace and presented him to the King, whom he found 'exceedingly attentive'.[29] Then came the invitation to Windsor Castle to bid farewell to Prince William, who urged him to follow his example and travel on the Continent to learn another language.

The Prince did not, however, look forward to the interruption in the career he was enjoying so much but he had no choice in the matter. On the thirty-first of the month, he left Greenwich, where the royal yacht *Augusta* waited to take him to Germany. Before embarking, he was entertained by the governor, Admiral Palliser, who had quarrelled so publicly with his superior, Admiral Keppel, during the Prince's first spell at sea. He was shown the Painted Hall and admired its murals but, when conducted round the pensioners' wards, criticised the system of housing some in comfortable 'show-wards', which were shown to visitors, whereas most lived in bleak dormitories, which outsiders never saw.

He remembered his shipmate in the *Prince George*, John Adams — 'the old commodore' — for whom he had found a place as a pensioner. The old man was delighted. 'Well, my Royal William!' he is reported to have declared, 'I am comfortably brought up at last and thanks to you for it. You promised me when you visited me in my berth after the action with the lubberly Dons that you would find a berth for me for life and I am now here safely moored. Thanks to you, my Royal William.'

The Prince was told that there were a dozen other pensioners who had fought in Rodney's action and he gave the governor thirteen guineas to distribute among them. 'I'll drink your health this very night, my Royal William!'[30] promised Adams and next morning duly appeared dressed as a 'yellow admiral'.

After dining with Admiral Palliser, the Prince boarded the *Augusta* and sailed immediately. Calling at Tilbury, he found that the commander of the fort was in bed. Not recognising the visitor, the sergeant of the guard remarked that 'bed is as good a place as he can be in, and so it is for everyone who has nothing to do'.

'Then present him with the compliments of Prince William Henry,' said the visitor, 'and tell him that he is now on his way to Germany and that he hopes on his return he shall not only find him *up* but also in a place where he has something to do.'[31]

With that, the Prince returned to the *Augusta* and sailed for the estuary, the North Sea and a stormy passage, which, anxious as he was to demonstrate his aptitude for seafaring, was much to his liking.

5

This Unallowable Passion

Prince William hated Hanover. His father's plan for the completion of his education was condemned to failure by his choice of companions for the volatile young man on the eve of his eighteenth birthday. To put him again under the direction of General Budé, the tutor of his early boyhood, was retrogressive, seemingly a return to the schoolroom. To give him the affable Captain Merrick only as companion and occasional aide-de-camp removed all the inhibitions of naval discipline.

However, his unhappiness was not immediately apparent because a busy programme had been arranged. On arrival at Hanover, he was greeted by his brother Frederick, who was obviously enjoying himself, working at his studies, hunting, gambling and finding himself at ease with the Germans. The brothers set out on a visit to Berlin and the nearby military town of Potsdam, William travelling under the name of 'Lord Fielding' and his brother, already something of a linguist, as 'Count Hoya'. On arrival they were presented to the elderly Emperor Frederick, who took them to watch military manoeuvres and reproved William for not having read *Candide*.

They continued their military training at Luneburg that winter and were promised a visit to Prague in the following year to attend the spectacular Imperial Review. But for most of their time they were to stay in Hanover studying and attending social functions. Each morning they were woken at eight and, after breakfast, they inspected the cream-coloured stallions at the stud and watched the drilling of Hanoverian soldiers. At dinner William found the Germans, whom he called 'The *Vons*', boring as there was no tradition of conviviality and conversation at the dinner-table.

Permissible entertainment in the evenings included the theatre and opera and even smoking and playing skittles in taverns. There were also gambling, heavy drinking sessions and prostitutes but any of that meant eluding the stern, sharp eye of General Budé. The old tutor was no fool, nor was he entirely humourless, and there were moments of fellowship. The two princes had nicknamed him 'Et cetera' because it was a term he constantly used. Once, on a visit to Heidelberg, William read out the bill of fare at a café: 'Punch, Rum, Curaçoa, Petit-lait d'Henry Quatre, Orgéat, Glaces, Sorbets, Marasquins de Zara, Nectar, Café, Riz, Kirche, Absinthe, *et cetera*', and said to Budé, 'There is an article in this bill of fare that I know is particularly agreeable to your taste.' The old man asked him to order whatever he thought he would enjoy, although he would prefer it not to be a 'made dish'.

'It is one, I own,' replied the Prince, 'that I never met with before, but perhaps you will glance at the bill and see if you give preference to any other. The article I have selected for you is the last one mentioned.'

The general wiped his spectacles, read the card and exclaimed, 'Why, your Royal Highness surely does not mean that I am to order *et cetera* for my supper?'

'Certainly I do. It is a kind of standing dish with you and as Heidelberg is celebrated for its wine it may perhaps be equally so for its *et cetera*.'[1]

Budé laughed and the ordering of *et cetera* became a standing joke. But such good humour between them was rare. After a few months of mutual tolerance, William confided in a letter to the Prince of Wales, 'You may remember I told you when I set off for Germany that it was likely Budé and myself should fall out, as he never has enjoyed my confidence. The affair has happened and we are now on such terms that must be very disagreeable to both of us. He has acted, or rather wished to act, in the same style as he did formerly. He was displeased if I went out alone. However I soon cut him short and have done exactly as I like best, and in measures where I want advice I have always taken Merrick's.'[2]

From William's point of view, Captain Merrick was a splendid companion, a man after his own heart, who enjoyed drinking, gambling and the opposite sex. He had demonstrated practical loyalty when the Prince, following his brother's example, had begun to gamble for large sums. But he had made the mistake of playing with a skilled and dangerous gambler, a Baron Hardenberg, a survivor of many gambling scandals, who specialised in luring rich innocents into play. True to form, Hardenberg allowed the Prince to win a large sum in order to entice him into raising the stakes. Noticing this, Merrick advised William to withdraw and he did so to the rage of his opponent, who thereupon insulted him and a challenge to duel ensued. Forbidding Merrick to fight on his behalf, the Prince found a British captain of the Guards, who was visiting Hanover, to act as his second and arrange a time and a place to meet with pistols. Happily, General Budé came to the rescue with his worldly *savoir-faire*, threatened Hardenberg with the exposure of his part in a past scandal in Berlin and induced him to apologise for his insult.

General Budé had his uses but, for the most part, he was a hindrance to his charge's chosen pastimes. Without the constant activity of a ship to occupy him, boredom coarsened William's tastes. His brother Frederick was happy with gambling and hunting wild boar, so it was in his elder brother George, Prince of Wales, that he chose to confide. Apologising for not having written more often, he asked, 'I did not like to do it, for what should I say? My amours, perhaps, with a lady of the town against a dead wall or in the middle of the parade, higher I have not as yet arrived. This can be no amusement to a young man in the real pleasures of London, nor can my private disputes with Budé amuse you. In short, Hanover is a dull place and very much given to scandal.'[3]

He knew that, soon after he had left London, George had moved into Carlton House, the mansion the King had given him in Pall Mall, overlooking its own gardens and St James's Park. There, he had heard, his brother was setting new standards in living fast and loose amid surroundings of unsurpassed splendour. But even the lesser satisfactions of London would have suited William in his present frustrations. 'Oh! I wish I was returned,' he wrote, 'England, England for ever and the pretty girls of Westminster; at least, to such as would not clap or pox me every time I f***ed.'[4]

But the consequences to William of encounters with prostitutes were less of a worry to General Budé than his affairs of the heart. As usual, he was falling passionately but romantically in love. Among the objects of his devotion were his mother's fourteen-year-old niece, Princess Charlotte of Mecklenburg-Strelitz; Maria Schindbach, the daughter of a prosperous merchant; and Caroline von Linsingen, the daughter of a Hanoverian general, who was to claim that they had been secretly married and who may have become pregnant by him. All such entanglements were reported to the King in greater or lesser detail and the only one to arouse agitation was the first, which brought a long but sensible letter from Queen Charlotte. 'Your attachment to my niece,' she told him, 'which you call *imprudent* in your own letter, does not for the moment surprize me, as you are of an age when young men are apt to fancy themselves in love with every sprightly young woman they see....' She said that as there was 'not the least probability of its ever terminating in anything else but flurtation (sic)', it was important that William should try to 'conquer this unallowable passion'[5] and never to declare his love to the girl herself.

Love and lust helped to pass the time but, soon after his arrival, the Prince had determined that his stay should be cut as short as possible and that he would try to return to the Navy. He knew that his father would never consider a change of plan – particularly as he was preoccupied with a political crisis at home, brought about by the fall of the government at the end of the war in America – and that the most hopeful course was to enlist the support of Admiral Hood. He was now in England and, it was reported, would be standing for Parliament in the general election, which was to be held in the early spring of 1784. He remained the King's favourite admiral and might be persuaded to tell him that, despite the peace, William was needed back at sea.

As he was leaving for Hanover, he had written to Hood, saying how much he hoped to continue his naval career but, realising it was too soon to ask for his release, did not ask for any intercession with the King. The admiral had replied with a verbose and flattering letter of seven pages, buried in which was the advice that the prince should be careful in his use of mockery.

'Not only the actions but every word of a Prince are noticed and remarked on,' he wrote, 'I am therefore led to express my most sincere wish that you will ever, Sir, be tender of an absent person and never turn anyone present into ridicule. We all have our little foibles, and, though they do not correspond with the polite, well-bred man, yet may be perfectly innocent and harmless, but no one likes to be held up as a Butt, and made a jest of, for the amusement of others.' He then immediately softened the gentle reproach by saying that he planned to send him a 'Mulatto cook and a very good turtle with him'[6] and a copy of the latest Navy list.

Soon afterwards, William wrote to ask Hood if he would intercede with the King, suggesting his return to the Navy. With profuse apologies, the admiral refused on the grounds that it was not for him to advise his sovereign on private matters. He then launched into another homily: 'Steadiness is a great and laudable characteristic in a Prince and whenever a regular system is laid down for his education it should be cheerfully submitted to rather than be departed from.'

But Hood was anxious to continue the correspondence and tried to entertain him with an account of a dinner at which he had been guest of honour at the Ironmongers' Hall in London. The tables had been decorated 'with Britannia and Neptune in their cars and the *Barfleur* and *Ville de Paris*, full rigged, both had all their sails bent, those of the former were full and swelling, as if in chace, standing after the latter, whose sails appeared becalmed. Each had the exact number of guns she carried, with men upon her decks, in the shrouds and upon the topgallant yards in the act of furling the sails. They were allowed to be as perfect and complete models as ever were seen and Your Royal Highness will be surprized when I tell you that every part was eatable, being made of almond paste. Where the long table joined to the other was fixed a Triumphal Arch with very curious and emblematic devices and, in the centre, my Arms were hung.'[7]

The letters from the King were very different in tone and content. Acutely conscious that the behaviour of his two sons in Hanover was being watched by his relations and the other German royal families, he insisted on being kept closely informed. Gratified that Prince Frederick was giving his younger brother 'an excellent example', he worried about William's wilful and contrary attitude and was determined that it should be reformed. The spate of reproving letters which had followed him across the Atlantic now continued across the North Sea, accusing him of 'persisting in doing what you knew would displease me and then thinking to get off like a child by saying you will not do the like again'.[8] Soon afterwards he was comparing William with his brother: 'His civility and propriety are remarked by all ... but I am sorry to say your manners are still compared to the frequenters of the forecastle,' and he again noted his son's 'love of improper company'.[9]

In reply, William held up a shield of polite, sometimes obsequious, blandishments such as: 'Promises I will not make, as your Majesty hints that my parents are not deceived by such things. Believe me, Sir, my intention was not to blind the eyes of my best friends, as I hope I may call my parents, for I well know that people of your Majesty's good sense were not to be deceived in that way.'[10]

Receiving little sympathy from his brother Frederick and none from his parents, William increasingly turned to his brother George, who was even more out of favour with the King than himself. Summarising his position, he concluded one letter, 'Being thus situated with Budé, and not being pleased with the phlegmatick way of the Germans, I wished to return, not to stay in London but to do my duty at sea. I accordingly wrote to Lord Hood and expressed my desire of his mentioning the matter to the King. His Lordship declined, as it would be a dangerous subject to speak to his Majesty. Somehow or other it got to the royal ears and I was informed my father did not approve of my coming home, nor of the tricks I have plaid here, though God knows I have not plaid many.'[11]

Soon after he told him of the next move: 'Yesterday morning I received a set down from the two persons that were concerned in begetting me. The female was more severe than the male ... I have not done anything I know to merit such a rebuke.'[12]

So it continued, with the King and Queen writing rolling barrages of reproving prose, the former even threatening to put a final end to his son's career in the Navy; William abjectly apologising and begging to be allowed to return to sea but confiding cheekily to the Prince of Wales and continuing to enjoy himself in the company of raffish English visitors to Hanover and any loose women he could find. He travelled in the spring, summer and autumn of 1784, visiting German principalities, Prussia, Silesia, Vienna, Switzerland and northern Italy before returning through Austria; in Berlin he is said to have been dismayed by the poverty he saw in slums such as he had never been shown in London. The winter offered more opportunities for the forbidden indoor activities and, since his allowance of pocket money from his father was said to be only £10 a year and he continued to gamble, he was also deeply in debt.

Prince Frederick, basking in parental approval and thoroughly at home in Hanover, was beginning to find his brother's escapades and excuses a nuisance, and on 1 April 1785 finally took up his cause with their father, if only to get William out of the way. So he wrote: 'But pardon me, Sir, if I add that there can never be any real alteration for the better in him till he has been kept for some time under severe discipline, which alone can be done on board ship, for his natural inclination for all kinds of dissipation will make him, either here or indeed in any place by land, run into any society where he can form to himself only an idea of pleasure.'[13]

As for William himself, he had on the same day written yet another letter of apology and explanation to his father, pleading, 'I was most extremely hurt by the last letter your Majesty thought proper to write to me. It gave me very great uneasiness to find my conduct had been so highly displeasing to my father.' Now, he continued, he was 'under the double misfortune of being on bad terms with my father and of being prevented from serving my Sovereign. I know of no method to avoid this fatal blow than by beseeching your Majesty to change my situation and recall me from Hanover....'[14]

On 6 May, the King replied, beginning in the familiar style of the angry god: 'I had hoped reflection must by this time have convinced you of the impropriety of your conduct ... but as you plainly shew sorrow at having displeased your parents, I am willing to flatter myself your future conduct will deserve approbation. I have therefore resolved that the *Augusta* yacht, which conveys Edward* on the 20th to Stade shall reconduct you, when you shall immediately pass the strict examination to become a Lieutenant and then be sent to sea; but that there may be no impropriety in your conduct whilst here, I intend you and Major-Gen. Budé shall, if I am at Windsor, come instantly there and, when I am in town, you shall be at the Queen's House, not St James's ... and that you will remember you are now to shew yourself the Prince, the gentleman, the Officer and not merely the sailor. Get command of yourself and then you can be of use to your profession; without it, your being brought forward would be a detriment to the Service. You will now be a Lieutenant but the next rise must depend on your future conduct not only on float but ashore.'[15]

Prince William hastened to reply, 'I was most agreeably surprised by the receipt of Your Majesty's orders to recall me to duty. I hope and trust that my being placed in an active situation of life will entirely

---

* Edward, Duke of Kent, the King's fourth son and fifth child.

alter my disposition and make my behaviour in all respects correspond with the intentions of my parents.'[16] His two years of exile had
not been entirely wasted for he could now speak some German and
French, he had met a variety of Continental royalty and he was more
experienced in human activities, military and diplomatic as well as
those of the tavern and brothel.

A few days later he sailed for England, and on the evening of 10
June arrived at Buckingham House, which was also known as the
Queen's House as it was his mother's residence in London. When
news of his arrival reached Carlton House, the Prince of Wales, who
was that night host at a magnificent fête in his new house and garden,
hurried along The Mall to welcome his brother and insist that he return
with him to the party. William had not yet seen the extravagances of
Carlton House, but the King forbade it, telling his eldest son it was
reported – 'Eh! What! Take William away? Take William away? He
shan't go, he shan't go! Just arrived from Hanover. Want to know how
things are going on there – fine stud, fine stud. Shan't go. Better with
his mother tonight.'[17]

A week later, the full Board of Admiralty assembled for Prince William's examination, instead of the usual panel of three captains. His
qualifications for a lieutenant's commission were in order, although he
had spent two of the obligatory six years' service on the Continent.
He was aged nineteen, as was necessary, and he could produce his
midshipman's journals and certificates of competence. Presiding over
the Board was the First Lord of the Admiralty, the formidable Admiral
Lord Howe, known as 'Black Dick' because of his saturnine face and
heavy, dark eyebrows. Yet all went smoothly and Howe later told the
King that his son was 'every inch a sailor'.[18]

Granted his commission, which all agreed he deserved, he was
appointed forthwith to be third lieutenant of the *Hebe*, a frigate of
thirty-eight guns, commanded by Captain Edward Thornborough and
currently engaged in operations against smugglers in British coastal
waters. Before leaving for Portsmouth, where his ship was lying,

he had time to attend the King's levée, which was being held at St James's Palace that day. He was dressed in his new lieutenant's uniform, was formally presented to his father by the Lords Commissioners of the Admiralty, and kissed his hand.

Next morning he attended a celebration breakfast given by the Prince of Wales at Carlton House and then travelled to Windsor for the night, before leaving for Portsmouth in Lord Howe's carriage. On board the *Hebe*, he was greeted by Captain Thornborough, one of the few captains to have risen from the ranks and known as a brilliant seaman, although semi-literate. He was told that the frigate was to sail at once for the Orkneys to join a light squadron, commanded by Commodore Leveson-Gower, engaged in survey work as well as chasing foreign fishing-boats out of British waters. He was delighted with his new ship, writing to his father, 'I have every reason to think the *Hebe* is the finest frigate in your Majesty's Service: she is an excellent seaboat in a gale of wind and can turn off from a lee shore vastly well ... I think her a very handsome ship ... she has tremendous masts and yards. I only wish she was better and stronger manned: our people are by no means seamen and there are few as tall or as stout as I am.... Her complement is not enough: instead of 250, she ought to have 300 men.'[19]

They sailed for Scotland at once, calling at Great Yarmouth and Hull. It was the first time William had seen his own country, other than the environs of the royal residences, the Portsmouth road and the naval ports, and he enjoyed himself. Off Yarmouth, he endeared himself to a boat's crew, whom, when pulling hard on the oars against a strong head sea, he encouraged by promising them that, once on board again, they would 'splice the mainbrace' and be given 'a little of the best of anything your Nibcheese has in his stores',[20] meaning that they would be issued with an extra tot of rum and some titbits from the purser's stores.

While ashore at Hull, the Prince was thrown from a horse he had hired and was taken unconscious to a nearby cottage by the officers who had been riding with him. As he lay prone and pale, with his long, fair hair untied, his companions told the old woman, who was trying to minister to him, that he was a young lady fleeing to Scotland in disguise with her lover and teased him about this when he recovered consciousness.

In one respect he was frustrated. As he wrote to his brother George of his jaunt to Yarmouth, 'I was on shore there but once and had no opportunity of getting hold of a girl: my next excursion was in Yorkshire, where I was going on horseback from Burlington [Bridlington] Bay to Hull and intended to lay two in a bed that night.'[21] But it was then that he had been thrown and lay in bed alone and unconscious.

On 5 July, the frigate anchored off Kirkwall, where he met Commodore Gower and was accorded a civic welcome as the first member of the royal family to visit the Orkneys. Ashore he was approached by an old shipmate from the *Prince George*, Lieutenant Moodie of the Royal Marines, whom he had once come close to fighting with his fists. He was finding it hard to live on his half-pay allowance, so the Prince promised to give him an annuity of £40 until he found suitable work and that he would help him to do so.

William was delighted when the commodore treated him like an adult, writing to George, 'I like Gower very much: he is a pleasant man and behaves towards me with the greatest politeness. He is no Digby: he lets me go on shore when and with whom I please ... I will let you know of the pilgrim's progress....'[22] As he got to know Gower better, he discovered he had a quick, hot temper and told his father in a letter: 'He is a most attentive and rigid officer, but unfortunately is passionate at times: however it is immediately over. I find myself very happy in my situation on board.'[23]

The *Hebe* was engaged in a little surveying, taking soundings in channels and anchorages, then cruised to Fair Isle and anchored off Stornaway on Lewis. He shot wildfowl, although he did not particularly enjoy shooting, and received loyal deputations from the local clans. His newly-acquired self-confidence gave him an awareness of his surroundings and an enthusiasm to expand his interests beyond his profession and his appetites. So he wrote a long and discursive letter to the King about his voyage and his experiences ashore.

Of the Orkneys, he wrote, 'Everything is miserable there beyond description; the common people go without shoes and stockings; what is remarkable is they speak nothing but English and that with less of a Scotch accent than they do more to the southward. We... then proceeded thro' the Pentland Firth to the Hebrides ... I think the inhabitants here are in a more miserable state than the negroes in the West Indies.... They do not talk English; it is not even understood here: they will talk Erse and wear the Highland dress.'

The ship had begun her return voyage down the west coast of Scotland and, continued William, 'The Highlands are prodigious mountains, more exalted as you approach to the southward: a Highland Chieftan came on board with a boy piper playing in the boat.'[24] After lying off Campbeltown but unable to land because of rough seas, they crossed to the coast of Ireland and anchored in Carrickfergus Bay. Loyal Ulstermen had gathered from Belfast to greet the Prince, but it was decided that he had carried out enough royal duties and must now be regarded as no more than a naval officer and keep his watch on board. So the ship ran down the Irish Sea to Milford Haven on the coast of Wales, arriving on 5 August.

The *Hebe* remained in the great Pembrokeshire harbour for a fortnight, carrying out another survey. There were entertainments ashore for her officers, with a dance at the ballroom in Haverfordwest and visits to the country seats of the gentry. Then the frigate sailed for Falmouth, where the Prince went ashore to be shown the Cornish tin mines, was served with steak cooked on tin skillets and told that revenue from the industry accrued to the Prince of Wales. At this he joked, 'This tin money will be very acceptable to my brother George.'[25]

Finally on 5 September, the frigate returned to Spithead and her captain was told that she was to be based at Portsmouth, where his royal lieutenant would be given the training in ship-handling which would qualify him for his next promotion to the rank of captain.

William was delighted with his new life and confident that he was at last finding favour with his parents. But such hopes were dashed by a letter from his mother, written early in August in reply to a jolly one he had written. He had made some flippant remarks about people he had met and she had taken this very seriously indeed.

'I am very happy to find by both your letters that you are perfectly well and so much amused,' she wrote, 'but cannot help saying how sorry I am that you continue still to harbour such unaccountable dislikes to those about you. Your reasons for liking and disliking are in general so trifling and frivolous that the best judgement one could form upon them would be that of youthful volubility, but when one knows you to be twenty years of age this very month, this excuse can no longer be made and severer judgements must arise, which can be no less than the want of a *good heart*, want of *understanding, ambition, vanity, wilfulness* and an uncommon share of caprice, which imperceptibly will lead you to be what you will be ashamed to hear, *a true trifling character*, which is the most despicable thing in the world....' So she continued for pages and ended by urging him that it would be better to 'have recourse to Budé's advice and follow it than to be directed by your own little nonsensical, volatile head'.[26]

It was a cold, cruel letter that would have undermined his new self-confidence had not he found new friends and a new and unexpected purpose in life. Once again he was expected to use the Commissioner's House in the dockyard as his base ashore and this was still occupied by Commissioner Martin, who had been kind to him when he had stayed there with General Budé five years before. Again he was made welcome and wrote to the Prince of Wales, 'I prefer the Portsmouth station on many accounts. My present situation is as happy a one as I could wish. Whenever the ship is in port I am on shore at the Martins' in the Dock Yard. I am treated as if I was one of the family: he has two daughters about my own age: we dance and amuse ourselves vastly well.'[27]

It was the first time William had known a family which did not rely upon inheritance for its comfort and standing; which was not constantly watching its manners in relation to royal favours, but was confident, cultivated and content. Commissioner Martin was a retired captain and his twelve-year-old son Byam, with whom the Prince had fought at their first meeting, was to follow suit and was now attending the Naval Academy at Portsmouth.

The Commissioner's daughters were William's contemporaries and he fell in love with one of them, Sarah. She was the opposite of the cosseted young ladies – or diseased whores – who had occupied him in Hanover. She was, as her brother Byam was to describe her, 'handsome, exceedingly attractive and interesting in her manners with an excellent understanding and a well-cultivated mind'.[28]

As an individual, Sarah Martin was as suitable a match as the Prince was ever likely to find, but the strictures of the Royal Marriage Act meant that she could not be considered as such until he was aged twenty-five and, even then, it would be a long and difficult procedure. The girl was aware of this but, more importantly, she was not in love with her ardent suitor although flattered by his attention. As for the Prince, he was determined that neither her father, nor his, should have any doubts as to the honour of his intentions. Doomed as the attachment was, the fair, ruddy-cheeked Prince and the handsome, intelligent girl were much admired when they danced a minuet together – 'abounding in bows and curtseys, full of grace'[29] – at a ball in Portsmouth.

The *Hebe* was putting to sea for short cruises when Lieutenant His Royal Highness Prince William Henry would be allowed to take command under the sharp eyes of Captain Thornborough and Commodore Gower. Once, when a storm delayed their return and the frigate had to shelter in the Solent off Cowes, William wrote a letter to Commissioner Martin, although almost within sight of his house:

'Since last Sunday we have not been at a great distance from each other, owing to the badness of the weather.... During my watches I frequently cast a longing look towards my worthy friends in the dock-yard. I hope you will believe me when I assure you I am not here with my consent but would much rather be under your hospitable roof. I look forward with pleasure to the time when we shall next meet and, still more so, when I shall command a guardship and then be able to devote more of my time to you.'[30]

His hope was that he could be given command of one of the guardships which lay at their moorings in the naval ports, ostensibly on guard and, of course, his would have to be at Portsmouth. Before falling in love, he had written to his father asking for the command of the fine frigate *Phaeton*, where he had heard there was a vacancy. But his father had replied sternly that a new captain had already been chosen for her and that, in any case, 'I should not have approved of your being so soon a Captain.... It is highly important you should be perfect in every branch of the Service.... It is by the regularity in your conduct as an Officer of the ship and a propriety of behaviour at all times that I can hereafter advance you to the rank of Captain; the object is to fit you for commanding fleets....'[31]

Another form of advancement was increasingly on his mind. His brother Frederick had been created Duke of York on reaching the age of twenty-one and given a greatly increased allowance and his own household. As he wrote obliquely to the Prince of Wales in November, 'I believe it cannot now be long before something must happen as I am of age next August. The King will in the course of the winter deter-mine in what situation I am to be after that period. I would wish to be employed until I was four or five and twenty years of age; in short, till my wildness was a little gone off.'[32]

Sometimes he even thought of abandoning his career and trying to shake off his royal chains. 'Was I to resign my commission, where could I live?' he asked George in a letter. 'You are as much distressed as I am; and what is to become of a young man of one and twenty years old, who has neither a profession nor money? A pretty situation indeed; add to all this a King's son. What shall I do? I have a letter prepared to Lord Howe with my resignation.'[33]

In desperation, he rushed to Windsor and poured out his unhappiness to his parents. On this occasion, the Queen was more sympathetic than the King, who found the sudden visit 'very unpleasant and unexpected'[34] and took immediate action, ordering his son to rejoin his ship, which was then to leave Portsmouth for Plymouth. As for the future, Prince William would return to American waters to keep him out of further harm's way.

In vain he pleaded against this decision, even telling his mother that another exposure to the immoral ways of the Americans would finally ruin his character. 'You suspect the American manners to be very vicious,' she wrote to him in another torrent of reproof, 'Alas, where is not vice to be found? I am so little acquainted with it in general that I cannot enter much upon that subject....

'You was at entering the Service as much Prince William and the King's son as you are now and, did you really set that value upon your person that proceeds from judgement, you would have shewn proper submission to your superiors and condescension to inferiors; but not familiarized yourself with the latter.... Upon your conscience, tell me you are not even now, and were then, your own enemy? One comfort there is left, which I recommend strongly to you and that is, *it is never too late to improve.*'[35]

In February, he had to say goodbye to Sarah Martin. 'I arrived at Martin's house at ten in the morning,' he wrote to George, 'Immediately after breakfast I retired with the girl and her mother. Everything that happened during my absence proves her affection for me. Neither of us could speak when I look leave of her.'[36]

While the *Hebe* still lay at Spithead he wrote a letter to her father and sent it ashore. The Commissioner replied gratefully, 'With a heart devoted to you, I trust you will do me the justice to believe that I feel most sensibly the noble and honourable part you have acted by me and my dear child: could I have foreseen the attachment you have been pleased to honour her with, I should certainly have removed her for a time from my house, that both your Royal Highnesses and she might have avoided the difficulties and distresses, which must necessarily be the consequences of it.

'She is, thank God, tolerably well; but blessed, Sir, as she is, with a superior understanding, she has with becoming fortitude guarded against the too tender impression a declaration so unexpected, and so much superior to what she could ever presume to raised her thoughts to, might otherwise have made, and which, had your Royal Highness's station in life been more at a level with hers, she would naturally have felt, where every gratification of mind and person conspire to captivate the heart…. It will afford us infinite consolation to be assured that the noble efforts you are making to subdue a passion that in the pursuit would have been attended with consequences fatal to your repose, as well as that of the object of your affection, from the impossibility that it could ever meet with the sanction of your Royal parents, are attended with success.'[37]

So the *Hebe* sailed from Portsmouth and Sarah Martin was taken to London for a change of scene. Unwisely, perhaps, William wrote a letter of introduction to his brother George: 'The worthy family are in town: do see them; speak kindly to them, consider my dearest S. is a shy girl: do not be surprised if she is at first reserved. Remember who loved her, who does still with all his heart.'[38] Yet Sarah Martin was unlikely to appeal to the Prince of Wales, whose taste ran to older, married women in smart society.

The family did not meet the Prince of Wales, but while in London did receive a message from the King and Queen that 'their Majesties … expressed the fullest satisfaction of the conduct of your family and lamented that any branch of theirs should have been the cause of disturbing for a moment its peace. They were delighted with … Miss S. Martin's proper behaviour and in justice to Prince William … they are in very good humour with him.'[39]

Although it was no longer acceptable for William to write to Sarah, he constantly wrote to her father, including such passages as, 'My heart bleeds for my poor unfortunate Sarah, whom God bless and give strength of mind to support this misfortune ... I must once more repeat – Dear Sarah! I feel for her more than I can express; she is an unfortunate and virtuous girl'[40] and, 'Few girls, after the declaration I made to her, would have behaved in the manner she has done. I both love and respect her. I find absence has increased my passion.'[41]

Steering westward, the frigate was so buffeted by a gale that she had to run for shelter in the lee of Guernsey. The governor of the island invited the Prince to dine and he reported, 'Few got up sober, for we were at the table and bottle seven hours and a half. I am sur- prized I was not drunk.' But he had recovered his old instincts enough to report to George, 'As for their women, I had not time to see any of them. I am told they are pretty.'

As they sailed towards Plymouth, he again had time to brood and became convinced that Lord Howe, as well as his father, was trying to ruin his career by sending him to America now that there was no war there. 'I am really unhappy,' he wrote again to his brother, 'Everything goes against me. I have been obliged to leave the girl I adore; my father will not allow me to live with the brother I am in intimate friend- ship with and he does not even shew me common justice. Frederick, who is only two years older than I am, has a Regiment of Guards and is a Lieutenant-General; besides this he has been allowed £5,000 ever since he has been in Germany....

'I see there is a storm brewing over my head which must soon burst. S. is all I regret; taking leave of her was a cruel thing; perhaps for ever. I may never see her again....

'Why then should I be banished to America? Let me at least choose my station, now it is peace. This however is a plan of Black Dick's.'[42]

For a month he languished at Plymouth without orders to move to another ship for passage to America, or any communication from

---

* Sarah Martin died in 1826, unmarried, at Loughton in Essex.

his parents, and his funds were running low. Then, just as his despair seemed to demand some desperate remedy, all was transformed. The King and Queen had been considering his prospects and had, at last, decided that some encouragement might prove effective. The First Lord of the Admiralty urged that he should work his way from third to first lieutenant and then spend some time as a ship's executive officer before being promoted to captain. But the King reversed his own opinion, over-ruled Lord Howe and decided that his son should be given his own command. So not only would he be promoted again after only ten months as a lieutenant and skip the intermediary appointment as commander but he would also miss the probationary rank of captain to become a post-captain on the permanent list. Henceforth his promotion through the higher ranks would – barring incapacity, or some gross breach of discipline – be automatic and subject only to vacancies. His promotion would date from 10 April 1786.

His euphoria was enhanced by the news that he was also to be given his first command forthwith. The ship was to be the *Pegasus*, a small frigate of twenty-eight guns, and he was to cross the Atlantic as her captain. He at once sent his father his 'most hearty and sincere thanks'.[43]

On the fifteenth of the month – a fresh, breezy day with distant haze – he boarded his ship at her moorings in the Hamoaze estuary and took command, entering in his log, 'At 8 a.m. being appointed to the command of His Majesty's Ship *Pegasus* read my commission as Captain to the Ship's Company and Isaac Schomberg's commission as 1st. Lieutenant.'[44] The first duties of the day were to scale the guns of rust and receive barrels of beer and fresh water from a tender.

He set about exploring the ship. Cramped as his and his officers' quarters would be, he was determined to behave as a captain should and show a proper mixture of aloofness and condescension. His father had reminded him of this and he wrote in reply, 'Respecting my conduct toward the officers of the *Pegasus*, I am fully sensible of the necessity of keeping them at a proper distance without pride, and can with truth say they themselves know the propriety of this and will, on their part, adhere to it. They are all of a certain age and behave with great propriety.' He stressed that his own quarters were simple – 'My cabin is the plainest in the service: the chairs are all of wood painted green.'[45] – and that he would keep careful accounts.

Wearing his new captain's blue uniform coat trimmed with gold lace, he held a celebratory levée in Plymouth and when he found that no officer below his own rank had been invited held another for lieutenants and dined with them, announcing, 'A jolly good day, my boys, we will have of it together.'[46] He was presented with the Freedom of the Borough of Plymouth and initiated as a Freemason in a secret ceremony at The George inn. A week after assuming command he made his presence felt in another way, mustering his hundred and fifty officers, ratings and marines in the waist of the ship to witness punishment. The culprit, a seaman named John Russell, received twelve lashes for 'contempt' and was thereupon discharged from the ship.

The Prince made a short visit to London to call at the Admiralty and say farewell to his family. He saw his brother amid the splendours of Carlton House, where he was told that its colossal cost had plunged him ever more deeply in debt, and there were rumours that the pair of them again spent a night roistering in fancy dress at Ranelagh pleasure gardens in Chelsea. Returning to Plymouth, he took his ship for a 'working-up' cruise to the coast of Normandy before the ocean crossing, and on his return he received his final orders.

On 20 May, he wrote to George, 'I am to spend this summer on the Newfoundland station, the winter in the West Indies ... the following summer in Nova Scotia and Canada and then proceed to Jamaica for the next winter and the remainder of the three years is to be spent on the different West Indian stations. I am very much pleased with this mode of my serving abroad till I get steadier....'[47]

Prince William had always been generous and an opportunity for patronage had arisen. Commissioner Martin had taken advantage of his repeated protestations of devotion to the whole family and had asked him to take his son, Byam, aged twelve and a pupil of the Naval Academy, to sea with him as a 'captain's servant', potential midshipman and candidate for a commission. So he was able to write inviting the boy to join his ship at Plymouth.

William's love for Sarah had already faded to a distant glow, for he had met another beautiful girl at Plymouth. So, as the *Pegasus* prepared to sail, there was another tender but less emotional farewell to be made. After he had enjoyed further entertainment ashore at other ports, he was confiding to George in a letter, 'At Plymouth I was fond of a most lovely girl, with whom I constantly danced, and ever since every woman appears insipid. I was more really in love at Portsmouth, but at Plymouth I enjoyed a higher gratification: do not imagine that I debauched the girl: such a thought did not once enter my head: the highest crime under Heaven, next to murder, is that of debauching innocent women; and is a crime I can with a safe conscience declare I have never committed.'[48]

There was another flogging – twelve lashes for 'neglect of duty' – to be ordered on 26 May before the ship was scrubbed and polished for the visit next day of the Duke and Duchess of Buccleuch and their 'two very ugly, red-headed daughters'. As the ducal party came alongside, the frigate was dressed overall with signal flags and her yards manned. To complete the spectacle, young Byam Martin was ordered to stand on the top of the tallest mast. 'I was stuck upon the main topmast cap with a gold-laced hat about as broad as the number of my perpendicular inches, with fine gold tassels hanging over the hat at each end,' he was to recall, 'I made as pretty a letter T as ever ornamented a piece of gingerbread.'[49]

It was the crowning moment of Prince William's ambition. At twenty he was a post-captain in command of his own ship and outward bound.

6

Farewell Discipline

On 3 June 1786, Captain His Royal Highness Prince William balanced his growing reputation as a disciplinarian by arranging for his ship's company to be paid two months' wages in advance. Next day, before they could hope to get ashore and spend it, the *Pegasus* sailed from Plymouth Sound.

In company with another small frigate, the *Rose*, commanded by Captain Henry Harvey, who was senior to Prince William, they set course for Guernsey to load cheap wine and fresh food before beginning the Atlantic passage. The ships arrived off the island on 5 June and the Prince went ashore to the thumping of saluting guns fired from the citadel and the other ships at anchor. Victualling was quickly completed and three days later the two ships sailed for Newfoundland.

During the voyage, which could be expected to take three weeks, William took stock of his ship and her company. They seemed happy enough and proud to be commanded by the King's son. He had been able to choose most, but not all, of his officers and captain's servants and he had resisted applications from those whose principal qualification was aristocratic birth, so that, as Byam Martin noted, 'we had not in the ship one single sprig of nobility'. Another frigate, he had heard, was 'so crowded with the bantlings of the aristocracy that one of the lieutenants of the ship, a rough hand but with some humour, had been reading the King's Speech to Parliament and, presently after, being officer of the watch he was desired to "wear ship" and in doing so he called out to the young noblemen and honourables stationed at the different ropes: "My Lords and gentlemen, shiver the mizzen topsail." [1]

Above all, he was thankful to be putting three thousand miles of sea between himself and General Budé, who had always seemed to be hovering and waiting to pounce like a haughty old eagle whenever he stepped ashore in Europe. Yet he was not quite free of his father's far-seeing eye and restraining hand. His first lieutenant had, he knew, been carefully chosen on the recommendation of Lord Hood and he feared that he might prove to be another Captain Napier, if not a General Budé.

Lieutenant Isaac Schomberg was certainly a 'man of family', albeit an unusual one. He was the nephew of a captain in the Navy and a celebrated physician, and his family had been related to the Duke of Schomberg, a notable soldier of fortune on the Continent, who had married an English-woman and settled in England at the end of the previous century. Twelve years older than the Prince, he had begun his career in the King's yacht *Royal Charlotte*, served in two flagships, seen action on several occasions and commanded a schooner on the Newfoundland station. Nobody doubted his skill as a naval officer but there seemed a tension and an air of self-importance about him that was expressed in his large, wary eyes and tight, thin-lipped mouth. Certainly William suspected that he had been privately ordered to keep an eye on his captain and try to prevent him from making professional mistakes, or social gaffes, while he was determined that Schomberg should remain his executive officer and nothing more.

After a fortnight at sea, the two frigates sailed into the colder, dank air of the north-west Atlantic. One night when Lieutenant William Hope was keeping the middle watch he felt 'a sudden and excessive chill' in the darkness and guessed what it might mean. A year before, his ship had been trapped and squeezed between two icebergs in the north Atlantic and they had been lucky to extricate her and escape. Now again he felt that ominous cold as 'an island of ice of huge dimensions'[2] materialised in the night. Ordering the helm over, Hope called his captain and the officers came tumbling up on deck to watch it glide past. Byam Martin estimated that it was five hundred feet long and three hundred feet high. As they neared the Newfoundland Banks, they entered a blanket of fog and each ship fired a gun every hour to give her approximate position, while sounding depths of forty to fifty fathoms. This had shelved to twenty-three on 25 June, when the fog rolled back and lookouts sighted distant outcrops of land, which were identified as the Bull, Cow and Calf Rocks of Newfoundland. Two days later they anchored among the fishing-boats in Trepassey harbour.

During a week at anchor, fresh food and water were loaded but William did not go ashore and took the opportunity to write to his brother. George was at Brighton in his newly-acquired Marine Pavilion, in what seemed another and increasingly desirable world far from the smell of fish and pinewoods. 'Pleasuring in England as you do, my dear friend, is by far a more preferable life to what a soldier or sailor is obliged to go through,' he told him. 'Since I have been here a most violent rheumatic complaint has prevented my going on shore, but the report of the gentlemen is very infavourable. Such a constant thick fog that there is no seeing a mile, no inhabitants to associate with; all drunken Irish fishermen; the English bathing-places, how elegant they are with the first company in the Kingdom. I hope when I return to have it in my power to go a little in the great world. There is so great a want of anything stirring that I do not know what to write about....'[3]

From Trepassey, they sailed along the south coast of Newfoundland to the anchorage at Little St Lawrence and thence to the large natural harbour at Placentia. While there, the Prince at first kept his ship's company under tight discipline and there were ten floggings – mostly for drunkenness – in less than a month. He went ashore to carry out legal duties as the governor's surrogate and won approval for the seemliness with which he conducted the funeral of one of his men, himself reading the service at the graveside.

Hearing of a widow in the little town with fourteen children for whom she had no means of support, he chose one of the boys to join the ship as a captain's servant, following another he had found at Plymouth in similar circumstances and taken aboard. Both waited on the Prince and were trained to stand behind the chair when he dined in his cabin. He did not expect either to use his patronage to follow a career in the Navy and promised to send them to school when the ship returned to England.

His magisterial duties were more demanding. Twice a week he had to go ashore and preside over a court until one particular case made it necessary to add another weekly session. This was a riot by three hundred Irish fishermen, who had protested against some fishing regulations with a drunken demonstration, when they assaulted the constables stationed at the little fort. Prince William at once went ashore with a file of marines, pursued the rioters, arrested the suspected ringleader, convened a court and sentenced him to a hundred lashes to be applied 'with the utmost severity'. Thereupon the Prince ordered all the inhabitants of Placentia to take the oath of allegiance to the King.

On another occasion, a man accused of 'a multiplicity of crimes shocking to mention'[4] was examined at a two-hour sitting and the Prince sent him to St John's, the capital, to stand trial for his life. He wrote a report on the growth of 'Popery' and recommended that, while Roman Catholicism should be tolerated, the ruined Protestant chapel should be rebuilt.

Ashore, Prince William was already the pillar of the constitution. He was also about to become the third in succession to the throne, without control by a regent, on reaching his twenty-first birthday.

On 21 August 1786, while the ship lay at Placentia, he celebrated his coming of age with a carousal and for a day discipline was forgotten. As a precaution, the master of arms, Mr Rumbold, the midshipmen and boys were told not to drink but everyone else was allowed to do so, the ship's company not only being given double tots of grog but allowed ashore to buy more.

The captain dined early with his officers and the sober young Byam Martin recorded, 'The interchange of condescension on the one part and of love and loyalty on the other was so often plighted in a bumper that by one o'clock scarcely one of the company could give distinct utterance to a word.

'By some means, I know not how (it was no easy matter), his Royal Highness contrived to crawl up to the main-deck, no doubt with the adventurous hope of being able to reach his cabin; but in an instant he was recognised by the seamen, all nearly as drunk as himself, who with unfeigned, irresistible loyalty, mounted him on their shoulders and ran with him violently from one end of the deck to the other ... I am sure I may say that his head passed within an inch of the skids [beams] several times and one blow, at the rate they were going, would inevitably have killed him.

'I was on the gangway at the time, looking down on them, and seeing the danger roared to the men to stop, but all in vain. I then threw my hat upon them with all the force I could to draw attention and I succeeded in getting the men to lower him.... It was altogether a strange scene, one that would have astonished the members of the Temperance Society.'[5]

On 6 September, the frigate sailed for St John's, to a formal welcome from Commodore John Elliot, who was both senior naval officer on the Newfoundland Station and governor of the colony. There was little social activity to amuse the Prince and the Newfoundland women were not noted for their looks or sophistication. One officer, who had attended the ball at St John's in celebration of the Prince of Wales's twenty-first birthday three years before, described how they had had their hair elaborately dressed, greased and powdered by the town's only hairdresser and those whom he attended first might have had to spend the night before the ball sitting upright so as not to disturb their coiffures.

Despite this unpromising environment, the Prince was content. At last his father had shown trust in him and given him responsibility, although Lieutenant Schomberg's constant watchfulness remained an irritation. But he was grateful and showed it by writing a long letter of the sort he imagined the King would want to read, cramming it with observations on the topography, industry, trade and customs of Newfoundland.

'The face of the country is truly deplorable,' he wrote. 'A small brushwood for the first five hundred yards in shore and then a most dreadful, inhospitable and barren country intersected by fresh water ponds, lakes and bogs: I am informed that the woods are very large, thirty miles from the sea and are of prodigious size and extent. Few people have ever visited the inland parts of the island so that they are scarce known; it is not even determined whether they are inhabited....'

He described the shoals of cod and herring in the fishing grounds on the Newfoundland Banks and the inland wilderness swarming with game, and continued, 'In the fresh water rivers and lakes there are plenty of salmon and trout and close along shore lobsters, flat fish and flounders in such numbers that in three hours I have with my bargemen caught enough to serve the ship's company.'

He reported that St John's, although relatively large with more than twenty thousand inhabitants, was 'very orderly from the number of magistrates and the number of military'. It was also prosperous from fishing and the export of dried fish. 'The trade at St John's is prodigious,' he wrote; as well as seventy trawlers, there were hundreds of boats employed in fishing and 'at present more than a hundred ships and brigs preparing to sail for the European markets with fish and several schooners loading for the West Indies.... It must give your Majesty great satisfaction....'[6]

Departing on 26 September for a nine-day passage to their next port of call, Halifax in Nova Scotia, the *Pegasus* ran into thick fog south-east of Cape Breton. A heavy swell was running when the banks of fog suddenly parted to reveal surf breaking on a sandbank ahead of the ship. This was Sable Island, a notorious hazard to shipping, so the navigation of the frigate's master was faulty. The helm had to be put hard over and they instantly plunged into even thicker fog but bearings had been taken and the ship was saved.

Halifax proved a more entertaining town than St John's, but William was not in a mood for jollity, or so he claimed, for he was hankering after the pretty girl with whom he had danced in Plymouth, Sarah Martin's memory having shrunk and faded. He wrote to his brother George, 'I have been in Newfoundland, a country of no amusements, but there I was happy: at Halifax, a very gay and lively place full of women and those of the most obliging kind, I wished myself back to the inhospitable shores, foggy atmosphere and rugged, barren cliffs of Newfoundland.'[7] There he could be alone with his romantic musings.

After a short refit, the ship sailed on 26 October, bound for her final destination, the West Indies. Two days later she was struck by a hurricane so cold that the seamen could hardly take in the sails to prevent her being dismasted. The surgeon, Jonathan Fidge, who had a reputation as a skilful helmsman of a sailing-boat, was so terrified by the 'indescribable violence of the wind and its accompaniments of hail, thunder and lightning, together with the leaning over of the ship'[8] that he resolved to take a practice ashore at the first opportunity.

When the storm abated, the weather warmed and then they were in the tropics where the unaccustomed heat made the men languid and irritable. The schoolmaster, Mr Mears, had long been called a madman behind his back by the midshipmen but now gave substance to their mockery. One afternoon while the Prince was sleeping on the sofa in his cabin with the stern windows open, he dreamt that Mears was about to murder him, woke with a start and there indeed was the schoolmaster, holding his captain's wrist with one hand and a knife in the other.

'Good God, Mears, what are you about?' cried the Prince.

'I was merely going to tell your Royal Highness that you would be likely to lose your life by sleeping here with the windows open,' replied the schoolmaster.[9] Mears had access to the cabin where he wrote the day's entry in the captain's log, so no action was taken. However, in the early hours of the next morning, the schoolmaster again appeared outside the captain's cabin, demanding entry to tell him that the ship was on the wrong course and in danger of running aground. Again he was sent away but, half an hour later, suddenly rushed for the door of the cabin gripping a carving-knife. This time no allowance for eccentricity was made and a marine sentry felled him with a blow. Fidge, the surgeon, was summoned, insanity diagnosed and Mears confined until he could be sent ashore to a hospital in a British colony.

After a fortnight's passage, they were off the wooded hills of Jamaica and anchored in Kingston Bay. Ashore in Port Royal there was cheap rum to be had; discipline slackened and, during their ten-day stay, there were six floggings on board and a marine was put in irons for sleeping on duty. The captain prided himself on running a 'tight ship' and an efficient one, and when he saw drunken seamen, or when the ship had been at risk through faulty navigation, he instinctively looked for someone to blame and his eye often fell on the first lieutenant. He, aware of this, would try to avoid cause for blame by becoming more of a martinet.

Even during the Atlantic crossing, the Prince had found that Schomberg 'wished to carry on the duty of the ship entirely and, particularly whenever I found fault, would reason and shew this was not wrong'. At Halifax he had even, he added, 'so far forgot himself as to advise me about punishments'. The Prince was at first reluctant to rebuke his experienced first lieutenant but now he did so, although 'very mildly', he claimed.[10] But soon after he told him sharply that he would be captain in his own ship.

Before making for the British naval base at English Harbour on the island of Antigua, the *Pegasus* called at Barbados, St Vincent and Dominica. On St Vincent, the chief of the native Caribbee Indians and his family were entertained on board, Byam Martin recording that 'His Majesty was accompanied by as curious an example of filthy royalty as the eye of curiosity could desire to see … the person of her sacred Majesty was the most disgusting of the whole party….

'After a plentiful dinner and unrestrained indulgence in their love of ardent spirits, the royal savages, our visitors on board the *Pegasus*, were so excited that their company became exceedingly disagreeable and even dangerous. The Prince therefore hastened their departure and, having presented the king with a fowling-piece and a very handsome pair of pistols, they took their leave just sober enough to get over the side with some help from our men.'

On being put ashore, Martin continued, 'Her Majesty and her daughters stripped to cleanse and cool themselves by bathing close to our launch, then busy filling casks with water. We were all made sensible of the advantage it would have been to us if this ablution had taken place previous to their visit.'[11]

While they were lying off the island, a French frigate arrived from Martinique with a pressing invitation for the Prince to visit the island. However, the King, well aware of the risk of sending his son ashore to be entertained, had forbidden him to enter foreign ports. William handled the problem with remarkable tact, giving a dinner party in his ship for the French officers and telling them that nothing would give him greater pleasure than to accept but that if he did so he would have to accept similar flattering invitations to visit all the Spanish, Dutch and Danish islands in the Caribbean and would have no time for his professional duties.

Off Dominica, early in December, another frigate was sighted approaching under full press of canvas. She proved to be the *Boreas*, wearing the pendant of the senior officer on the Leeward Islands Station. The British ships employed there were usually divided into two squadrons: the southerly based on Barbados and the northerly on English Harbour in Antigua. However, Rear-Admiral Sir Richard Hughes, the Commander-in-Chief, who was based at Barbados, had recently sailed for home and the whole command had temporarily devolved upon his deputy, who commanded in the north and to whom Prince William would now be responsible. This was his friend Captain Horatio Nelson.

Since they had parted at Windsor Castle three years before, Nelson had been active. First, he had followed William's advice to learn another language by spending his leave in France. Then, early in 1784, he had been given command of the *Boreas*, a small frigate mounting twenty-eight guns, like the *Pegasus*. Ordered to the West Indies, he had found, instead of warfare, an unexpectedly difficult peacetime problem. Since the American colonies had won their independence, they had lost the preferential trading rights they had enjoyed with other British colonies. This was as unpopular in the West Indies as in the United States and was frequently flouted by both American traders and British merchants. It was Captain Nelson's duty to enforce the Navigation Act, which had been passed to put an end to such illegal trading, and this was making him as unpopular as the law itself.

It had been his major preoccupation for many months past, but a more recent one was his search for Prince William. He had been informed that the *Pegasus* and her royal captain were to come under his command and were sailing south from Halifax, but he had no idea where they were. A further preoccupation was his new-found love for a charming widow, Fanny Nisbet, the niece of John Herbert, the President of Nevis, a beautiful island within sight of his base at Antigua. With two failed courtships behind him, he had met her – and her infant son, Josiah – after the end of a sentimental attachment to a married woman at English Harbour, and now they were engaged to be married. In November he had told her about his new subordinate as he awaited the arrival of a ship that might have news of him.

'This Prince hunting is a bad sort of business,' he had written from English Harbour, 'I am anxiously looking out for the *Berbice* that I may know where to find the Royal sailor.'[12] Then, on 1 December, he wrote again to say that the ship had just arrived from Barbados, that he had heard the *Pegasus* was off Dominica and that he was sailing immediately to join her there. His orders were to escort the Prince with his ship and himself, much as he had on the royal visit to Havana. But now there was a change in their relationship for the Prince was aged twenty-one and Nelson was only eight years older. Both were naval officers, both had been in love; they liked each other and their friendship was resumed with warmth and mutual sympathy.

In his wooing of Fanny Nisbet, Nelson was as courtly and old-fashioned as his appearance had seemed to William at their first meeting off New York. So he was amused and slightly shocked to note the Prince's mixture of calculated charm and ruthlessness of manner in the round of levées, balls and dinner parties at which he had to be in attendance.

'Our young Prince is a gallant man,' he wrote to Fanny, 'Some ladies at Dominica seemed very much charmed by him. He is volatile but always with great good nature. There were two balls during his stay and some of the old ladies were mortified that His Royal Highness would not dance with them, but he says he is determined to enjoy the privilege of all other men, that of asking any lady he pleases.'[13]

He was too delicate to mention that the royal sailor had a fondness for telling coarse jokes, whether or not ladies were present, but he did tell her, 'Mrs Parry dined at table the first day at the Government House, but never afterwards appeared at dinner, nor were any ladies at Governor Orde's dinner.'[14] The Prince himself was bored by all but young and pretty women and by men who became flustered when presented.

He confided in Nelson his own lost loves in England and insisted that he be told about Fanny. As sentimental as he could be vulgar, William was delighted and amused by his friend's reverent account of his fiancée and showed it by proposing what was taken as a flattering honour. Nelson wrote to Fanny, 'I can tell you a piece of news which is that he is fully determined and has made me promise him that he shall be at my wedding and says he will give you to me. He has never yet been in a private house to visit and is determined never to do it except in this instance.'[15]

Their two ships sailed from Dominica and on 14 December entered the landlocked basins of English Harbour beneath the batteries and barren hills of Antigua. The little dockyard had been expanded and fortified for almost a century in what had long been a 'hurricane hole', where ships could shelter from storms. Now warships could be refitted and careened during the hurricane season in late summer and there were stocks of timber, masts, yards, rigging, canvas, ordnance and provisions in the storehouses. A few paces from the quays, slip-ways and capstans on the waterside were weather-boarded, white-painted houses on stone foundations, in which the senior dockyard staff and visiting officers had their quarters. Above, on a little hill, stood a handsome house called 'Windsor', where the commissioner of the dockyard lived and where Nelson had sighed over Mary Moutray, the charming young wife of the elderly commissioner, two years before.

The *Pegasus* was not only in need of smartening for her next cruise – her hull was to be washed and painted, mastheads and yards blackened and rigging tarred – but Captain Nelson reported to the Admiralty that she was hardly seaworthy. Not only was she leaking and her ironwork corroded but, when she was examined in the dock-yard, it was found that the seams of her sides had so opened and their metal bolts were so rusted that she could only have been given a summary inspection when last in dock.

Her captain was anxious that this should be remedied as quickly as possible for he wanted to resume his tour of the islands. In particular there was a lady he wanted to meet again at one of his recent ports of call, and Nelson wrote to Fanny that they might 'sail for Barbados, where a foolish female is ready to resign herself to His Royal High-ness'.[16] But first there was entertainment at St John's, the capital of Antigua, and on Christmas Eve Nelson wrote an exhausted letter to Fanny from English Harbour: 'We returned last night from St John's and I fancy many people were as happy to see His Royal Highness quit as they were to see him enter St John's, for another day or two's racquet would have knocked some of the fair sex up. Three nights' dancing was too much and never broke up until near day. Miss Athill is the belle of the island and of course attracted His Royal Highness's attention. I will tell you much when we meet, for you know the danger of putting too much upon paper. I could not have supposed that there had been near the number of females on this island as appeared at the balls, and all being in their best clothes made them look tolerable well.

'You will wonder I have been able to get through all this fatigue. I have not more than twice or thrice been in bed till morning and have rode a great deal in the day, but so far from doing me harm everybody tells me they never saw me look so well. I am reconciled to the business as I really love to honour the Prince, otherwise I could not have gone through with it ... as an individual I love him, as a Prince I honour and revere him.'[17]

Despite the evidence that Prince William was of the same flesh as his rowdiest sailor, Nelson's inbred reverence for the institution of monarchy remained unimpaired. He was also grateful to him for his support over the unpopular stopping, searching and occasionally impounding of American merchant ships ordered by the Navigation Act: one entry in the log of the *Pegasus* read, 'Fired two Main deck guns shotted at a Merchant ship to bring her to.'[18] His company ashore ensured that Nelson was not ostracised by colonial society for his implacability over this issue as he sometimes had been.

For his part, the Prince was receiving further education. 'It was then that I particularly observed the greatness of Nelson's superior mind,' he was to recall, 'The manner in which he enforced the spirit of the Navigation Act first drew my attention to the commercial interests of any country. We visited the different islands together; and ... we fought over together the principal naval actions of the American war. Excepting the naval tuition received on board the *Prince George* ... my mind took its first decided naval turn from this familiar intercourse with Nelson.'[19]

Their friendship survived yet another round of parties as the worthies of Antigua entertained the Prince. 'How vain are human hopes,' wrote Nelson to Fanny on the first day of 1787, 'I was in hopes we would be quiet all this week. Today we dine with Sir Thomas, tomorrow the Prince has a party, on Wednesday he gives a dinner at St John's to the regiment, in the evening is a mulatto ball, on Thursday a cock fight, dine at Col. Crosbie's brother's and a ball, on Friday somewhere, but I forget, on Saturday at Mr Byam's, the President. If we get well through all this I shall be a fit for anything.'[20]

Even at English Harbour there were convivial evenings because Nelson, the Prince and the other captains with ships in port had formed a little mess at the senior officer's house and would dine there together. When even this did not offer enough privacy, the Prince asked that a handsome new house, built on stone foundations and surrounded by wide verandahs, should be built for his use on the far side of the harbour, opposite the dockyard, and this was begun. [Later named Clarence House, it still stands.] In order to keep the usual distance between themselves and their officers they had, as he put it, 'settled to ask no officers whatsoever, at which my Lieutenants were hurt, as they were by not being asked to go to St John's. I perceived this immediately and paid particular attention to my behaviour when on duty, to treat them with kindness and politeness and civility. However Mr. Schomberg so far forgot himself as to speak to me with disrespect.'[21]

Nelson had become aware of the tension between captain and first lieutenant when the Prince had written in a letter of 'your friend Schomberg, as he calls himself, but I don't believe you know much of him'.[22] But squabbles were commonplace in the tropics where the heat, humidity, mosquitoes and alcohol left nerves raw and sensitive. He still had a high opinion of Prince William, writing to his brother in England, 'I wish that all the Navy captains were as attentive to orders as he is.'[23] To Captain Locker he wrote, 'he has his foibles as well as private men, but they are far over-balanced by his virtues. In the Professional line, he is superior to near two-thirds, I am sure, of the List; and in attention to orders and respect to his superior officers, I hardly know his equal: this is what I have found him. Some others, I have heard, will tell another story.'[24]

They would indeed. For the *Pegasus* was no longer the happy ship she had seemed when first commissioned. As recently as September, a captain who visited her off Newfoundland had noted that her officers 'gave the Prince a very high character and the men seemed fond of him' and that the captain himself seemed 'very sensible, but talked a great deal and that altogether he was much of a gentleman'.[25]

Indeed, the impression at Court in London was that he was happy and successful. His sister Augusta passed on news of him to another brother, Augustus, after she had had a letter from William, writing, 'He says he is as happy as the day is long and that the *Pegasus* is his whole and sole delight and pleasure. He has a little Band of musick that serves to make his ship's company dance and he says, "*I doat to see my men happy.*" Everybody speaks well of him and I believe him as I always did a very hearty, good, honest, English tar, liking better a hammock than a bed and plain salt beef than all the fine dishes and luxury that townspeople fare upon; he always wears his uniform and no curls and yet looks as well dressed and more of a man than any of the fashionable powder *monkies*.'[26]

But to his ship's company he no longer seemed the same man. Now he was aloof, bad tempered and more of a martinet than his first lieutenant had even been. As Byam Martin wrote later, 'A change took place in the conduct of our royal captain on reaching the Leeward Islands Station ... it was as discreditable to him as it was unjust and disagreeable to all on board. I may safely affirm that there was not a person in the ship who did not wish earnestly to do whatever might be most pleasing to the Prince and best promote his credit as our captain.'[27]

The officers, who had been forbidden by their captain to accept any social invitations ashore, discussed and argued the possible reasons for his moods. Some said it was the influence of Captain Nelson, but as they got to know him better that was discounted. Another factor might have been the combination of tropical heat with late nights and hard drinking. They were not to know that the Prince was worried about money. He had found that his annual allowance of £3000 had not lasted his first six months in command and wrote to a friend at court, pointing out that 'His Majesty did not consider that it is expected of me to give a dinner to the people in office in the different islands and plantations and if he would but pay these extraordinary expenses I should then be able to make both ends meet…. If he would but allow me a certain proportion more, I shall be enabled to live as gentleman, otherwise I must resign the command of my ship and lead a private life.'

But he admitted in this confidential letter that he was not leading the kind of life of which his father would approve. 'I have been in constant round of dissipation from my first arrival in the West Indies,' he wrote, 'and I am afraid it will continue as long as I remain in these seas…. My time I spend pleasantly enough; tho' I have had two or three severe complaints in my stomach. The people here say I ought to drink more wine; but I do not agree with them on that subject. You will, of course, hear of the addresses, fine presents, fêtes and balls the gentlemen in these islands have given me. So long as it does not hurt my health it is well and good, but I am afraid I shall fall a sacrifice to this feasting.'[28]

It was not only feasting, nor the excess of alcohol. Soon after his arrival in the West Indies, Fidge, the ship's surgeon, was treating him with mercury for 'a sore I had contracted in a most extraordinary manner in my pursuit of the *Dames des Couleurs*',[29] he confided to George in a letter. Indeed, venereal disease – albeit in a relatively mild and treatable form – became, together with prickly heat, boils and fevers, one of the recurrent health problems he associated with service in the tropics.

The factors contributing to his irritability and intolerance – including the ambivalence of his position as royalty, the carping of his parents although he was now an adult, and the apparent impossibility of establishing a normal relationship with a girl of his choice – were brought together in his confrontation with his first lieutenant.

Mutual resentment and professional rivalry had always been more than a possibility and had steadily grown.

The point of contention was often the frigate's order book. Although considered unnecessary by many captains – particularly those who worked closely with their officers – it was accepted practice that standing orders could be entered in a book, which would always be available for consultation. Indeed this could be a necessity in a large ship where officers were constantly changing.

In the little *Pegasus*, the captain had begun dictating orders for recording on arrival at Placentia and by the beginning of 1787 there were many pages of neatly-written instructions. At first, the orders were sensible, even if they were mostly matters which could have been left to the common sense of the ship's officers. For example, on 5 November it had been noted 'In order to keep the lower deck perfectly cool and clean, it is my directions that while the *Pegasus* remains either in warm weather, or in the West Indies, that the Fore-mast men do dine on deck....'

But a month later, a note of irritability became apparent. 'From my having seen the Ship's Company laying about asleep at night on the decks and on the booms, out of their hammacoes in their cloaths,' it was written, 'it is my positive orders that the Seamen and Marines do not lay about in that shameful and scandalous manner ... and they may depend upon being most severely punished if they are caught asleep in the open air with their cloaths on, unless they have the watch on deck.'[30]

Elaborate instructions were laid down for the order book to be studied by all officers and midshipmen and for it to be available at all times. Gradually the Prince took to dictating the orders to his clerk instead of explaining them to his officers. Many were so obvious that there was no need to issue them, such as his order that 'No officer is to read in bed by candlelight' because of the risk of fire. Others were obviously enlightened but should have been unnecessary in a well-ordered ship, like, 'No Seaman or Marine or other person is to be struck, or otherwise ill-used, by any Officer or Gentleman.' More were the repetition of accepted opinion, such as, 'It is expected that Men going on shore, on leave, bring no disgrace on themselves or the Ship by drunkenness, or riotous behaviour, but carry themselves soberly and respectfully.'

Yet others were ludicrous, particularly when ordered by a captain known for his noisy volubility, swearing and hard-drinking. One such ran, 'The officers are to use every means in their power to prevent that but too common and absurd practice of Seamen in making a noise on every occasion when the duty of the Ship is carrying on by *Huzzaing, Hallowing*, etc.' Another declared, 'As it is but the too frequent practice on board his Majesty's Ships to make use of that horrid expression *Bugger*, so disgraceful to a British Seaman, if any person shall be heard using this expression they may be assured they will be severely punished.'

The order which was the cause of the first direct confrontation with Lieutenant Schomberg was to do with the drying of clothes. Washing could only be hung up to dry from lines, which could be tied to the rigging but must on no account 'impede His Majesty's service'.[31] While the ship was at Halifax, the captain ordered a seaman and a marine to be flogged for hanging up their wet clothes to dry between decks. The first lieutenant objected that the punishment was too severe. As the captain saw it, 'the intent of these words were that if *we* punished for every trifling offence, *we* should make ourselves unpopular and be constantly punishing.' To the Prince, Schomberg's giving his 'sentiments unasked' was an act of 'disrespect'.[32]

Other issues followed. One was the first lieutenant's failure to collect sheets from the hospital at Antigua for the ship's sickbay, for which he accepted blame but explained that there had been so much else to do and there had been only two boats available. But when the Prince spoke sharply to him about this failure – calling up to him from a boat alongside the ship and so presumably within the hearing of others – Schomberg's cool manner infuriated him.

On 12 January, Prince William wrote to Lieutenant Schomberg, 'From my situation in the World, more is expected from me than from any other Captain in his Majesty's service.... I have more to do with you from your situation in the Ship as first Lieutenant than with any other of the officers; it is incumbent on you to promote and rigidly follow all directions and orders you may from time to time receive from me as your commanding officer.... I am sorry to say that in your general conduct ... many and various have been the objections made by you to what I have thought conducing to the better disciplining of H. M. Ship under my Command ... likewise your negligence in not complying with my orders....'

He told him that he had considered putting him under arrest for 'disobedience of orders and neglect of duty' after his response to the rebuke over the sheets. 'I was happy I did not take that step,' he continued, 'as Courts Martial upon officers are things of a most disagreeable nature and ever to be avoided if possible, more particularly so in a ship commanded by a Person of so elevated a situation in life as Providence has thought proper to place me in ... I hope you will consider this letter ... as an admonition to you: there are few officers in his Majesty's service more zealous, or more conversant with the duty of an officer, or blessed with better sense than you, and I hope that for the future I shall find your conduct in these respects altered, otherwise I must, though ever so reluctantly, be obliged to bring matters to a disagreeable issue.'[33]

Next day, Schomberg replied in a long and courtly letter, accepting blame for the incident of the sheets but maintaining, 'I have ever made it my study by an unwearied and indefatigable attention to the duty of the ship to merit and deserve your Royal Highness's approbation and not to have unintentionally incurred your displeasure. The visible changes in your Royal Highness's conduct since the *Pegasus* arrived in English Harbour might have drawn from me the expression which you allude to ... a consequence of the observation your Royal Highness made use of previous to it – "that of late there seemed to be nothing but difficulties, objections, etc." These pointed reproofs, Sir, from an officer of your distinguished rank must make me feel most sensibly so undeserved a rebuke....'

The Prince did not consider this 'as respectful as it ought to be' and wrote a sharp reply, which concluded, 'I have now, sir, to inform you as your Commanding Officer and as Captain of H.M.S. *Pegasus*, I shall be obliged, though ever so reluctantly and against my inclination, to bring you to a Court Martial for disobedience of Orders, Neglect of Duty and disrespect to me as your Commanding Officer, unless you make me full and ample concessions for your impropriety of conduct.'

Schomberg considered the options and decided it was preferable to face a little humiliation before his captain and a few lieutenants rather than the almost certain ruin of his career, whatever the outcome of a court martial. So he asked the second lieutenant, Mr Hargood, to announce his decision. 'I then sent for him into the cabin,' the Prince recorded, 'where, before his brother officers, he made a full and ample apology for his past misconduct, upon this I reinstated him in his command.'

Peace did not last. The captain had insisted that his officers consult the order book before taking almost any action and on 22 January he had reminded his first lieutenant that boats must not be sent ashore without his own express permission. Soon after, he was surprised to see one leaving the ship and to be told that this had been authorised by Mr Schomberg. He berated the first lieutenant, who was standing on the quarterdeck and the next day entered in the order book the accusation, 'From Mr Schomberg's neglecting to inform me yesterday of his sending a boat on shore ... I think proper to recommend the reading of these orders with attention by the Officers and Gentlemen, as for the future, I shall make them accountable for their conduct in disobeying my commands or orders....'[34]

The Prince dined ashore and, on returning to the ship that evening, found a note from Lieutenant Schomberg, telling him that, in order to vindicate his name, he had written to Captain Nelson, as senior officer, demanding a court martial. Nelson was horrified. Although aware of strains on board the *Pegasus*, he had not realised that they had reached breaking point. He and the Prince had been planning another cruise to the islands of Grenada, Monserrat, Nevis, St Kitts and the Virgin Islands and consequent rounds of entertaining. Now, suddenly, he faced a challenge to his tact and judgement.

He could not refuse the request for a court martial, although this would inevitably exacerbate the incident and call into question Prince William's fitness for command. On the other hand, he was unable to convene a court martial because he could not assemble the necessary quorum of captains from the few ships within call. Whatever sympathy he felt for Schomberg, he did not want to undermine his captain's authority. He therefore took the only course he felt was open and wrote to the Prince, 'I have the honour of acquainting your Royal Highness that in consequence of a letter I have this day received from Lieutenant Schomberg ... I have thought it proper to order him under an Arrest and beg you will grant him such indulgence, or lay such restrictions on him, during his Arrest, as his behaviour shall appear to you to deserve.'[35]

Nelson then wrote to Schomberg, telling him of this decision, and adding that a court martial would be arranged when possible. He also issued an order that officers should not demand court martials 'to investigate their conduct on a frivolous pretence'[36] and, if they did, they would be charged under the Articles of War.

On reflection, Nelson was more exasperated with Schomberg than with the Prince, with whom he maintained a cheerful friendship and, soon after Schomberg had been confined to his cabin, wrote to Captain Locker, 'His Royal Highness keeps up strict discipline in his Ship and, without paying him any compliment, she is one of the first ordered Frigates I have seen. He has had more plague with his Officers than enough: his First Lieutenant will no doubt be broke. I have put him under Arrest.... In short, our Service has been so much relaxed during the War, that it will cost many a Court Martial to bring it up again.'[37]

With Lieutenant Schomberg temporarily out of sight and mind, Nelson and the Prince began their cruise at the end of January. For both of them, the climax was to be their arrival off Nevis in March, for it was then that Nelson was to be married to Fanny Nisbet and the Prince was to 'give away' the bride. William enjoyed teasing his friend about the wedding, and Nelson, both flattered and irritated, wrote to Fanny, 'What is it to attend on princes, let me attend on you and I am satisfied. Some are born for attendants on great men, I rather think that is not my particular province. His Royal Highness often tells me he believes I am married for he says he never saw a lover so easy, or say so little of the object he has regard for. When I tell him I certainly am not what is (vulgarly) no I won't make use of that word commonly called love. He is right, my love is founded on esteem, the only foundation that can make love last.'[38]

The cruise continued, exhausting Nelson with late nights and an excess of food and drink. Meanwhile the Prince continued his banter, insisting that Nelson marry when planned and not try to change his mind. 'His Royal Highness has been with me all this morning,' he wrote to Fanny early in March with flustered excitement, 'and has told me that as things have changed, if I am not married this time we go to Nevis, it is hardly probable he should see me there again, that I had promised him not to be married unless he was present and that he did it to show his esteem for me and should be much mortified if any impediments were thrown in the way to hinder his being present. He intends it as a mark of honour to me, as such I wish to receive it. Indeed his behaviour to me has ever been that of a friend instead of a person so elevated above me. He told me this morning that since he has been under my command he has been happy, and has given me to understand that there is no doubt whenever he may be placed in a high situation that I will find him sincere in his friendship. By keeping in his esteem there is no doubt I shall have my right in the Service if nothing more.'[39]

His liking for the Prince was strengthened over a very different court martial from that in their minds. A seaman had deserted from another ship at English Harbour, had been tried and given the obligatory sentence of death. Nelson wanted to save him from hanging and the Prince agreed to exercise royal prerogative in granting a reprieve, while the condemned man's captain agreed to his discharge from the Navy. On the day set for the execution, all the preliminaries for hanging were ordered and then the seaman was told that he was free. Nelson was later to be reprimanded for discharging him, but pointed out that on sentence of death he had been deprived of his identity so could be given a new life.

On 11 March 1787, Horatio Nelson and Fanny Nisbet were married at Montpelier on the green slopes of Mount Nevis, high above the sea. In the shaded rooms of the plantation house and in the dappled sunlight of the garden beneath the spreading branches of a great silk-cotton tree, the ceremony was performed by the rector of the parish. Prince William gave the bride to the groom and then proposed the toast to the future health and happiness of 'the principal favourite of the island'.[40] Few heard the only sombre note when one of the naval guests walked away and muttered, 'It is a national loss that such an officer should marry; had it not been for that circumstance, I foresaw Nelson would become the greatest man in the Service.'[41]

Three days later, Prince William wrote to Lord Hood, telling him that Lieutenant Schomberg had, after several weeks under arrest, apologised again and that he had replied that 'he should have proceeded with more caution and temper at first and that he had taught me a lesson never to forgive an officer.'[42] He then wrote to Nelson, urging him to bring Schomberg to trial as quickly as possible. It was still impossible to convene a court martial, so Nelson decided that the *Pegasus* should go to Jamaica, where Commodore Gardner, the senior officer, should have enough captains available.

Early in May, this was suggested to Prince William. He was particularly eager to go because his ship's company had become sickly in the close confines of English Harbour and he himself was suffering from a recurrent fever, which a change of environment might benefit. So he sailed westward and arrived off Kingston on the twenty-sixth of the month.

In a covering letter to Commodore Gardner, Nelson explained the problem of the court martial, but was careful not to make accusations against Schomberg. 'I therefore, in order to prevent Lieutenant Schomberg from being again, as set forth in his letter, unjustly accused, ordered him into Arrest,' he explained, adding of the dispute itself, 'His Royal Highness, I can have no doubt, gave the orders alluded to, although Mr Schomberg might have misunderstood them.' His own complaint was that the lieutenant's request for a court martial could set a tiresome precedent. 'If this was to be allowed, farewell Discipline,' he concluded.[43]

Meanwhile, the *Boreas*, after a short refit at English Harbour, sailed for England in June, his wife and little stepson following in a merchant ship. For the time being, Captain Nelson would no longer be present to influence the Prince. But Lieutenant Schomberg had accompanied him to Jamaica under guard, and seemed likely, like a curse, to continue to do so.

7

Those Damned Women

The *Pegasus* remained an unhappy ship and her midshipmen spoke mockingly of their captain's quarters as 'the Court'. For several weeks only the youngest had been invited to dine with him as it was thought that the older boys had a liking for Lieutenant Schomberg, as indeed they had.

'The invitations to the royal table were confined to a few of the younger members of the fraternity,' noted Byam Martin, himself now a midshipman, 'and for a short time I was of the number, till it came to the knowledge of the Prince that I had been guilty of the great crime of visiting my kind imprisoned friend ... for Schomberg's excellent little library was always free of access to those who desired to profit by it, but I was always glad to go to him when I could. I was rather a green hand, unskilled in the sycophancy of the courtier....'[1]

The older officers were actively harassed. Before leaving English Harbour, they were not even allowed to go ashore for a walk without entering their names, the time of leaving the ship and time of their return, in a book provided for the purpose. One, Lieutenant Hope, whose sympathy for Schomberg had been noticed by the Prince, was not only reprimanded and ordered to apologise but transferred to the *Boreas* before she sailed without being given his certificate of service which he needed in order to be paid.

Nor was it only the officers who suffered. A Hanoverian artist arrived with a letter of introduction from the governor of Dominica, and was invited to stay on board the Prince's frigate while sketching picturesque tropical scenes but fell out with his host. Whether or not this had anything to do with Lieutenant Schomberg, the captain lost his temper and ordered the German to be spreadeagled over a gun and flogged across the buttocks with a cat-o'-nine-tails. As angry as he was hurt, the outraged German left at once for St John's and began legal proceedings, in consequence of which the Prince had to pay him several hundred pounds, ostensibly for medical treatment.

None of this diminished the Prince's indignation over Schomberg, who remained with him in the little ship as a constant reminder of mutual resentment that had grown into a critical confrontation. Not only was the Prince still determined that his first lieutenant be brought to trial, but he had broadcast his exaggerated account of the affair so that it was the talk of the well-informed in London and throughout the Navy. He had not only written at length to Lord Hood, whose protégé Schomberg had been – and this had come to the attention of the First Lord of the Admiralty, Lord Howe – but he had written thousands of words about it to the King and to the Prince of Wales.

On paper the affair seemed absurdly inflated, as indeed it was, and there was worry that if Schomberg were acquitted, or only reprimanded, by the court martial, the Prince's reputation might suffer more than that of the accused. To reduce the tension, it was suggested that Howe might quickly send replacements for the disaffected officers to the West Indies. Such exasperation seems to have been shared by Commodore Gardner in Jamaica for he brought the matter to a head swiftly and tactfully.

'Everything is now settled,' William wrote to his brother George on 10 June, 'Schomberg has left the ship. Upon my arrival at Jamaica I immediately waited upon Commodore Gardner with Nelson's letters and my narrative. He at once was sensible of my peculiar situation in being the only witness to support the charges.' So, instead of convening a court martial, Gardner suggested that he should accept an apology from Schomberg made in the presence of two other captains.

He agreed and ended his letter, 'I accepted his apology.... He is gone home.... On Monday next I sail for America.'[2]

He sailed for Halifax a sick and embittered man. At Jamaica, recurrent fever and pains in muscles and joints had been followed by prickly heat and infected boils. He could not eat, sleep was difficult and the treatment prescribed by Fidge, the surgeon, who had himself been invalided from the ship and sent back to England, had been ineffective. Only the cooler northern climate seemed to offer any hope of relief.

He remained worried about his father's view of his troubles because there had been no letter from him since the arrival of one dated 4 March of the preceding year. 'It is near two years since I saw him and I have on certain points asked his advice, but he never honours me with an answer,' he wrote to George, 'I can by no means find out whether my conduct is satisfactory or not.'[3]

His letters to the Court treasurers, appealing for an increased allowance, had been unsuccessful and he told his brother of the unpaid tradesmen's bills he expected to arrive from London every time a bundle of letters was brought on board. But he maintained that he was determined to remain a naval officer: 'I have not in the least any idea of resigning: on the contrary, I glory in the Service and it will ever be the height of my ambition and always my wish to be employed.' Even if he did return to London, there would be nothing for him to do: 'Was I in your situation to live with you, we both well know how little that would be relished.'[4]

He missed Nelson's company, for now there was no one with whom he could relax. 'The kinder a Captain behaves to his officers the less he is respected, at least I have found it to be the case,' he wrote to Lord Hood. While Schomberg had been in the ship, he had forbidden the midshipmen and captain's servants to mix with the lieutenants but now, he said, he allowed them to do so again, 'but if I ever meet with disrespect or disobedience from the officers, that minute, the youth entrusted to my care shall not mix in with them'.[5]

The *Pegasus* had sailed from Jamaica, past Cuba and up the coast of America to Halifax, where they had arrived on 27 July after a voyage of fifteen days. But the cooler climate had not improved his health, 'on the contrary the cold affected me violently in the neck and shoulders and the inflammation was so high as to make me delirious.'[6] After a few days he sailed for the ruins of the former French fortress-city of Louisbourg and then up the St Lawrence river to Quebec.

While there, he wrote two long letters to his father, describing his voyage, giving a lyrical account of Canada at the most beautiful season as the leaves of the woods above the river turned red and gold in autumn: 'As for the province of Canada, it vastly surpasses all accounts I can give your Majesty of its magnitude, beauty and fertility: the Province in extent is larger than all Europe: the views in summer are magnificent and where in England the eye commands a view of ten miles, in Canada for many leagues the corn and sky appear to meet. The ground is rich and if the industrious Englishman tilled it, instead of the lazy Canadian, it would be inestimable.'

He described meeting Indians, who, he told the King, had greeted him as 'one in whose veins flowed the same blood as in the body of their Great Father in the East, meaning your Majesty.... The Indians not only love your Majesty but they go further in adoring, their respect being so wonderfully great for everything that relates to your Majesty.'[7]

Any contentment that William might have felt in such surroundings was disrupted by a letter from Nelson, which had clearly been written after much reflection on his voyage to England and posted in Portsmouth on his arrival. Like others involved, he had had time to consider the furore over Schomberg and had come to the conclusion that the blame for it had to be shared between the lieutenant and his captain.

It was a long letter, written with extreme courtliness, and it began, 'If to be truly great is to be truly good ... it never was stronger verified in your Royal Highness in the instance of Mr Schomberg.... Resentment I know your Royal Highness never had, or I am sure will ever bear any one: it is a passion incompatible with the character of a Man of Honour. Schomberg was too hasty certainly in writing his letter; but now you are parted, pardon me, my Prince, when I presume to recommend that Schomberg may stand in your Royal Favour as if he had never sailed with you; and that, at some future day, you will serve him. There only wants this to place your character in the highest point of view. None of us are without failings: Schomberg's was being rather too hasty; but that, put in competition with his being a good Officer, will not, I am bold to say, be taken in the scale against him.'

Having asked the Prince to substitute patronage for antagonism, he assured him of his own devotion. 'More able friends than myself your Royal Highness may easily find, and of more consequence in the State,' he explained, 'but one more attached and affectionate is, I am bold to say, not so easily met with. Princes seldom, very seldom, find a disinterested person to communicate their thoughts to. I do not pretend to be otherwise: but ... I am interested only that your Royal Highness should be the greatest and best man this Country ever produced.'[8]

It did not prompt the desired response and William wrote brusquely in return, 'With respect to Schomberg, I must confess myself surprised that you should recommend him after what I have so often said, and in what we do both agree, namely the never forgiving of an officer for disrespect; rest assured I never shall, and particularly Schomberg ... I am by no means of a revengeful temper: what I did I did for the good of his Majesty's Service and most certainly shall do again; but this affair has so stamped my character in the service that I trust and hope it will be the only act of severity I shall ever be under the disagreeable necessity of performing.'

He did agree to send Lieutenant Hope his certificate of service in the *Pegasus*, but with some reluctance. Then he ended his letter on a harsh note: 'In my own ship I go on pretty well. I have had two court martials, one on the master-at-arms, who was broke and received a hundred lashes, and the other on a seaman, who received fifty lashes on board his own ship. Believe me, dear Nelson. Yours sincerely, William.'[9]

In mid-October, the *Pegasus* left Quebec, sailing down the St Lawrence with a small squadron bound for Halifax. She was still an unhappy ship. Not only did her captain keep aloof and dine alone but had put an order in writing that when he reprimanded his officers they were not to answer back. One of them, Samuel Stillingfleet, who was still a midshipman at the age of twenty-six, almost brought about a repetition of the Schomberg incident. On 21 October, as the ship was emerging from the mouth of the great river, he wrote a letter to his captain, which read, 'I think it my duty to acquaint your Royal Highness in what a disrespectful manner I heard Lieutenant Church speak of your Royal Highness publicly on the quarterdeck in the River St Lawrence when he took charge of his Watch, after making sail with all hands, because your Royal Highness found fault with the manner in which it was done.'[10]

Confronted with this, Church wrote to the captain denying that he was responsible for making 'the most foul and disrespectful asperations against your Royal Highness'[11] and demanded that he be tried by court martial to clear his name. The Prince did not want a repetition of the recent furore and disregarded this amid the bustle of social activity at Halifax, where they arrived on the twenty-sixth.

On his first night ashore, he dined with the Governor, John Wentworth, and his young American wife. The latter enjoyed a reputation among the officers of the garrison of being 'a most charming woman but, unhappily for her husband, rather more partial to our sex than her own', which was quickly recognised by the Prince. Soon after, when Governor Wentworth was away, it was rumoured that 'a mutual passion subsisted between his Royal Highness and her'. This time the passion was sexual rather than romantic.

His amorous adventures were not confined to Mrs Wentworth. On his second day in Halifax, he had met some bored young Army officers and with one of them, a subaltern named William Dyott, began roaming the town, visiting 'all the young ladies' and became 'perfectly acquainted with every house of a certain description', where they enjoyed 'some pretty scenes'. Soon, noted his new companion, 'he would go into any house where he saw a pretty girl'.

Dyott did not consider him a heavy drinker, although recording that he could finish two bottles of Madeira, his favourite drink, in a day. But he enjoyed persuading others to get drunk, proposing endless toasts – 'Dyott, here's a bumper toast', or 'Dyott, your good health and your family' – and whenever he noticed an empty glass he would call out, 'I see some of God Almighty's daylight in that glass, Sir; banish it.' On one occasion, Dyott noted, 'He took very good care to see everybody fill and he gave twenty-three bumpers without a halt.'[12] A naval friend writing at this time to William's former shipmate Richard Keats told him, 'He really speaks of you with much seeming regard … *drunk* as well as sober.'[13]

He cut a fine figure in his uniform, 'about 5 foot, 7 or 8 inches high, good complexion and fair hair', as Dyott described him, 'I never … saw him in the smallest degree lose his dignity, or forget his princely situation.' But he was affable and enjoyed his rowdy evenings. While conscious of social and military rank, he would mix with junior officers, apparently on terms of equality, but was quick to check the familiarity he prompted. 'His character is, where he takes a liking he will be very free,' noted Dyott, 'but always guarded and if ever any man takes the smallest liberty, he cuts instantly.'

He loved dancing although, as Nelson had noticed in the Caribbean, he never bothered with the middle-aged but 'danced with all the pretty women in the room'. Next morning Dyott would, like Nelson, record the jollities of the preceding night; 'He is very fond of dancing; we changed partners every dance…. The last dance before supper at the Governor's … his Royal Highness, Major Vesey and myself and six very pretty women danced Country Bumpkin for nearly an hour. We went to supper about one,' or, 'We had a very pleasant ball; Country Bumpkin, the same set, and a devilish good supper. We danced after supper and till four o'clock. He dances vastly well and is very fond of it. I never saw people so completely tired as they all were. I saw his Royal Highness to his barge and ran home as fast as I could.'

Despite his recent troubles in the *Pegasus*, he was proud of his ship and invited friends on board. In his cabin, which one found 'rather small and neatly furnished', they would be served with 'a most elegant dinner'; a guest remarking, 'I did not think it possible to have had anything like it on board ship. Two courses, removes and a most elegant dessert. Wines of all sorts, such Madeira I never tasted.' The Prince's own favourite dish was cold turkey.

He delighted in showing off the ship and his sailors and, for the benefit of visitors, would make the coxswain of his barge dress in each of the uniforms he had designed for different climates and occasions. 'His own barge's crew most elegantly dressed and the handsomest caps I ever saw,' ran one description, 'Black velvet and, all except the coxswain's, with a silver ornament in front and the King's arms most elegantly cast. The coxswain's was of gold and his Royal Highness told me it cost fifty guineas.'

His affair with the governor's wife was causing something of a scandal, for it was noticed that he was constantly at her house, particularly when her husband was away. He would change there for dinners and balls but they would leave in separate carriages. 'The ladies of Halifax are a little scrupulous of their virtue,' noted Dyott, 'and think it in danger if they were to visit Mrs Wentworth.'[14]

The Prince himself feared that word of the affair had reached London because in October he wrote obliquely to the Prince of Wales, 'My father's conduct towards me is inexplicable,' for he still had received no letter. But when he did, 'there is every reason to suppose he will write his sentiments about Schomberg and at the same time speak also on the rest of my conduct … between ourselves a certain affair is likely to take place that will spoil the whole. Those damned women cause me more uneasiness than enough.'[15]

Perhaps the King had learned of the scandal. Perhaps in order to disengage his wayward son from his entanglement with the wife of the colonial governor, he countermanded his previous orders to prepare for a return to Jamaica. Certainly the Prince announced early in November that he was under new orders to sail for England. The reason given was alarm about a diplomatic confrontation with the Dutch over access to the Scheldt, for which a stronger naval presence might be needed. Yet no such orders were seen by others and the rumour circulated that either the Prince had been recalled by his father so as to reimpose discipline, or that he had decided to return without orders; the former possibility seeming the most likely.

Yet William was in high spirits on the night of his farewell party at Halifax. 'In the course of my experience I never saw such fair drinking,' recorded the indomitable Dyott, 'I think it was the most laughable sight I ever beheld to see the Governor, our General and the Commodore all so drunk they could scarce stand on the floor, hoisted up on their chairs with each a bumper in his hand; and the three times three cheers was what they were afraid to attempt for fear of falling. I then proposed his Royal Highness and a good wind whenever he sailed with the same ceremony. He stood at the head of the table during both these toasts and I never saw a man laugh so in my life.... When he had drunk the last the old Governor desired to know if we had any more, as he said if he once got down he should never get up again. His Royal Highness saw we were all pretty well done and he walked off. There were just twenty dined and we drank sixty-three bottles of wine.'[16]

The *Pegasus* sailed out into the Atlantic, taking a northerly route so as to avoid the western approaches to the Channel, because, her captain explained, enemy cruisers might be waiting, should war have broken out. On 3 December, they reached Cork and were accorded the customary civic welcome, the subaltern commanding the guard of honour mounted by the 76th regiment being a certain Arthur Wellesley [the future Duke of Wellington].

While in Cork harbour, the frigate's mainmast was struck by lightning and some of its iron hoops knocked off. Another thunderbolt was a letter that reached her captain from his old friend and patron Lord Hood telling him that he had appointed his enemy Isaac Schomberg to be first lieutenant of his flagship, the *Barfleur*. He wrote in reply, 'After the intimacy and friendship, which I was in hopes had subsisted between your Lordship and myself, and after my having laid all the particulars relative to Schomberg before you, my Lord, I would never have supported your Lordship would have countenanced him ... I want words to express my feelings on this subject; was any brother officer of mine to require a Lieutenant to quit his ship, I should, my Lord, be the last person to take such a man on preferment. Your opinions relative to Mr Schomberg have been from the beginning very different from mine and now your Lordship has given the Service very convincing proof of your approbation of Mr Schomberg's conduct.'

It was an extraordinary letter for a captain of twenty-two – albeit a prince – to write to an admiral and a peer of sixty-three. He compounded what must have been seen as gross impertinence by taking exception to the First Lord of the Admiralty's criticism of his treatment of Lieutenant Hope, concluding, 'There is nothing in this world I feel so sensibly as an attack on my professional character, under which I now labour by your Lordship's support of Schomberg and Lord Howe's disapproving of my conduct about Mr Hope. Much as I love and honour the Navy, yet, my Lord, I shall beyond doubt resign if I have not a satisfactory explanation from both your noble lordships.'[17]

Realising that he could expect no sympathy from his father, whom he was about to ask for both a larger ship – he had already applied to the Admiralty for the command of a ship of the line, the *Foudroyant* of eighty-four guns – and a larger allowance, he tried to enlist the support of his brother, telling him of Hood's action and complaining, 'I am not a little hurt ... I knew from the beginning of this business that Lord Hood had disapproved of my conduct throughout this unpleasant affair but I never could have expected his Lordship would have so soon and in so publick a manner have marked his disapprobation.'[18]

Hood replied with his customary courtliness, saying, 'I flattered myself I had so thorough a knowledge of your Royal Highness's humanity and condescending goodness of heart, that you could not wish the ruin of any man.' He explained that Schomberg had not intended to offend him and that he was, in fact, 'a very excellent officer and a sensible, well-behaved man'. Not even Hood's assurance that he 'would never cease to pray for your Royal Highness's Health, Glory and Happiness[19] could disguise his contradiction of the Prince's opinion and demands.

From Cork, the *Pegasus* was ordered to Plymouth, which was far enough from London to inhibit visits to London. Sailing into the Sound, past Drake's Island, below the citadel and batteries and the steep, green hills of Devon, the majesty of the Royal Navy again became apparent. Instead of commanding a frigate, lying off some Canadian or Caribbean port and being flattered and fawned upon, his command now shrank into insignificance beside the great ships of the line, the dockyard, storehouses and magazines and the power they represented.

Whether or not this reminded him that he had gone too far in his reproach of Lords Hood and Howe, he now wrote to Hood again, slightly softening his reproach. He still claimed to be 'vastly hurt' by Hood's appointing his enemy to his own ship 'without having previously consulted me' and that he was subject to 'infinite uneasiness, for it is the general topic of converse that Lord Hood supports Mr Schomberg in opposition to Prince William'. He added, however, that 'upon cool reflection, Mr Schomberg is too contemptible an object for me to break off my connection with your Lordship, but I must entreat his name may never be mentioned.'[20]

Hood replied by return of post with the usual cornucopia of flattery embedded in which was one sharp point: 'How was it possible, Sir, as you are pleased to suggest, that I could consult your Royal Highness in the business?'[21] He could have intended to mean that this would have been impossible since they were on opposite sides of the Atlantic, or he could have meant that it was not appropriate for an admiral to ask the opinion of a captain before appointing an officer.

Christmas was spent at sea in a gale but no greetings had reached him in Ireland from his parents and he wrote to George that if he had to visit them 'my Christmas box, or New Year's gift, will be a family lecture for immorality, vice, dissipation and expence and that I shall meet with the appellation of the prodigal son.'[22]

The Prince's orders were that his ship was to refit at Plymouth for further foreign service and, for this, his first choice was the Mediterranean, where he had not yet served. He was still determined to run a 'tight ship' and, on the day of his arrival, ordered that, while in port, all officers should be on board and that three officers were to be on deck all night. These were rules which – it soon became apparent – did not apply to him. Yet, despite the tensions and frustrations, he was for the time being happy to be where he was.

Despite the distance from London and the enticing revelry at Carlton House, Plymouth was well-suited to William's dual activity. The naval dockyard and his professional life would be separated geographically, as at Portsmouth, from the town and its social scenes. The whole was set among steep little hills and around bays and inlets, so giving an air of privacy to whatever he chose to do with his time.

After passing from the Sound through the narrow mouth of the Hamoaze, the river opened into a wide anchorage and on its eastern shore was the dockyard; between that and the barracks stood the busy, rather squalid, sailors' town called Dock, all surrounded by fortifications. Nearby, across an inlet, lay another little town, Stonehouse, and the Marine Barracks, facing two small bays which opened on to the Sound. Farther east, about a mile and a half by road from Dock and sheltered by the high bluff of The Hoe and the ramparts and bastions of the citadel, lay Plymouth itself. The old seaport had been built around Sutton Pool, a small, almost land-locked harbour that recalled

English Harbour and the 'hurricane holes' of the West Indies. The narrow streets of the town ran down to Foxhole Quay facing the harbour and there stood the handsome house of the Winne family, where William was anxious to make his first social call.

The attraction was Sally Winne, the pretty daughter of a Plymouth merchant, George Winne. She, it seems certain, was 'the lovely girl' to whom he had lost his heart before his departure nearly a year and a half before, because his arrival at Foxhole Quay was expected. Two days after Christmas, her father took a small leather-bound notebook, wrote at the top of the first page, 'Memorandums' and noted, 'Plymouth, Thursday, the 27th Dec., 1787 – His Majesty's Ship *Pegasus*, commanded by His Royal Highness Prince William Henry arrived here from Cork, when the Prince sent his Purser, Mr Whitehead, to enquire after the Health of my Family and to say that so soon as the Prince had waited on the Admiral he would be with us, which he was accordingly soon after the departure of Mr Whitehead, who breakfasted at my House. The Prince also dined, drank Tea, supped and slept this night under my roof.'

The object of William's interest was the belle of Plymouth. It was said that her face had caught the eye of a visiting artist, John Hoppner, who sketched her wearing a straw hat and leaning on a windowsill. When Hoppner had said that he wanted to publish the portrait as an engraving, George Winne had refused permission as this had not been asked when Hoppner had drawn his daughter; so it was printed as a portrait of the theatrical character 'Sophie Western', keeping the sitter's initials.

Her father was under no illusion that his daughter might marry the Prince for he, like the fathers of William's other loves, was aware of the Royal Marriage Act. But a romantic attachment could bring other benefits to the family and, in particular, he himself aspired to being appointed Agent Victualler, or principal contractor for provisions to the Navy at Plymouth. With this in mind, he set about making Sally's suitor more than welcome.

Next morning, the Prince returned to his ship after breakfast but early on the morning after, a Sunday, Winne was recording, 'Rec'd a letter under the Prince's own hand saying he would dine with me this day, which he did accordingly, also drank tea and supped with my Family.' On the Monday he was back to dine, drink tea and sup with them and, as his host noted, 'Stay'd up till after 2 o'clock to see in the New Year.'

There were several more visits during the first week of 1788, and on the following Sunday exciting news arrived. 'H.R.H. P.W.H. dined with me this day and we meant to have drank Tea, supp'd and slept at my house, but receiving letters informing him that his brothers the Prince of Wales and the Duke of York were on the road to pay him a visit, the Captain Elphinstone soon after arriving, confirming this news, the Prince left me soon after dinner.'

Next morning, the Prince, accompanied by Captain Elphinstone, travelled to Ivy Bridge to await his brother. They did not arrive and the next day he heard that they had not left London until Sunday but expected to arrive by nightfall on Wednesday. Their motive was not only a fraternal greeting, for all three brothers would have preferred to arrange an extravagant reunion in London. The two royal dukes were travelling to Plymouth for a political purpose. Both were locked in opposition to their father. The Prince of Wales's enormous debts, arising from the extravagant courts he was creating at Carlton House and at Brighton, seemed to have been settled by an increased allowance from the Civil List and a huge new grant from Parliament. But his involvement with Mrs Fitzherbert, a Roman Catholic widow with whom he went through a form of clandestine marriage, and fast living with politicians and gamblers, ran up more.

Both were seen as political opponents by the King because of their support of the Whig faction, but the amusing, hard-drinking politicians were more of an attraction than their policies. Both needed more money but, as there was opposition to this, they were in need of their younger brother as an ally. So they travelled to Devonshire to recruit him with flattery and sympathy.

William was as flattered as they had expected. On Tuesday, while awaiting his brothers, he sent a message to Winne, asking him to cancel the Plymouth Assembly, which was to be held at the London Inn the next evening and promised to compensate the landlord. Instead he hurriedly arranged a ball in honour of his brothers to be held that same night in the Long Room at Stonehouse and ensured that word of it was spread among the worthies of Plymouth.

The arrival of the three royal brothers was as dramatic as it was unexpected. At eleven o'clock on Tuesday night their carriages rolled through the streets of Plymouth past new classical and old gabled façades lit by oil lamps and flares. They did not stop but swept on to the rough little town of Dock, where they were to be lodged.

The Prince of Wales cut an extraordinary figure amongst the robust seafarers, shipwrights, farmers and merchants. Tall and good-looking, albeit overweight, puffy and marked by a decade of debauchery, he was extravagantly dressed in the height of the fashion he himself set. His manners were exquisite when he chose and his wit and mimicry brilliant, if barely comprehensible to his hosts who were not conversant with the gossip and scandals of London.

The Long Room was crowded with Plymouth society, the ladies resplendent in ball-gowns and plumes. Afterwards an exhausted George Winne wrote in his memorandum book: 'The Ball at the Long Room was very numerous and splendid. The dances at the request of Their Royal Highnesses commenced at about 9 o'clock, and 1½ hours afterwards the Three Princes entered the Room, the Band immediately playing 'God Save the King'. Prince William then taking out my daughter, began the dance and afterwards being introduced by her Partner to H.R.H. The Prince of Wales. She was honour'd in like manner by him, when he had declined dancing with any other lady.... The company broke up at 2 o'clock on Thursday morning, the P. of Wales first ordering at his own expense a Ball for the next evening.' Before leaving, he paid compliments to Mrs Winne 'in a singular manner' and thanked her and her husband for their 'attention to his Brother William', also 'engaging himself to dance the next night with our daughter'.

When the music struck up again that evening, Winne recorded, the Long Room was 'equally numerous as on the preceding one, but the visitors more genteel. The P. of Wales and the D. of York declining to dance this night (the former making a personal excuse himself and repeating the same by his Brother P. William on account of the cramp in his leg, etc.).' William opened the ball by dancing with another young lady – 'agreeable to a previous appointment' – but 'very soon afterwards making choice of my daughter, he danced with her the remainder of the night'. Finally, the princes left at one o'clock the next morning showing 'every mark of being highly pleased with their entertainment'.

Friday morning was spent 'viewing the Marine Corps and Barracks, the Royal Hospital, and the Citadel at Plymouth' and they rode at Mount Edgecombe and Maker Heights on the Cornish shore of the estuary. Then to the thumping of a royal salute from the batteries, the visitors set off for London, accompanied as far as Ivy Bridge by their brother, who returned for tea with the Winne family at Foxhole Quay. The three days had been thrilling, and George Winne noted, 'The joy expressed by all ranks of people by Illuminations, Ringing of Bells, display of Colours, Bonfires, etc., etc., was very great.'

More had been achieved in private by the two elder brothers, who had persuaded the younger to join their coalition in opposition to their parents, in the hope of more help to pay their debts. William also showed willingness to join the Prince of Wales in supporting his Whig friends and, in turn, the Prince of Wales promised to urge that William should, like Frederick, be granted a dukedom.

The Prince then resumed his attendance upon the Winne family, visiting them almost every day for a meal or tea and sometimes staying overnight, one of Winne's servants sometimes meeting him with 'a lanthorn and surtout coat'[23] to escort him to their house. The Prince was gracious to his host, inviting him on board the *Pegasus*, to social occasions ashore, and on 18 January, the King's birthday, he break-fasted with the family and danced with Sally – and only with Sally – at the Long Room.

Among his visitors at this time was Captain Nelson, whom he had invited to Plymouth partly for the general celebrations surrounding his presence but also to discuss unpleasant consequences from their time in the Caribbean: both their enforcement of the Navigation Act and frauds which Nelson had had to investigate. The Prince had written to his friend, who had been staying in London, and he had travelled with his wife to Bath, where she had stayed while he continued to Plymouth.

'I found Prince William everything I could wish – respected by all,' he told Captain Locker in a letter, 'Those who knew him formerly say he is a most altered young man; and those who were prejudiced against him acknowledged their error. The *Pegasus* is allowed by every one to be one of the best disciplined ships that ever came into Plymouth. But the great folks above now see he will not be a cypher, therefore many of the rising people must submit to acting subordinate to him, which is not so palatable; and I think a Lord of the Admiralty is hurt to see him so able after what he has said about him.'

This was presumably Lord Howe, who was unhappy about the Schomberg affair. Over this, Nelson now took the Prince's side, add-ing, 'He had wrote Lord Hood what I cannot but approve.' William returned the admiration, saying that 'Captain Nelson ... though a young man, has a sound judgement.'[24]

When Nelson returned to collect his wife at Bath and take her to his father's parsonage in Norfolk, where he was to begin his unem-ployment on half-pay, the Prince resumed his double life: seeing to the smartness of his ship and enjoying domesticity with the Winnes. Because of his courtship, he drank less than usual but his hostess ensured that he ate well; when he arrived one morning with a hare and a pheasant for Mrs Winne, her husband recorded, 'We had the former for dinner and the latter for supper.'[25] On another occasion, he gave Mrs Winne and Sally curiously inappropriate presents: engravings of the deaths of General Wolfe and Lord Robert Manners,* bought at a local auction.

In return, they made him comfortable and, when he stayed overnight, ensured that whatever newspapers were available were ready for him to read before breakfast. Now that he had been visited by the Prince of Wales, these newspapers and the monthly journals cocked an eye towards him. Blameless as it was by his standards, his dalliance with Sally Winne made amusing gossip and for the first time his amorous adventures appeared in print. Indeed, the popular satirist, Dr John Walcot, writing under his pen-name 'Peter Pindar', made fun of his sojourn at Plymouth,

> A town where, exiled by the higher pow'rs,
> The Royal tar with indignation lours;
> Kept by his sire from London and from sin,
> To say his catechism to Mistress Wynn.

Such good-natured teasing, and even a mild breath of scandal, did not worry her father, for his own ambitions seemed to be well-advanced. He had first mentioned his suitability for the appointment of Agent Victualler to the Prince before he had sailed for the West Indies nearly two years before; now the present contractor was ill and a vacancy seemed likely. At his prompting, William wrote to the Prince of Wales in March, 'From the friendship and intimacy that subsists between Mr Winne and myself, you will I hope stand his friend concerning the appointment of Agent Victualler at Plymouth.'[26]

Soon after he wrote more fully, 'From the friendship and regard you will know exists between my friend Winne and myself, you will I hope excuse me that I trouble you again on the subject of his appointment to the Agent Victuallership at Plymouth: the time now draws near for a vacancy: the present possessor of the post is exceedingly ill and on his way to Bath.... Now, my dear brother, exert your interest

---

* A dashing young captain in the Navy, killed in action in 1782.

for the sake of my friend Winne; he is really an honest, respectable man and from whom, as well as from his family, I have received the greatest civility and friendship. At this present moment I am with them in their house.'[27]

He then wrote about 'my worthy friend Winne' to the Devonshire Member of Parliament, John Rolle, 'Two years since, I promised Mr Winne to use my influence in procuring him the Agent Victuallership at this port. Mr Tonkin, the present Agent, is at the point of death. It is now therefore time for me to request you will apply to Mr Pitt and your other ministerial connections for the appointment of Mr George Winne.... His character, I may safely say, will bear the strictest enquiry and he is a very fit person for the place, being well versed in business and accounts.'[28]

Rolle sent a copy of the letter to the Prime Minister, as requested, but the Prince's influence was not so potent as was imagined, for word was about that he had joined his brothers in support of the Whigs and so in opposition to Mr Pitt's Tories. Winne did not, of course, know this and was in high hopes of being chosen. The appointment carried an annual salary of £200 but that was only the beginning of the benefits; all the provisions he would order for the Navy could pass through his hands and his account books and the possibilities of profit seemed limitless.

Nor was this the only service the Prince performed for the family, for in February the Winnes' nineteen-year-old nephew Jonathan joined the Navy under his patronage. As he was a little old to be rated captain's servant, he was entered as 'Master's Mate' in the *Pegasus*, with the same opportunity for promotion to midshipman and an eventual commission.

William's own most immediate worry was that he might be posted away from Plymouth and Sally. His ship was fitting out for service overseas but the Mediterranean seemed an increasingly unlikely destination, as did the East Indies, to which he had heard a squadron was bound, and which sounded exciting. So the West Indies station was probable once again. He had, however, reason to plead exemption on grounds of health and consulted his former surgeon, Fidge, to whom he had given fulsome testimonials when invalided home. Fidge was in Plymouth and, at the Prince's request, gave the opinion required.

In the West Indies, he wrote, the Prince had been 'repeatedly seized by sudden Attacks of Fever ... which did not leave his Royal Highness till his having returned some time to America ... I may add that we lost some of the strongest men in the ship, who died in the West Indies from the same cause.'[29] He sent the surgeon's report to the Prince of Wales, asking him to make what use of it he could. 'The Mediterranean is certainly my wish,' he wrote, 'but old square-toes will not approve of my going there.'[30] The First Lord of the Admiralty, whose old-fashioned footwear – so different from the elegant pumps worn by the royal dukes – he mocked, had already ignored a succession of requests from the Prince for promotions and appointments, but he hoped that the Prince of Wales might achieve more.

So William explained that the appointment which would suit him best would be the command of a frigate patrolling between Torbay and Land's End, which would allow frequent visits to Plymouth. Failing that, the command of a guardship lying in the Hamoaze would be ideal, so he boldly wrote again to Howe, asking for this and adding – so as to seem avid for activity rather than a quiet life at moorings – that he wanted to take part in a forthcoming exercise at sea by the Squadron of Guardships. But he was not optimistic and there were rumours that his appointment to another command on a foreign station might be imminent. 'The more, I am afraid, we have to do with Lord Howe, the worse it will be,'[31] he concluded sadly.

So, in preparation for a parting from Sally Winne, he had his portrait painted in miniature for her and sent a lock of his hair to George in London with instructions to have it mounted in a gold locket set with diamonds. It was obvious that his next appointment, like all the others, would depend upon his father and he wrote to George, 'I understand the old boy is exceedingly out of humour and I am in hourly expectation of a thunderstorm from that quarter. Fatherly admonitions at our time of life are unpleasant and of no use; it is a pity he should expend his breath in such fruitless labour.'[32]

The prince: an engraving of Prince William Henry aged twelve, after a painting by Benjamin West, published when he first went to sea.

The midshipman: Prince William on board the *Prince George*; painted by Benjamin West, probably in 1780.

His first battle: an enemy ship blows up during Admiral Rodney's engagement with the Spanish fleet off Cape St. Vincent on 16th January, 1780; by an unknown artist.

Admiral Lord Hood, the mentor, who supervised Prince William's early career; painted by James Northcote.

Admiral Robert Digby, the first naval guardian, who took
Prince William to sea in his flagship.

Captain Horatio Nelson, the
friend; detail from the portrait
begun by John Rigaud in 1777
and completed in 1781.

Lieutenant Isaac Schomberg, the
enemy, who was appointed first
lieutenant of the frigate *Pegasus*.

The sweetheart: Sally Winne as "Sophia Western", a character in *Tom Jones*; an engraving after the portrait believed to be of her by John Hoppner.

Captain Prince William Henry; the miniature by Richard Cosway, given by the sitter to Sally Winne.

"Nauticus: Those Lips were made for Kissing, Ladies!" A caricature of the Prince as a sailor ashore.

"The Battle Royal": a caricature of the three princes, visiting Plymouth in 1778, amused by a brawl between "Big Bess", a sailors' trollop, and an Army officer.

Dorothy Jordan: the Duke of Clarence's favourite portrait of his mistress and
favourite actress, painted by George Romney, and owned by their
descendants until 1990.

"Neptune reposing after *Fording* the *Jordan*." In a caricature of 1791, Dorothy Jordan wakes beside her lover, thinking, "What pleasant Dreams I have had tonight! ... Yet if this be a dream, I would not wish to wake again."

The Duke of Clarence supports Mrs. Jordan, indisposed on stage by one of her many pregnancies, while the Prince of Wales applauds and the audience jeers. "Blast the Lubbers! I wish I had them lash'd fast to the main rigging. I'd give them a dozen apiece!" her lover declares in this caricature of 1791.

"*La Promenade en Famille* – a Sketch from Life." James Gillray lampoons the Duke of Clarence and Mrs. Jordan as they move their family from Richmond to Bushy in 1797.

Their destination: Bushy House, seen during the Duke of Clarence's lifetime in an engraving after a painting by Henry Ziegler.

"An Illustrious Character" – the discontented Duke of Clarence, unemployed and in debt, seen by Gillray in 1802.

The last scene: Dorothy Jordan acting in Cheltenham on the night she was summoned to her final meeting with the Duke of Clarence.

Meanwhile his persistent but gentle courtship continued. Early in March, he escorted Sally and her brother to the Plymouth Assembly and danced with her throughout. He was now living in lodgings at Dock, where he liked to entertain; George Winne gave him a live turtle when he gave a dinner for the port admiral and some captains. This was to celebrate the announcement of his next appointment, which was to command the frigate *Andromeda*. Mounting thirty-two guns, she was bigger than the *Pegasus* and the captain's quarters were more roomy. Also, he was to take his entire ship's company with him, including William Hargood as first lieutenant and George Church – now forgiven for Midshipman Stillingfleet's allegations – as second.

He took command on 13 March 1788, but did not stay on board his ship for long. 'This day H.R.H. Prince William, after breakfasting at my House, went on board his Ship and returned afterwards and dined, drank Tea and supped with my Family and at 11 o'clock was drove to his lodgings at Dock.'[33] The log of the *Andromeda* showed that he had gone on board with his ship's company for the commissioning ceremony and the frigate had been moored alongside a hulk to begin loading tons of iron and shingle ballast. More amusement was to be had at Foxhole Quay. The following weeks were passed agreeably with supervising – often from a distance – the provisioning of the ship, preparing her rigging and sails for sea and overhauling the armament. Her captain had decided that she should be the smartest frigate in the Navy and set his men to work scrubbing, painting and blacking her mastheads, yards and blocks.

It was not only the ship that was smartened. The Prince's Hanoverian delight in uniforms had been heightened by the gorgeous appearance of his brothers among the plain blue, white and gold of the naval uniforms, and he amused himself adapting these for his own officers. They were incredulous and embarrassed when told what they would be called upon to wear and Midshipman Byam Martin described this with his customary verve.

'It was his Royal Highness's pleasure undoubtedly that there should be a uniformity,' he wrote, 'but the dress was of his own imagination and quite at variance from that which the Service prescribed. Old and young, tall and short, all were to be alike; the boy of twelve years old was to be rigged out as a man, and so squeezed into a tight dress as to leave no chance of growing, unless, perchance, nature's efforts should prove more than a match for the tailor's stitches.

'Only conceive a midshipman with white breeches so tight as to appear to be sewn upon the limb – yellow-topped hunting boots pulled close up and strapped with a buckle round the knee ... a pig-tail of huge dimensions dangling beneath an immense square gold-laced cocked hat; the tail thickened by introducing between the hair a leather thing the shape of a large carrot, and this ribboned over had a most formidable appearance; but to complete the head-dress the side hair was allowed to grow to a great length and being frizzed down and well stuffed with powder and pomatum, terminated in a large curl, leaving just room for it to work clear of the shoulder.

'Add to all this a sword about two-thirds the length of the little body that wore it ... in all the pride and pomp of a man thirteen years old and about four feet, ten inches high. Such was the dress conceived and adopted by our royal captain.'

Soon after the officers had been so dressed, the Duke and Duch-ess of Buccleuch came on board and the ship was dressed overall and her yards manned. Midshipman Martin had to stand on the cap of the maintop-masthead; he found the ascent difficult in his tight new breeches and recorded, 'I am sure it could never have been accom-plished but for the fortunate bursting of the breeches in divers places, whereby the limbs gained greater freedom of action. But ... I found the rents in the lower garment admitted more of the sharp north-west wind than was agreeable during the two hours I spent aloft.'

Another of his duties was to command the barge awaiting his cap-tain's return from Foxhole Quay. 'This waiting was dreadfully tedious,' complained Martin, 'for notwithstanding the customary punctuality of the Prince, it was sometimes hours after the appointed time before he could happily tear himself away from this beautiful young woman.' The midshipmen were wistfully admiring of her. 'Neither the malevolence of envy nor the breath of slander could taint her reputation,' declared Martin, although she was 'pushed forward by the unprincipled broker- ing views of her father … everyone whose opinion was worth having admired the propriety of her conduct under circumstances so calcu- lated to disarrange a mind less fortified by good principles.'[34]

Sally and her Prince were occasionally on public view when danc- ing, at military reviews and once at the theatre. On 28 April, the family accompanied the Prince to see a play called *The Midnight Hour* at the theatre in Dock and, as her father noted, 'all sat together in the box bespoke by the Prince. The house overflowed with the genteelest company ever seen together.' A few days later, he invited the Winnes on board his new ship for 'a noble cold collation' and the masts and yards were manned in their honour.

Although, in May, the *Andromeda* was ordered to anchor out in the Sound, the visits and festivities continued. On the fourth of June, the Winnes watched the celebration of the King's birthday with salutes fired by the guns of the Citadel and the muskets of the militia, drawn up on the Hoe. Looking seaward, they could see that 'H.R.H.'s ship … in the Sound was dress'd and the day being remarkably fine with a fresh breeze she made a most noble and gaudy appearance.'

Four days later, they celebrated another birthday – Sally's twenty- first – by dining with William on a haunch of venison. To George Winne's mortification, the Prince had to send to his ship for half-a- dozen bottles of champagne to toast Sally as there seemed to be none in the house. 'But thank God I had a small remnant left in my *sanctum sanctorum*,' noted Winne, adding smugly, 'that I thought bet- ter than his, altho' his was made him a present by H.R.H. the P. of Wales.'[35]

This prolonged dalliance had been noted by William's family, whom he had not visited since his return to England. Letters arrived from two of his sisters, Augusta and Elizabeth, now aged twenty and eighteen respectively, who knew more of his future plans than he did. 'You are going to sail away without taking a last leave of your little Gussy,' wrote the former, 'I own I am very much hurt.'[36] The latter wrote 'a few lines to assure my dearest William that no one can be more hurt than I am to think that you have been so long in England without having the happiness of seeing you ... Augusta and me are always very much together, all the sailors' songs we can get to sing we have....'[37]

There was another cause for concern at Court. Ever since his brothers' visit, William had been wondering how he could return their favours and had decided that he could do so by taking up active Whig politics. Hearing that there was a vacancy in the Totnes constituency, he began making enquiries about standing for election as its Member of Parliament. It was probable that as a prince of the blood he was ineligible, but the fact that he was showing interest and if elected would presumably join the Opposition was discovered by both the Prime Minister and the King, and gave both a practical reason for wishing him far away.

The reaction of the King to his son's amorous and political activities was more robust than his daughters'. Later Byam Martin heard what the King was supposed to have said: 'What, what, what – William playing the fool again? Send him off to America and forbid the return of the ship to Plymouth.'[38]

As Martin soon became aware, 'No sooner said than done; out came the royal mandate in the shape of an Admiralty order and a bitter pill it was. It came like a clap of thunder and was rendered the more astonishing as it reached us just at the moment when the Prince was in an ecstasy of delight.' William was staying at Foxhole Quay on 9 June when, as George Winne recorded, 'H.R.H. P. William being call'd for this morning between the hours of 4 and 5, he got up and was immediately attended by my family with whom he breakfasted. The information brought to the Prince was that Admiral Leveson Gower was off the harbour,'[39] and that his presence was required.

There was a flurry of activity and a sudden sense of doom as all knew that the *Andromeda* was to join the admiral's squadron and that they would be going to sea. They sailed for a cruise to the Scilly Islands before returning for what he knew would be only a short respite. In vain he wrote to George, 'Has not Frederick, without asking, a Regiment of Guards, so why refuse me so small a favour as a guardship?'[40]

The squadron was back in the Sound on the twenty-sixth and William came ashore. He was in a strange mood and, while at the Winne's house that evening, summoned for his amusement two dwarfs from a travelling freak-show: 'Mr Harris and Miss Morgan, two very remarkable little people, who at this time were shown as such at the London Inn, Foxhole Street'.[41]

In his depression, he did not reply to a letter from Nelson, who was staying in London on his way to obscurity in Norfolk. Congratulating the Prince on his new command, he had written, 'Your Royal Highness knows everything relative to a single Ship; and it can only be by commanding a Fleet which will establish your fame, make you the darling of the Nation and hand down your Name with honour and glory to posterity.' After more flattery, he got to the point: he was unemployed, seemed about to become a gentleman-farmer of modest means and was in need of money and position. He hoped that Prince William, after all his effusions of esteem, might be able to help.

'There may be a thing within reach of your Royal Highness,' he continued tentatively. 'Therefore, trusting to your goodness, I shall mention it. The Princess Royal must very soon have a Household appointed her. I believe a word from your Royal Highness would obtain a promise of a situation in her Royal Highness's Establishment not unbecoming the wife of a Captain in the Navy; but I have only ventured to say thus much, leaving the issue to your better judgement.'[42]

Nelson could not know that his friend was in no position to ask favours of his eldest sister, Princess Charlotte, let alone suggest that the wife of the companion of his wild West Indian days should become her lady-in-waiting. In any case, William's premonition fully occupied his mind. On 29 June, he again spent much of the day with the Winnes but next day his host noted, 'This morning news being that Admiral Gower's Fleet being going to sea, P. William arose and went on board.... N.B. the whole of Admiral Gower's Fleet took their departure from Plymouth this day to go on a cruise, as before for about a fortnight, or three weeks.'[43]

Whatever Sally Winne's hopes might have been, they had come to an end.

8

A Time of Dissipation

On the morning of 1 July 1788, a barbaric ceremony was performed on the upper deck of the *Andromeda* as she sailed past the coast of Cornwall. Just before the frigate had left Plymouth Sound, a file of marines had come aboard to reinforce the detachment responsible for enforcing the discipline of the ship. Anyone who thought that this might now be tightened would have been right.

During her long stay in port, punishment by flogging had been no more or less than expected in a ship of her size, except that the usual sentence was now twenty-four instead of twelve lashes, which was the most a captain was supposed to order without permission from higher authority. Perhaps some thought that the ship's company had become more orderly, while others might have wondered whether the captain was reluctant to order more punishment, which would be seen and heard from the shore and might come to the notice of the sensitive beauty of Foxhole Quay.

Certainly, on the first morning out from Plymouth, as the squadron dipped through the rising swell five miles south of Falmouth steering for the Atlantic, the captain mustered the crew to witness punishment. Behind ranks of armed marines in their red coats and pipeclayed cross-belts, the ship's company watched as the boatswain's mates took fifteen men, made them fast, one by one, to a wooden grating, rigged upright, and laid open their backs with a cat-o'-nine-tails. Ten seamen and five marines – one in ten of the ship's company – were flogged: six of them with twenty-four lashes, the rest with twelve, for the usual shipboard crimes of neglect of duty, disobedience and fighting, mostly related to drunkenness.

Prince William, having established his authority in his new command, now looked forward to returning to Plymouth at the end of the cruise later in the month. But he was not to do so. While homeward-bound, off the Lizard headland, another ship, the *Edgar*, fired a gun to attract attention and hoisted a signal that she carried orders for the *Andromeda*. William scribbled in a hasty note to the Prince of Wales, sent ashore by the ship which had brought him the despatch, 'This instant I have received an order to proceed to America without anchoring ... I all along was afraid of it. Excuse me if I write but a few words, my time being so short.'[1]

He also found time to write a brief but fulsome letter of explanation to George Winne and, with that, ordered the ship's master to lay a course for Nova Scotia. On the evening of the next day, the Winnes were reading his farewell, 'the most friendly letter to be imagin'd ... informing me of his being ordered to Halifax and the West Indies without so much as coming to an anchor, or taking leave of my family'.[2]

During the month it took the frigate to reach her first destination, her captain devoted much time to drafting and re-drafting a long letter to the King. This began, 'The unexpected manner in which your Majesty thought proper to order the ship I have the honour to command to America, obliges me, though very reluctantly, to express my sentiments on the subject in a more explicit manner than I have ever yet done. In the present situation, from the manner in which I was ordered, it is plain that the step originated solely in the breast of your Majesty....'

He stressed the danger to his health from service in the West Indies – admitting that past illnesses there had included venereal disease – and explained his reasons for wishing to remain in home waters: 'London, believe me, Sir, is the last place in your Majesty's dominions I wish to visit,' he continued, 'I do not deny my partiality for Devonshire: my connections there are such as I am by no means ashamed of....'

It was the manner in which the order had been given that particularly angered him. 'After having been three weeks at sea and returning in sight of the Lizard and then to find unexpected orders to proceed abroad without anchoring, is I must confess in time of peace very hard.... With respect to myself I cannot help feeling it, but the situation of the officers and men under my command is very different.... The men are in a peculiar hard position ... the most part of them are married, and have left their wives and families unprovided for, having made no provision for them during our absence. I cannot help mentioning the satisfaction I received from the conduct of the officers and men on this occasion.'

He concluded by stressing that the letter was 'by no means dictated by passion, heat or disappointment, but to be the language of my thoughts when cool, sedate and temperate and likewise that the language is comfortable to the respect due from a son to his parent.'[3]

Arriving in Halifax on 18 August, William immediately addressed a letter to Foxhole Quay and a month later George Winne – still vainly awaiting news of his appointment as Agent Victualler – received the news of his safe arrival 'after a passage of four weeks from Land's End, during which voyage he had suffer'd much from extreme Heat and a slow nervous Fever'.[4] He entered this in his little book of 'Memorandums', conscious that this was probably the end.

If William felt a sense of *déjà vu*, this was justified. Most of the major movements for him and his ship seemed to have been to get him away from women; twice those concerned – Sarah Martin and Sally Winne – had been charming girls, who under other circumstances would have made him good wives. Instead, as he saw it, he had been torn from their arms and thrust into the embrace of loose women and diseased prostitutes on the far side of the Atlantic. This time he had the enthusiastic Mrs Wentworth as a foregone conclusion and, on landing, went straight to her house. Her husband was away but he was too late, for another lover was in favour. As he wrote to his friend Captain Keats, who also had experience of Halifax, 'Your friend Wentworth is inspecting the woods of New Brunswick … in the meantime Madam is amusing herself with an officer and has, I am sorry to say, thrown off all remaining decency.'[5]

He was to emulate her, helped by the fact that his senior officer was now Captain Charles Sandys, acting as the commodore of the small squadron at Halifax, whom Midshipman Martin described as 'one of those vulgar, drunken dolts who bring discredit on the Naval Service'.[6] Even Nelson, who was ready to see the best in anyone under criticism, had written of him two years earlier, 'Between Bacchus and Venus he is scarcely ever in his senses. I am very sorry for him, but his heart is good, but he is not fit to command a man-of-war.'[7] When the Prince paid his formal call on him in the *Dido*, 'he found the sot in his bed, drunk'. Midshipman Martin, who was no prude, thought that, 'It was truly disgusting to witness the scenes which took place during the time we remained in such bad company.'[8]

Four days after his arrival, William's twenty-third birthday was marked with the hoisting of the royal standard and a royal salute of twenty-one guns. A series of parades, receptions and dinners continued for a week, to reach a climax with a ball on board the *Andromeda*. On one of these occasions, at least, the Prince matched his superior officer's tendency. Dining at the Chief Justice's house, his friend Lieutenant Dyott noted, 'I never saw a man get so completely drunk. He desired the General to order the whole garrison up the Citadel Hill to fire a *feu de joie*; but his Highness was not able to attend it, as he was obliged to go to bed.'[9]

As usual, he made a quick recovery and was on his most polished behaviour for the ball in the frigate. 'The quarterdeck was divided at the mizzen-mast,' Dyott recorded, 'between it and the main-mast was for dancing, and abaft it for supper, the whole covered in with a frame and canvas and lined with white colours and blue festoons.' The Prince 'paid the greatest possible attention to everybody' and his officers were 'the most genteel set of young men I ever saw'.

After the dancing, 'the colours that divided the quarterdeck were drawn up in festoons and displayed the most completely elegant supper I ever saw. At the end of the deck were two transparent paintings, the one representing the Scottish motto and thistle, the other St George's Cross and the Garter. Upwards of sixty people sat down to supper at a table in the shape of a horse-shoe. The supper was chiefly cold, except soups and removes, with partridges, etc., champagne, hock, etc. We remained more than an hour at supper and it was wonderful to see the attention his Royal Highness paid to every one present, not neglecting a single midshipman. We danced till three o'clock, when the champagne began to operate with some of the gentlemen and the ladies thought it near time to go ashore. I never spent a more joyous night.'[10]

A month later, another entertainment was held in the *Andromeda* to celebrate the anniversary of the King's coronation. This, too, began with the firing of a royal salute and then the frigate's log recorded in the customary dry, factual style the time of the Governor's arrival and the number of guns fired in salute. It concluded the twenty-four-hour entry: 'By order of Commodore Sandys saluted and drinking public toasts with 168 guns at different periods.'[11]

More detailed accounts were given by Lieutenant Dyott and Midshipman Martin. Dyott noted that, as the company were assembling, the garrison ashore and the squadron in the harbour fired royal salutes and, after the twenty guests sat down to 'a superb dinner', the *Andromeda* fired salutes of twenty-one guns when each of the first eight toasts were proposed. 'We got pretty tipsy,' he confessed.[12]

Martin maintained that had it been arranged by Lieutenant Church, as would normally have been the case, the occasion would have been conducted with decorum, but the 'worthless commodore and his libertine captains' were in charge. The ship was lying out in the anchorage and the fresh breeze, which had made the embarkation of the guests a test of their resolution and their hosts' seamanship, increased to a gale. So it was not until eight o'clock next morning that they were able to be got ashore without the ladies' dresses being soaked.

During the long party, Commodore Sandys led the drinking and (as Martin put it) was 'at an early period of the evening in a state to be quite insensible to the increasing violence of the wind'. He was also unaware of tragedy. 'He, with all his sins, could not be reproached with hearing the minute guns of a ship in distress about five miles below at the entrance of the harbour.... As if to mock their distress we were firing frequent salutes to complement any favourite toast.'[13] Meanwhile, the ship at sea foundered with the loss of all hands.

During his stay at Halifax, according to Dyott, the Prince showed a new delight in military ceremonial. 'His Royal Highness was pretty constant to the parade and, I think, would prefer our profession to his own,' he said. 'It is astonishing how he remembers and knows almost all the officers of any rank in the army. If any officer has ever been presented to him, he never forgets his name or his character.'

William was enjoying himself as the focus of patriotism, which was given piquancy because none of his admirers knew he was in disgrace and had been banished by the King he was representing. To keep the social tempo at this pitch, he entertained lavishly, ashore as well as in the ship. At one dinner party ashore, described by Dyott as 'the most elegant thing I ever saw', fifty-five dishes were offered for first course and thirty-five as the second; in another, on board ship, there was 'a famous feed and champagne *à l'abondance*'. This was expensive: during six weeks at Halifax he estimated that he spent between £400 and £500.

Whether or not he had given up touring the brothels, Dyott made no mention of this in his diary. When the time came for him to sail for the West Indies in October, his friend did record his split character: generosity and charm mixed with coarse hedonism: 'Take him altogether, I think I never saw or heard of a finer character,' wrote Dyott, 'He is, I will venture to say from experience, as honourable a man as ever held a commission in the British service. He has a generous and noble spirit and will, I am convinced, render an essential service to his King and Country. I had the honour, I may say, of living with him for three months and in that time one may be able to judge of a man's character. I believe I shall never spend three months in that way again, for such a time of dissipation, etc., etc., I cannot suppose possibly to happen.'[14]

The Prince was well aware of this dichotomy, writing to his brother, 'I am sorry to say I have been living a terrible debauched life, of which I am heartily ashamed and tired. I must in the West Indies turn over a new leaf, or else I shall be irrecoverably ruined. This country affords no necessary thing worth relating: drinking is the only occupation ... I have made a determined resolution to abstain from excess of all kinds.'[15]

The *Andromeda* had been on one cruise and returned to Halifax before sailing for Jamaica and arriving at Port Royal in mid-November. Going ashore with his first lieutenant, without ceremony and unannounced, he made his way to the public rooms for drinks and a game of billiards. A party of Army officers at the tables invited him, in a friendly, casual manner and without introductions, to join them. At the end of a game, the Prince turned to his opponent, the senior colonel present, and asked him to be kind enough to parade his regiment at daylight as he wished to inspect it. The colonel's amazement at such a request from a captain in the Navy, junior to and younger than himself, was resolved by mutual introductions and much subsequent *bonhomie*.

England seemed as far away as it was, but occasional packets of mail brought his memories into poignantly sharp focus. His principal informant was George, to whom he confided, 'I must inevitably be in debt and God knows who will pay them. The day will come when I am afraid my father will [bring] everything up in a horrid manner. The storm is gathering and must burst over my head.'

He had been disappointed to hear that George Winne had not been chosen as Agent Victualler, but he thanked his brother for 'having interested yourself for my good and worthy friend Winne; though unsuccessful, believe me, dear brother, I feel the obligation equally.'[16] The prospects of meeting with anything but disappointment and reproof in his own country seemed remote.

William delighted in Jamaica, despite the threat of its climate to his health. Unlike the provincial colonists of Halifax, the sugar-planters, merchants and ship-owners of the island were rich, and loved and entertained in lavish style. On arrival, he travelled through the fields of sugar-cane to Spanish Town to receive a loyal address from a deputation from the House of Assembly. The Executive Council voted a thousand guineas to have his star of the Order of the Garter set in diamonds, and let it be known that they would welcome his appointment as Governor. He had particularly endeared himself to them through his endorsement of slavery. Whenever he was conducted through the sugar fields or factories, the Negro slaves seemed healthy and cheerful and, now as on earlier visits, he concluded that they were probably happier there than in Africa.

On 15 December, the *Andromeda* sailed from Kingston Bay bound for Barbados. Remembering Nelson's example in enforcing the Navigation Act, and finding a little action diverting, he was on watch for illegal traders; on Christmas Day he noted in his log, 'Fired a shot at a brig to bring her to'.[17] Then on arrival at Barbados on 16 January 1789, he heard dreadful news that was confirmed over the coming days as merchant ships arrived from England, and by a letter from his old uncle, the Duke of Cumberland. The King was not only ill, but mentally ill.

In October, while William had been feasting at Halifax, the King had been seized by pains, cramps, convulsions, fever and a sequence of violent but seemingly unconnected symptoms. Purgatives were administered, and laudanum to ease the pain, but he grew worse and showed signs of dementia. His doctors were bewildered and in November two of them gave the Prime Minister, Mr Pitt, their opinions that the King was 'in a perfectly maniacal state'[18] and that 'the disorder was no other than direct lunacy', from which he might 'never recover'.*[19] If this was to be the case, the solution to the constitutional crisis would be a regency and the Prince of Wales expected to be called upon by Parliament to act, if only temporarily, as Prince Regent. But Pitt demurred, ostensibly on the grounds that the King's mental illness was not yet known to be chronic.

Despite his differences with his father, even mutual antagonism, William was distressed and wrote an emotional letter of sympathy to his brother George asking for more news of 'the best of Kings and fathers'. When he had heard of 'the dreadful situation ... the shock I first felt was great', he told him. 'I follow the dictates of my heart,' he continued, 'Sincerely do I love this good and worthy man and long may he with his usual firmness reign over us. The poor Queen! what a situation for her.' His brother, he thought, must be 'by now in the situation of Regent, for which, I make no doubt, you will be loved and respected by everybody.'[20]

His ship was ready to sail for home at an hour's notice and he begged for orders to do so. These should be sent both to the Leeward Islands and to Jamaica, he asked, because he had to continue his cruise. While awaiting instructions, William sailed for Antigua, where he lay for three weeks in Foremast Bay and visited old friends. He continued to Dominica and Grenada before the expected orders from the Admiralty reached him at the beginning of April.

As if borne on wings of ambition as well as favourable winds, the frigate crossed the Atlantic in three weeks, sailing past Plymouth, for even more enticing prizes seemed to wait in London. She anchored at Spithead on 29 April and the Prince went ashore immediately. At Portsmouth, he was told the latest news. The King had made a remarkable recovery, the crisis was over and a service of thanksgiving had been held at St Paul's Cathedral the week before.

---

* The King's illness is generally accepted to have been porphyria, an hereditary metabolic illness with symptoms of insanity.

So Prince William hurried to London, where his life took a new tack and, as Byam Martin put it, he 'commenced his foolish career as a politician'.[21] Three days later, he arrived at Windsor to an unexpectedly affectionate welcome from his parents. The King was weak but convalescent and the Queen looked skeletal, having lost so much weight through worry about her husband and the exhausting quarrels with her eldest son over the need for a regency. Gradually William learned the details of the violent confrontations of the past six months.

As soon as the King had become mentally deranged, the Prince of Wales had pressed his case for taking office as Prince Regent. He was due to ascend the throne eventually in any case, but to take power now would enable him to pay his gigantic debts and help his friends, notably the Whig politicians, whose chances of replacing the Tories in government seemed as remote as ever. In this he was supported by the Duke of York, his fast-living friends and, of course, the Whigs. In opposition to his hopes were his mother, who maintained that her husband would recover and did not trust her elder son; the Prime Minister, Pitt, and the Tory administration, who realised what their political prospects would be if the Prince of Wales were allowed to become surrogate sovereign. A furious political storm developed, with the Prince of Wales insisting that he be granted unlimited royal powers; later he agreed to some constraints: that he would not, for example, create peers outside his own family. But that would at least enable him to enoble his brother William.

It was with such rewards in mind that the three brothers resumed their intimacy. William exchanged the familiar surroundings of wood, hemp and canvas for his brothers' world of Siena marble, rosewood and ebony; chandeliers, looking-glasses and ormolu. Together, they attended routs and dinners at Carlton House, grand Whig houses and the faction's favourite club, Brooks's in St James's Street. William particularly enjoyed an entertainment given by the Spanish Ambassador at the Ranelagh pleasure gardens in Chelsea to celebrate the King's recovery. A huge tent of white satin fringed with gold was rigged inside the great Rotunda and the guests gossiped, listened to music and ate from solid gold plate. He himself returned such hospitality with a party at Willis's Rooms in honour of his brothers. Swagged with red and white roses and blue silk, the room was also decorated with enormous transparencies of their coats-of-arms and another, designed by himself, of a flag and anchor with the words, 'United For Ever'.

These were only immediate, fleeting satisfactions. His brother George had determined to reward him with suitable rank as soon as he took control of patronage, and the first steps had already been taken when the Prime Minister insisted that enoblement had to await the King's recovery. When this was finally announced, the recommendation was ratified as being inevitable and possibly prudent in view of William's recent political plans, the King sighing, 'I well know that is another vote added to the Opposition.'[22] But it would be exercised by a member of the House of Lords and not by the member for Totnes in the more politically potent House of Commons.

So three months before his twenty-fourth birthday, Prince William Henry was created Duke of Clarence and of St Andrews, and Earl of Munster in the Irish peerage. He was granted an annual allowance of £12,000, although the King was said to have suggested £14,000 and the Prime Minister to have reduced it; even so this was thought to be sufficient for the comfortable, dignified life of a duke.

He was also given an apartment in St James's Palace, a few minutes walk from Carlton House, and there was a suggestion that he could make use of a country house, probably The Lodge [now known as White Lodge] in Richmond Park, although the Duke, as he now was, would have preferred the similarly-named house in Greenwich Park, which was closer to ships and naval dockyards.

Inevitably, as the country was at peace, there would be a lull in his naval career, but he planned to resume it as soon as possible, combining it – as did Lord Hood and other senior officers – with politics. He was to relinquish command of the *Andromeda* when she was paid off in June, but hoped to keep his ship's company together because, despite his pride and aloofness, strict discipline and occasional brutality, he had commanded an efficient ship and had engaged some at least of her crew's loyalty. He was certainly attached to them and hoped they could accompany him to his next command, which should be a ship of the line. So, to further their careers he made various recommendations, asking that his first lieutenant, Hargood, be promoted to commander and that his old friend Keats be confirmed as post-captain and given a suitable command.

Then it was said that he himself was about to be promoted to flag rank, which would mean that, while he would no longer be eligible for the command of a ship, he could expect, as a rear-admiral, to command a squadron. His euphoria at the thought of this was dashed by a remark made to him by his first naval mentor, Admiral Digby, and then by hearing of others he was said to have made. He had recently dined with the admiral and they had spent a jolly evening together, but on their next meeting Digby had implied that he thought such promotion would be a mistake. He had added that he deplored the idea of his involvement in politics. Later he had apparently remarked to a mutual friend that William still had a habit of disparaging others behind their backs.

The Duke thereupon cut Digby on the next occasion they attended the same function in London. This was so obvious to all that the admiral wrote him an aggrieved letter. Asking why his formerly gracious behaviour had so changed, he wrote, 'Perhaps you have taken offence at my saying to you that I was sorry you was to have your Flag; I was so indeed but on your account chiefly; I think it will deprive you of much pleasure and the Nation of much advantage. I look upon it as laying yourself up in ordinary.'

What the admiral meant was that, as a flag officer, he would be eligible only for major commands and, when these were not available in peacetime, he was likely to be unemployed – as it were, laid up in reserve – whereas as a captain he would in all probability be given command of another ship at sea. He then dealt with the criticism of political involvement. 'If your Royal Highness has been offended at the friendly advice I gave on our first meeting, viz., to rejoice that you had been absent during the last Winter and cautiously to avoid engaging in *any party, I am sorry* but I must glory in it still.'

Finally he came to the question of personal conduct. 'I have said that if you went on abusing bodies of people you did not know before mix'd company and taking pains to make enemys, you would too easily succeed and that you wou'd damn your character irretrievably in a month (pardon the expression). But I have never said it but to your particular friends, who wish you well as I do. Ask *any one* of them if what I say is not a truth; Princes do not always hear such truths, nor do they all like to hear them.'[23]

Such blunt words were also being spoken behind the Duke's back. For all his good humour, generosity and ebullience, there was seen to be an element of cruelty in him. This was not only occasional roughness and rudeness – as when he remarked of an irritating lady guest, as he left the room, that she would benefit from a touch of the cat-o'-nine-tails – but more wounding behaviour. He was a man who, as Lieutenant Dyott had noted, would encourage familiarity and, when he had had enough, would deliver a snub. He could be charming when it suited him but his choice of friends seemed to be dictated by what the individual concerned could offer in return. He would continue to admire Captain Nelson, of course, but now that he was unemployed and living in the remote Norfolk countryside, there was no need to invite him to London for a levée or suggest that his wife might be suitable as a lady-in-waiting in his sister's household.

As a naval officer, he was known as a disciplinarian commanding an efficient, if not always happy, ship. Yet the quarrel with Lieutenant Schomberg* and his treatment of Lieutenant Hope were the talk not only of the wardrooms of the fleet but of the Board Room at the Admiralty. Lord Howe, the First Lord, Lord Hood, another member of the Board, and now Admiral Digby, were highly critical of him. His dabbling in Whig politics, even if it were no more than dabbling, had

---

* Isaac Schomberg was promoted captain in 1790 and became Deputy Controller of the Navy in 1808; he wrote a history of the Royal Navy and died in 1813.

irritated the Prime Minister and angered the King. So any thought of promoting him to flag rank was set aside and the Admiralty decided to consider him for another captain's appointment in due course, probably commanding a ship of the line.

It was now politics rather than morals which were to alienate him from his father, but money was to be the trigger for the familiar exchanges. On 28 May, William had written a courtly letter to the King, thanking him for quadrupling his allowance but adding that, while he would endeavour to remain solvent, 'I think it my duty not to incur the risk of deceiving your Majesty by giving expectation that I can live within the present income and at the same time maintain the character and mode of living inseparable from the relation I bear to your Majesty and my situation in the country.'[24]

The reaction was a sharply-worded letter telling him to be grateful for what he had been given, learn to live within a perfectly proper income and, once again, to mend his ways generally. He replied at length, pleading that he was only wondering whether the King might make his allowance one of £14,000, which he gathered had been the original intention, rather than the lower amount which had been agreed by Mr Pitt. But it was not the question of money which gave the King's letter its rancour, he knew.

William deplored 'the marked disapprobation which I am unfortunate enough to find your Majesty express of my conduct and behaviour since my arrival in England'. He denied having been guilty of 'a line of conduct void of kindness to your Majesty' and linked himself with his brothers in his protestations of innocence. 'I do not presume to judge of the proceedings of my brothers, or of the political differences of parties during your Majesty's late unfortunate illness,' he wrote, 'but my knowledge of the Prince of Wales and the Duke of York compels me to avow my firm conviction that they could never have been influenced by any sentiments other than those of true love and duty towards your Majesty....'[25]

The tension was relieved by the King's departure for further convalescence at Weymouth, where sea-bathing had been prescribed by his doctors. In the event, he preferred sailing, and the Admiralty provided a ship of the line and a frigate for the purpose; still hoping to please, William sent his barge's crew from Portsmouth to ferry his father out to the ships. After their first sail in the frigate, the Queen wrote to her son Augustus, 'We row frequently in ten oar cutters. Our rowers are those of the Duke of Clarence; they are very smart fine dress'd men.'[26]

Indeed they were rowing in the bay on 14 July 1789 as the Paris mob was storming the Bastille. Events in France – notably the attempts by the National Assembly to form a democratic constitution in belated emulation of British political development, it seemed – were being watched with excitement and admiration by the Whigs in England. The Duke of Clarence was interested only insofar as his elder brothers' clever friends were fascinated by events across the Channel. Now that his ship had been paid off he was far more interested in trying to set up his own suitably-endowed establishment. He had been upset again by his father's refusal to allow him the household officers of his choice. All three captains in the Royal Navy – Pole, Christian and Elphinstone – were thought unsuitable by the King, who eventually relented in part and permitted him to engage Pole as a Groom of the Bedchamber and Christian as an equerry. William preferred the company of naval officers, and anyone presented to him who could mention some connection with the sea was greeted heartily. When Fanny Burney, by now a novelist, was introduced as the sister of a naval officer, he declared, 'As long as she has a brother in the Service, ma'am, I look upon her as one of us. Oh, faith, I do! I do indeed! She is one of the corps.'[27]

The unemployed Duke of Clarence seen by Gillray as "A True British Tar",
complaining, "Damn all Bond Street Sailors I say, a parcel of smell-smocks!
They'd sooner creep into a Jordan than face the French – damme!"

Gillray's vision of the "Promis'd Horrors of the French Invasion" with William Pitt
being flogged and the Prince of Wales and the Duke of York being flung from
the balcony of White's on which the Duke of Clarence is about to be stabbed.

The beached sailor: the Duke of Clarence painted by James Northcote.

The imported bride: Princess Adelaide, Duchess and future Queen,
painted by Franz Winterhalter.

The lost friend. James Gillray draws Emma Hamilton as Britannia bewailing the dying Nelson, who is attended by King George III, while the Duke of Clarence appears as a sailor presenting a captured French flag.

The only naval action the Duke of Clarence saw in the "Great War" was a re-enactment of the Battle of the Nile by model ships on the Serpentine in Hyde Park during the peace celebrations of 1814.

"The toast is 'The Navy!'" An engraving after a flattering portrait by M. W. Sharpe shows the Lord High Admiral proposing the toast on board a ship, which, as the rolled and stowed hammocks show, is cleared for action.

The enemy: Vice-Admiral Sir George Cockburn, the senior naval member of the Lord High Admiral's Council; detail from a portrait by J. J. Halls.

The friend: Vice-Admiral Sir Edward Codrington, Commander-in-Chief in the Mediterranean, painted by Sir Thomas Lawrence.

The victory: the destruction of the Turkish and Egyptian fleets at Navarino by the British, French and Russians in 1827. But the victory was not welcomed by the politicians and not taken seriously by the public.

The pioneer of submarines: Captain Tom Johnstone, the Channel pilot, smuggler, spy and inventor; the only known portrait.

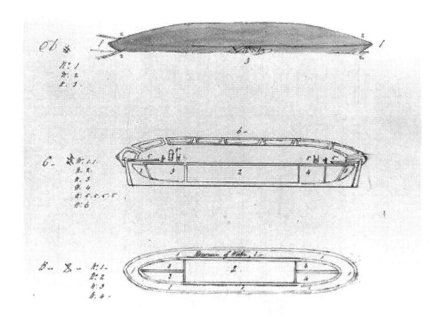

Plans for a submarine propelled by paddle-wheels drawn at the beginning of the 19th century by Lieutenant William Innes Pocock, Royal Navy.

The King as his subjects saw him in 1830: the robust and dutiful coastguard, a caricature by William Heath.

The King as he saw himself: the benevolent, fatherly admiral,
painted by A. Morton.

The accession: "Captain Cl——nce taking Command of the Ship British
Constitution", a caricature of 1830 by William Heath. The King and Queen
inspect the ship's company, which is calling for reform of the Navy, while the
guard of honour is commanded by the Duke of Wellington.

"The British Broadside, or Reform Triumphant." King William blows away the House of Lords, while a sailor cries, "I told you, Messmates, he would turn out True Blue", in a caricature of 1832.

The ship of state sails on: after the death of the King, Queen Adelaide sails in the Mediterranean on board H.M.S. *Hastings*; an engraving of 1838 after a painting by O. Borland.

He was also involved in his brothers' attempts to raise huge loans to finance their high living in London, and inevitably he joined them in their unpopularity. As a naval officer serving overseas, he had escaped the outrage provoked by the extravagance of the Prince of Wales. The most sharply pointed criticism came from the pens of caricaturists such as Gillray, Rowlandson and Cruikshank. Once his brothers had visited him at Plymouth, he had become fair game. George was drawn as the bloated, coiffed dandy; Frederick as the corpulent, corseted red-coat; and he was now the porcine, doltish Jack Tar. Londoners at all social levels found the caricatures funny and as they were hung in the windows of print-shops – the most famous of them in St James's Street near Brooks's Club – they were free entertainment.

The press, too, scented blood and the leader of the pack had been *The Times*. When the King had recovered his sanity, its proprietor, John Walter, had savaged his sons. 'The insincerity of their joy is visible,'[28] the newspaper had jeered. Even William, who had been absent throughout, was mocked as having returned from the West Indies without orders in the hope of becoming First Lord of the Admiralty. Walter was sued for libel, found guilty and sentenced to two years' imprisonment (he was released after eleven months) and fined £100 for libelling the Duke of Clarence.

It was a relief to escape from the watchful, malicious eyes of the capital for the summer season. The house in Richmond Park was too remote for William and he chose to rent another, Ivy Lodge, a handsome house on the riverside in the fashionable town itself. Richmond suited him: it was smart yet relaxed; frequented by the *haut monde* yet delightfully rural; it was a short drive from London and close to the Portsmouth Road should duty call.

His new neighbours included the dissolute Duke of Queensberry, who had lost his position as a courtier for favouring a regency during the King's illness; the artistic Lady Diana Beauclerk – born a Spencer, the favourite grand-daughter of Sarah, Duchess of Marlborough, and known to her friends as 'Lady Di' – and an old sailor, Vice-Admiral Sir George Pocock, who had made a fortune from prize-money at the capture of Havana in 1762 and had lived for a quarter of a century in comfortable retirement across the river at Twickenham. One of the most entertaining was Horace Walpole, the elderly wit and author, who also lived at Twickenham in his Gothic mansion, Strawberry Hill, and cast an urbane eye over riverside society.

The Duke of Clarence moved to Richmond in August, and his first public appearance was to attend a regatta on the Thames to celebrate his twenty-fourth birthday. It was a delightful spectacle, which he watched from the balcony of The Castle tavern in company with the pick of the local grandees, including Walpole, who described it in a letter.

'The day had been coined on purpose with my favourite south-east wind,' he wrote, 'The scene both up the river and down was what only Richmond upon earth can exhibit; the crowds in those green velvet meadows and on the shores, the yachts, barges, pleasure and small boats and windows and gardens lined with spectators, were so delightful that when I came home from that vivid show I thought Strawberry Hill as dull and solitary as a hermitage.'[29]

As always, William enjoyed lively nocturnal company and missed it at his new home. So, as Walpole recorded, 'His Royal Highness, to divert loneliness, has brought with him a Miss Polly Finch, who, being still more averse to solitude, declares that any tempter would make paradise more agreeable than a constant *tête-à-tête*.'[30] She was a *demi-mondaine* from Mayfair who had been won away from her former lover, as the press was eager to report.

'His Highness has with him a sweet little Finch, to whom he seems much attached,' reported *The Oracle*. 'The bird took to flight from a well-known house in Berkeley Street and has lately been seen hovering about a royal apartment at St James's from three until twelve, or later.' The paper then described how 'the notes of a *Finch*' had been heard 'on Richmond Hill to the animating thunders of the British Navy.'

It was hardly a love-match for, the report continued, she seemed to be 'a Finch, who, from the price, may properly be denominated a *gold Finch*'.[31]

As the pair settled down at Ivy Lodge, the Duke aroused two distinct reactions. One was that of Horace Walpole, who described 'this young prince, who never drinks or games, and is extremely good-humoured and well-bred', possibly with a touch of sarcasm. If Richmond needed a Parliamentary candidate and he had not been enobled, he continued, 'he would certainly be elected there. He pays his bills regularly himself, locks up his doors at night so that his servants may not stay out late and never drinks but a few glasses of wine.'[32] Indeed, it was said, 'the Duke of Clarence is so popular among, and so happy with, his Richmond neighbours that he talks of passing a great part of the winter with them.'[33]

But, when he was not on his best behaviour, there was another view. Another elderly wit, George Selwyn, noted his predilection for telling coarse jokes in mixed company: '*Il tient des propos trop indé-centes* – thinks that sort of discourse will give him the reputation of wit. It may, on the forecastle deck, but our Richmond ladies do not relish it.' They might have overlooked his keeping a mistress – realising that the Royal Marriage Act presented almost insurmountable obstacles to finding a suitable bride – but Selwyn doubted whether she was happy as '*un oiseau de cage*, although fed and caressed by a prince'.[34]

In fact, she was bored. Unable to accompany her lover to most social engagements as his consort, she found his company heavily masculine when they spent the darkening autumn evenings together. As she could not play billiards with him, he read aloud to her from John Campbell's *Lives of the Admirals*. After she had endured two volumes of naval biography, she discovered that there were two more and that was too much. Towards the end of the year, Polly Finch flew back to London and William later returned alone to his rooms at St James's Palace. He did not remain lonely for long.

At about this time (the date and the place were not recorded) the Duke of Clarence met an enchanting woman. Others had found her so: she was a successful actress, a charming comedienne, who 'spoke her lines as if she had just thought of them'.[35] Although lacking Sally Winne's conventional prettiness, she had a generous, lively face with gentle eyes, set wide, and a humorous mouth; as attractive off-stage as on, she had a memorably infectious laugh which echoed her warmth and humour. As the essayist William Hazlitt put it, 'There was no one else like her. Her face, her tones, her manner, were irresistible. Her smile had the effect of sunshine and her laugh did one good to hear it. Her voice was eloquence itself: it seemed as if her heart was always at her mouth. She was all gaiety, openness and good nature. She rioted in fine animal spirits.... She was Cleopatra turned into an oyster-wench, without knowing that she was Cleopatra, or caring that she was an oyster-wench.'[36]

Another contemporary writer, Leigh Hunt, thought that 'though she was neither beautiful, nor handsome, nor even pretty, nor accomplished, nor 'a lady', nor anything conventional or *comme il faut* whatsoever, yet was so pleasant, cordial, so natural, so full of spirits, so healthily constituted in mind and body, had such a shapely leg withal, so charming a voice, and such a happy and happy-making expression of countenance, that she appeared something superior to all those requirements of acceptability....'[37]

She was more than acceptable to William. Whether they first met at Richmond, where she was living with a lover, and where the elegant little Theatre Royal attracted the most celebrated performers as audience as well as cast, or whether it was at the splendid theatre of the same name in Drury Lane, where her greatest triumphs were applauded, is not known. What is known is that he loved going to the theatre and it is thought that he went backstage to congratulate her on her performance.

It has been suggested that while they were together in her stuffy little dressing-room, she gave him a glass of warm wine because, as a New Year present on 1 January 1790, he gave her a pair of silver-plated wine-coolers,* perhaps as a hint of more such meetings to come.

There were to be many more. He was to realise that he had found his ideal partner in Dorothy Jordan.

---

* The two wine-coolers, still in the possession of their descendants, are inscribed, '*His Royal Highness the Duke of Clarence to Dora Jordan, New Year's Day*, 1790.'

9

What Girl but Loves the Merry Tar

The idea of a love affair with an actress was exciting to the Duke of Clarence as to all young men of his stamp. By definition she was desirable, not only because she was almost certainly attractive and amusing, but because she would be desired by most of the other men in her audiences. There was a sexual piquancy about her profession, which shocked their elders and delighted them, in that she was probably intelligent and elegant, with the appearance of 'a lady', but exhibited herself on stage in what could seem a mild form of prostitution.

This theory seemed to find substance in the life of the famous actress, Mrs Jordan. Firstly, that was not her real name, which was Miss Bland. She had picked her stage surname after crossing the water – 'the Jordan' – from Ireland and had assumed marital status to cover the presence of her illegitimate children. Yet this was misleading: Dorothy Jordan was neither flighty nor promiscuous, but as good-hearted and jolly off the stage as on.

The illegitimate daughter of educated parents – Francis Bland, son of an Anglo-Irish judge, and Grace Phillips, daughter of a Welsh clergyman and herself an actress – Dorothy had been born in London on 22 November 1761. Four years older than the Duke, she was also more mature, having had to make her way through emotional shoals such as he had never had to navigate. As a pretty young actress in Dublin, she had been seduced by the domineering manager of her company, Richard Daly, and had escaped his clutches by fleeing to England in 1782, pregnant and destitute.

Joining another company, she soon made a mark as an *ingenue* with a talent for comedy. Accompanied by her mother and infant daughter, Fanny, she toured in the provinces before finding acclaim in London. By 1786, she was regarded as the equal of, and rival to, Sarah Siddons, the tragedienne, but as Mrs Jordan was anything but tragic the two complemented each other. In that same year, while performing at Drury Lane, she met a young lawyer with a fondness for the theatre, Richard Ford. She became his mistress, lived with him and bore him three children over four years. He spoke of marriage, and she sometimes called herself 'Mrs Ford', but he never proposed, probably because he had political ambitions and marriage to an actress might have proved a handicap in polite society. It was while living with him at Richmond that she met the Duke of Clarence.

Soon after their first meeting she appeared at Drury Lane in a farce called *The Spoil'd Child*, which opened in March 1790. She played the part of 'Little Pickle', a girl who disguises herself as a sailor. So dressed, she sang a winsome little song, which must have won William's heart:

> What girl but loves the merry Tar,
> We o'er the ocean roam, sir.
> In ev'ry clime we find a port,
> In ev'ry port a home, sir …

He was much taken with her, but, flattered though she was, she remained faithful to Richard Ford, who was handsome if ineffectual; she adored their children and still hoped for marriage. Even so, flirtation with the King's son was enjoyable and, as an actress who flirted with her audiences, it was easy to captivate this susceptible naval officer.

He was fascinated though not as yet in love, but she seemed as unobtainable as she was desirable and that was a spur. The attraction was sharpened when duty suddenly called him back to sea. A crisis had arisen on the other side of the world in an anchorage in the Pacific known by name to few naval officers and visited by fewer still. Ownership of the settlement at Nootka Sound, on the coast of Vancouver Island, was disputed by Britain and Spain and in May the Spanish had seized some British ships there. When the news reached Europe – and even Nelson was able to read about it in the *Norfolk Chronicle* – the danger seemed not only of war with Spain but with France as they were bound together by a treaty of mutual support. The Royal Navy was making ready for action, ships were being brought forward from reserve and officers recalled.

The Duke was told that his services would be required and, in distant Norfolk, Captain Nelson hoped for employment and wrote to his friend for help in being nominated for a command. He complied, mentioning Nelson's name to the First Lord of the Admiralty, the Earl of Chatham, the Prime Minister's elder brother. Nelson travelled to London in the hope of seeing the First Lord and, as he put it, making 'use of every interest to get a Ship, ay, even a boat, to serve my Country, but in vain'. Lord Chatham was too busy to receive him and, bewildered, Nelson concluded, 'there was a prejudice at the Admiralty against me, which I can neither guess at, or in the least account for.'[1]

Even more shocking was his reception by Lord Hood, who had been so friendly in American waters and seemed a future patron, and whom he now visited at his house in Wimpole Street. Nelson never repeated their exact conversation but later revealed that Hood had 'made a speech never to be effaced from my memory, viz.: that the King was impressed with an unfavourable opinion of me'.[2] This was undoubtedly true because Hood was still a favourite at court, where he was frequently consulted on naval affairs, and was also a member of the Board of Admiralty.

What hurt Nelson so deeply was that he had almost made a religion of his devotion to the monarchy and to the King in person. There were two probable reasons for the royal disfavour. One was that word had reached London of Nelson's implacable enforcement of the Navigation Act in the Caribbean and the consequent financial loss to many prominent British officials and merchants who had been disregarding it. The other was that he had been Prince William's superior officer and companion during the period he was known to have behaved so badly; it being forgotten, perhaps, that these lapses had taken place during Nelson's absence from the immediate scene. Bewildered and bitter as he was, he told himself that he must have made political enemies and maintained, 'Neither at sea or on shore, through the caprice of a Minister can my attachment to my King be shaken.'[3]

The knife was turned by the news that the Duke of Clarence had been appointed to command a ship of the line, the *Valiant* of seventy-four guns. He wrote a letter of congratulations from his father's parsonage: 'I have seen by the papers of the *Valiant's* arrival at Spithead: I hope she turns out everything your Royal Highness expected of her. My not being appointed to a Ship is so very mortifying that I cannot find words to express what I feel on the occasion: and when I reflect on your Royal Highness's condescension in mentioning me to Lord Chatham, I am the more hurt and surprised.'

Although he had not seen the Duke during his visit to London, he declared his friendship for him with a touch of desperation: 'The attachment, which I trust has never been found to vary, since I first was introduced to you by Lord Hood, had invariably for its object one point – nothing else for myself did I ever presume to solicit – that I might have the distinguished honour of being one of your supporters in a Line of Battle: then it would be shown that no person had your Fame more at heart than myself. I dare not venture a wish that your Royal Highness should trouble yourself again in my behalf.'[4]

Yet such was his despair that he could not resist writing to the Duke a few weeks later on his twenty-fifth birthday: 'May many revolving years give me an opportunity of congratulating you on its return',[5] he wrote, and expressing his concern at the unspecified indisposition which, he had heard, prevented him from attending the Prince of Wales's birthday party at Windsor shortly before. He need not have worried about the Duke's health, which was excellent; on his brother's birthday he had again been drinking tea and supping with Sally Winne and her family in Devon.

On 13 May 1790, a fresh and breezy day, the Duke of Clarence arrived at Plymouth to take command of the *Valiant*, and an hour later his purser, Mr Whitehead, called at the house on Foxhole Quay to tell the Winnes that they could shortly expect another call. Thereupon, George Winne took out his little book of Memorandums, left a couple of pages blank and then wrote the date and the news. An hour later, William, after a brief visit to his ship, arrived for tea, stayed to supper and it was not until midnight that he called a chaise to take him to his lodgings at the Fountain Inn at Dock.

Next morning, Mr Winne visited the Duke at the inn and, as he recorded, 'shew'd him an advertisement I had got printed by his desire inviting Seamen to enter on board the *Valiant* and the publication H.R.H. approved of'.[6] At four that afternoon, the Duke went on board his new ship to take formal command, inspected her and ordered that she be moored alongside a hulk while preparing for sea. Then, as the *Valiant* had been given priority in manning, seventy men were drafted to her from the *Cumberland*. 'We are miserably off,' her captain complained, 'No provisions and very few men … by scrapings and various other methods I have a hundred shabby sheep.'

There was plenty of work to be done, but nothing beyond the capacity of her first lieutenant, so the captain, content that 'both officers and men work with great spirit',[7] spent much time ashore, often at Foxhole Quay. He was no longer in love with Sally, for his thoughts were now with Dorothy Jordan in London, and he felt no need to be faithful to either. So, on his third day at Plymouth he wrote to the Prince of Wales about his first day in command of a ship of the line, adding, 'Now for my amusements … I first got tipsy with my brother officers and then compleated it at Winne's who, together with his family, beg to be remembered. Last night I followed those passions my godfather and godmother [the Duke and Duchess of Cumberland] would not renounce and retired into the arms of a chaste Irish whore, whose breath was impregnated with gin and tobacco. The whole day I dedicate to my duty....'[8]

During the coming days and weeks, as the ship was slowly made ready, he became bored. 'We are all here very dull and busy fitting out,' he wrote, 'The *Valiant* does not advance as quickly as I could wish for want of men. Provisions are at last arrived.' So, despite the proximity of Sally, he thought wistfully of London. 'I dare say the town is very gay and lively,' he wrote to George. 'The newspapers give fine accounts of your proceedings at masquerades, fêtes, balls and various other gay and fashionable amusements. Dullness here reigns altogether, but what is worse than all, not a woman fit to be touched with the tongs, not a house to put your head in after dark. It is what the French very properly call *La Misère*. The only thing bearable is our mess of Captains, which is composed of a variety of diversified, strange, out-of-the-way characters; in short, if it were not for the duty of the ship I should perhaps hang myself.'[9]

The Winnes had no inkling of his discontent, for he seemed almost as attentive as formerly. There were dinners and tea parties, at which Sally would, of course, be chaperoned by her mother, and a ball at the Long Room at which she was attended by her father. When they had met the day before, William had asked Sally to be his first partner, had sent her flowers the next morning and he danced with her, and her alone, until he left for Dock at midnight. So George Winne was sufficiently encouraged – despite his failure to become Agent Victualler – to cultivate the Duke to the maximum. It was to some avail, it seemed, because a dropped hint resulted in his young patron writing to the Prince of Wales to ask if he would give 'my good friend George Winne'[10] Tremmerton Castle, near Saltash, which was his property and currently untenanted. This expectation also came to nothing, but demonstrated that it would still be worth trying to keep in favour.

On 17 June, the *Valiant* sailed for Spithead to join the fleet assembling under the command of Admiral Samuel Barrington in case it should be needed to fight the French. Approaching the Isle of Wight, orders were received to enter the Solent by the westerly passage past the Needles because of deteriorating weather. Told that the ship's master had never taken a ship of the line through that narrow channel, the Duke announced that he would navigate himself and did so successfully. They arrived to find the anchorage crowded with twenty-one ships of the line and twenty-one frigates, and at last it seemed that William's ambition of finding glory in a line of battle might be fulfilled. The fleet looked magnificent, lying between Hampshire and the Isle of Wight with sunlight reflected on lively water whipped by a brisk breeze, but William soon became aware of a lack of confidence.

'We are two and twenty sail of the line at Spithead, tolerably fit for sea,' he told George in a letter, 'but thirteen hundred men are requisite before we can sail for any good purpose. In the *Valiant*, I want forty-seven seamen and nine marines; very few of the ships want less than ninety; in short, we ought not to sail for some time…. What can be expected from an undisciplined fleet short thirteen hundred men? Let me know whether we are to have war or peace; this state of suspense between both is exceedingly unpleasant.'[11] He continued to run a tight ship. During the weeks before sailing from Plymouth there had been only five floggings on board but one of these had been with thirty-six lashes and two with twenty-four. His officers were not specially chosen as formerly and he had not enough men for the work, but all knew their captain's readiness to react violently to any appearance of slackness.

At the end of June, the fleet sailed for Torbay, the anchorage from which an enemy fleet approaching up-Channel could be intercepted. Life at anchor there was even more depressing than at Spithead. One problem was that the other captains were all of Tory inclination and well knew of the Duke's Whig sympathies. 'I am by no means pleasantly situated: on the contrary, very far otherwise,' he told George.

'The officers, I mean the Captains, do not like me and I evidently perceive I am one too many in all their societies; in short, I live almost entirely secluded from the Fleet. Party runs very high and they are sadly disunited.'[12]

His own ship's company was, he liked to think, happy, despite the manning problems, and he wrote to his father, whom he was anxious to impress with his professionalism, 'On board the *Valiant* I kept everybody employed from five in the morning till nine at night.' His shortage of ratings had been alleviated by a draft of thirty-six men from the *Scipio*, but they should 'more properly to be called wretches; excepting the gunners and the quartermasters, I have not a man in the ship either as old as myself or has been as long at sea.' Many of the recently enlisted men, who were new to the sea, he had himself recruited in Richmond and Roehampton, and he found his ship's company amenable.

'Certainly I cannot say too much of the attention of the officers, but if the men had not of themselves been well inclined, no discipline in this short time could have effected the good order we are now in. At present they are very healthy; they have been very sickly, but by smoking their health is reestablished and I only lost one man.... It is a very great satisfaction to see through the whole Fleet the good humour and happiness of the men. I trust, should your Majesty think a war should be declared, that ... the *Valiant* will do her duty: she is a charming ship and I am more and more pleased with her and everybody on board of her.'[13]

Social life could be brought to the ship from shore. As soon as George Winne had heard that the *Valiant* was in Torbay, he bustled over to Paignton, on its shores, to arrange lodgings for his family including, of course, Sally. Another round of mutual entertainment began ashore and afloat and, to his credit, William was as attentive as ever to the family. He took George Winne on board the flagship *Barfleur* to meet Admiral Barrington and presented him to his grandest visitor, the Duke of Cumberland, his uncle and the nephew of

'Butcher' Cumberland, the conqueror of the Scottish rebellion of 1745. He was known as a generous rake and a bad influence on the Prince of Wales; it has been his marriage to a beautiful and witty wife, who was also 'vulgar, noisy and indelicate',[14] that had prompted the King to introduce the Royal Marriage Act, which bedevilled his sons. With the approval of Admiral Barrington, William had sent a cutter to collect him from Weymouth, where he had been staying with the King, and he expected some 'fine fun'. He was greeted with full ceremonial and entertained for twenty-four hours on board the flagship and the *Valiant*, with which he was delighted, writing to the Prince of Wales, 'I must say a finer ship or ship's company I never saw so perfectly in the minutest part exact; it does your brother great credit.'[15]

In mid-August, Lord Howe arrived to take command of the Channel Fleet. The Duke of Clarence, who had reason to be wary of the stern professional, now aged sixty-four, had mixed feelings about him. He had already written to George, 'I am individually glad that his Lordship is coming, for though I know him to be an unpleasant Commanding Officer, yet I am sure he is a man of honour.'[16] He may have been, but he was also demanding and, on arrival, ordered the fleet to sail immediately. This proved impossible because of various shortages on board the ships, and it was several days before Mrs Winne and Sally, watching from the cliffs, saw the magnificient sight of the Channel Fleet standing out to sea. They were alarmed because George Winne had been invited on board the *Valiant* that morning and they had not seen a boat bringing him ashore before she sailed. But he had stayed aboard to enjoy what was 'of all the sights which I have hitherto beheld this has exceeded the whole',[17] as the line of battle of the Channel Fleet made sail accompanied by nine frigates, two fireships, a hospital ship, two brigs and four cutters. As they passed Brixham, he climbed down the side and a boat took him ashore.

However, his host saw the spectacle through a jaundiced eye and complained to his eldest brother in a letter, 'The propriety of sending two and thirty sail of the line attended by five Admirals and a large body of frigates and other attendants, either during a profound peace, or during a negotiation with a certainty to end in pacific measures, speaks in my humble opinion for itself. Ten of these ships of the line are so badly manned and so dreadfully managed that the least wind will render them useless: besides the summer is now over and we are to expect gales of wind. We have not the most distant idea of the time of this extraordinary cruise. There is no difference of opinion on that subject: everybody is equally astonished. It is ridiculous to see how far vanity can lead a stupid old fool eat up with the gout and other bad humours: I, God knows, have been long enough at sea to hate it. I think his Lordship ought to be surfeited. Whenever I can with decency, I shall apply for leave of absence and never shall take another ship till shot have been exchanged in anger. Six weeks or two months at the utmost will, I trust, bring me back to the quiet and peaceable regions of Richmond.'[18]

But 'Black Dick' Howe, living up to his stern reputation, was determined to keep his ships at sea, patrolling between the Lizard and Ushant, until he had worked them into a state fit for action. Well might William again complain to his brother that after 'tumbling and tossing these ten days to no purpose' he was 'exceedingly tired of this cruize and very anxious to return'. Finally, when the admiral had heard – but his captains had not – that the threat of war had passed, he turned up-Channel again and entertained some of his officers, including the Duke of Clarence, now suitably shaken out of their lethargy, to dinner in his flagship.

'We are half way up the Channel but I am afraid not a bit the nearer landing for that,' he wrote to George, 'Do let me know whether it is peace or war. Am I to have any chance of being again amongst Christians, or am I to linger the rest of my life with the Philistines? Till a shot is fired in anger I do not go to sea again. The dinners at Carlton House are full as pleasant as those with Black Dick in his cabin.'[19]

At last, on 13 September, half the fleet – including the *Valiant* – put into Plymouth, while the other half sailed on to Portsmouth and Mr Winne took out his Memorandums book again. Although his ship was to stay in the harbour, William went ashore with his baggage immediately and moved into the Winnes' house, where he stayed, delighted to have his feet on land and a pretty girl at his side, until Sunday, 24 October. On that fatal day, George Winne made the final entry in his little book: 'This morning my nephew Jno. Winne landed at Plymouth from H.M. Ship *Valiant* (now in the Sound) and called H.R.H. the D. of Clarence agreeable to his Instructions rec'd from the 1st Lieutenant of the *Valiant*, that Ship, together with the *Vengenace, Bombay Castle, Egmont* and *Carnatic*, being then getting under sail for Spithead....'

William bade farewell to Sally, knowing that it was final. Their love affair had been demure, mostly conducted across a dining-room table, or over tea-cups, but she had been delighted to bask in the admiration of his beaming Hanoverian face and was flattered to be the object of universal envy when he would dance all night with her and her only. She cannot have expected marriage, so the courtship had been an end in itself and there had always been the expectation of financial favours for her father. When George Winne recorded in his Memorandums that the *Valiant* had arrived at Spithead, two days after she had sailed from the Sound, he put the little book away. Sally would have to look for another suitor.*

Meanwhile the Duke of Clarence stayed aboard his ship at anchor off Portsmouth until 22 November, when he took the *Valiant* into the harbour as a thunderstorm provided a magnificent, if mocking, simulation of a royal salute, and she was paid off five days later. He returned to London to find the Court in mourning for the death of his uncle, the Duke of Cumberland, whom he liked to remember as having had 'the best heart in the world'.[21] His immediate interests were at Carlton House and in Drury Lane: he had joined his two elder brothers in rais-

---

* A year later Sally Winne married the Anglo-Irish Colonel Ralph Gore. One of their sons, Arthur, an Army officer, was killed in action just before the Battle of Waterloo in 1815; his mother, who was herself dying, had a vision of him lying dead on a battlefield.

ing a loan of £300,000 to pay their debts and, of course, he was avid for Dorothy Jordan, who was still delighting her audiences as 'Little Pickle'.

She was still living with Richard Ford and, although she had tried to use the Duke's attention to provoke his jealousy and so a proposal of marriage, he had not responded. Now William had returned, a handsome, breezy figure in his captain's uniform, adding further theatrical glamour to the scene backstage at Drury Lane. She too realised that, even if she left her lover, William could be no more than another because of the Royal Marriage Act. However, a royal mistress would certainly be offered a regular income and special, if irregular, social standing. So, although she did not surrender, his advances were not rebuffed.

That William was regarded as no more than an ardent admirer was demonstrated in December, when Dorothy spoke lines in the epilogue of *The Greek Slave* in which she was playing the leading part. They were lines she could not have spoken were she seriously involved with a prince:

> How strange! methinks I hear a critic say,
> What, *she* the serious heroine of a play!
> The manager his want of sense evinces
> To pitch on *Hoydens* for the love of princes!
> To trick out *Chambermaids* in awkward pomp –
> Horrid! to make a Princess of a Romp.

Piquancy was added to William's delight at being ashore by the announcement of his promotion. On 3 December 1790, he was raised to flag rank as rear-admiral and would henceforth be eligible for the command of a squadron but not of an individual ship. His tailor added gold braid to his uniform and the twenty-five-year-old admiral cut a dash at London parties and in a box at Drury Lane and imagined that he would – after an interval for rest and recreation – do so again at sea.

This was less likely than he expected and Admiral Digby's pessimism was already being justified for he was still out of favour with his father and the Prime Minister and both distrusted naval officers who dabbled in politics. Senior admirals – particularly Lords Howe and Hood – had forgotten neither the Schomberg affair nor his impertinence in letters to his superiors; his habit of belittling them and others had also reached their ears.

Some of his near-contemporaries admired him – Captain Nelson among them, but he, of course, venerated royalty – for at times he had commanded an efficient ship. But others judged him ruthlessly and all the more harshly because of his privileged position. Even Byam Martin, who had some affection for him, could declare, 'He was deficient in almost all the qualities necessary for a person in high command. An unguarded way of speaking upon all subjects and to all persons made him very unsafe to be trusted with any confidential duty. A flightiness and want of sound judgement left him without any settled opinions upon any point, and he was turned and twisted just according to the advice of the person who happened to be last with him; it was therefore better he should be on shore than at sea.'[22]

That he should be on shore at the beginning of 1791 was not surprising for, despite the revolution in France, there was no immediate prospect of war and the Navy had not been mobilised. William continued to enjoy civilian life – often in his splendid new uniform – and in March took another house close to that still shared by Dorothy Jordan and Richard Ford in Richmond. This was Petersham Lodge, standing among ornamental trees half a mile upstream of Richmond Bridge and across the river from Admiral Pocock's house at Twickenham.

The siege of Mrs Jordan was brief: her lover had not proposed marriage and the Duke had proposed the next best thing. During the spring or summer, she and William became lovers and she moved to Petersham Lodge with her four children. In September, she played 'Little Pickle' at the theatre in the Haymarket, close to Carlton House and, as both William and the Prince of Wales were in the audience, the gossip-writers began to speculate in a welter of *double-entendres* and puns.

One whispered in print, '*A favourite comic actress*, if old Goody Rumour is to be trusted, has thought proper to put herself under the protection of a *distinguished Sailor*, who *dropped anchor* before her last summer at Richmond. As she resolutely held out, however, at that time, though the assault was vigorously pushed, perhaps this is only a flying report; and the lady thinks there is more security in a private *ford* than in the *open sea*.'[23] Another reported his success: 'We hear from Richmond that an illustrious Youth has passed the Ford, yet is not likely to be pickled by a legal process.'[24] The caricaturists had even more sport. William in his naval uniform had, with his elder brothers, become part of a comic trio and to this was added the nation's favourite comedienne. An added bonus was the name of Jordan for it was also current slang for a chamber-pot, and that became a regular feature of the caricatures, whether under the lovers' bed or crowning the Duke of Clarence. In one caricature, published as early as October that year, entitled, 'Neptune reposing after Fording the Jordan', the couple are shown in bed together. William is asleep in the arms of Dorothy, who is waking from a dream of paradise. Under the bed is a chamber-pot inscribed, 'Public Jordan. Open to All Parties.'

Dora – as he called her – was the ideal mistress. Although four years older, her theatrical skills enabled her to act whatever part was required: coquettish or dignified, witty or sympathetic. She was both alluring and maternal and the Prince of Wales had already set the fashion in choosing older, motherly mistresses. She was, in fact, a devoted mother and made it clear that her children had first call on her considerable earnings from the theatre.

She was accepted in London society as Polly Finch had never been, and even the King was said to approve of his son's choice, although considering the proposed financial settlement too generous. 'Hey, hey – what's this, what's this, what's this?' he was reported to have said, 'You keep an actress, they say. Ah, well, well; how much do you give her, eh? A thousand? A thousand? Too much, too much! Five hundred quite enough, quite enough!'[25]

For the first time, he was involved with a mature and responsive woman with ideas and needs of her own. She would thank him for a present, saying, 'It is the most beautiful and most *to my taste* of any thing I ever saw'; she loved him as an emotional equal ('If I may judge of *your* love by *my own*, I am sure I may with truth say, never *two* people loved so well'); and she sought his help in facing gossip and adverse publicity, asking him whether he had 'any influence over the people that manage the newspapers', continuing, 'I never take any in, but I have been told that some of them have been very severe on me, *unjustly so*, by asserting that I had totally abandoned my children. This is a charge that has hurt me extremely....'[26] He responded with love and support, particularly by treating her children as his own.

She took charge of their domestic arrangements, redecorating the apartment in St James's Palace in gaudy theatrical style, and even having a heraldic anchor – to symbolise the naval connection (and perhaps their new-found emotional stability) – on the doors of her carriage.

The Prince of Wales, who had admired her on the stage, gave the seal of his approval, seating her at his right on social occasions and treating her as his hostess when William entertained. Living in a modest imitation of his brother's style was expensive and the Duke's debts rose to some tens of thousands of pounds. Even when Dora's earnings amounted to more than was required for her children's needs and could meet some of theirs, the repayment of interest varied between £3000 and £5000 a year. This was not high living by ducal standards but it was enough to bind them closely to the public image of the extravagant, decadent royal dukes. The mockery directed at them by journalists and caricaturists entertained the less affluent, but it was also symptomatic of deeper, more dangerous currents.

The French Revolution, like the American, had echoes in England. The issues were not so drastically clear-cut but they were there, awaiting their champions. The Whigs had broadly supported both causes, although unease over the violence in France was beginning to alienate the gentler idealists. But a new radicalism was stirring throughout the country and had found a focus in a philosophical treatise, *The Rights of Man*, by a former Norfolk corset-maker, Tom Paine. The first half was published in 1791, with the second following a year later, and it was arousing radical, sometimes revolutionary and republican ideas, and alarming those who had much to lose.

The new ideas were spread by a variety of 'corresponding societies', which held meetings and corresponded with the like-minded in other parts of the country. The government was alarmed and several prominent radicals were arrested on charges of treason and imprisoned. The Duke of Clarence was concerned but confused: while joining his elder brothers in supporting the Opposition, he read the news from France and heard the rumours from the English provinces with alarm.

Domestic life with his mistress continued its agreeably placid way until August 1792, when his private life was upset by Dora's miscarriage and he heard that the Paris mob had stormed the Tuileries and imprisoned the King. He felt it his duty to speak out against threats to the institution of monarchy and did so in the House of Lords.

Among the letters of congratulation he received was one from an old friend, Captain Nelson, still in rural retirement, restless and unemployed, except for helping to work his father's little farm, gardening and hare-coursing with his brother. In September the Duke replied, thanking him for his support and declaring that it was 'the duty of every citizen to prevent, if possible, that confusion which might throw our Kingdom into the wretched, deplorable state of France'.[27]

This prompted a reply in which Nelson wrote of the growth of the radical corresponding societies in Norfolk: 'I think very soon every individual will be called forth to show himself, if I may judge from this County, where Societies are formed, and forming, on principles certainly inimical to our present Constitution both in Church and State....

Sorry I am to believe that others give a countenance to these Societies, who ought to conduct themselves otherwise ... I have been staying some time with my relation, Lord Walpole [Lord Walpole of Wolterton Hall, a distant cousin], near Norwich; at which place, and near it, the Clubs ... avow that till some of the Nobles and others in Parliament are served as they were in France, they will not be able to get their rights.'

He then complained that his repeated pleading for a command at sea had been ignored at the Admiralty, 'which has always been the way I have been treated' but that this in no way effected his loyalty to the King, 'which will never end but with my life'.[28] The Duke replied with bland reassurance, 'Though at present the armament is confined to small vessels, I much doubt whether any fleet will be equipped and still less do I see any chance for any rupture between this country and France. At the same time, this pernicious and fallacious system of equality and universal liberty must be checked, or else we shall have the most dreadful consequences.... Should matters between the two countries grow serious, you must be employed. Never be alarmed. I will always stand your friend. I wish you would write me word how you and Lord Hood are at present.'[29]

This prompted another, much longer, letter from Nelson, written at the Parsonage, Burnham Thorpe, on 10 December 1792. He began by explaining that he had not been in touch with Lord Hood since his application for employment had been refused so brusquely nearly two years before. Then he returned to the question of the radical societies, at first maintaining, in the manner of the Tory gentleman-farmer of modest means he now was, that the Norfolk magistrates should 'take away the licences from those ale-houses who allow of improper societies meeting at them, and to take up those incendiaries who go from ale-house to ale-house advising the poor people to pay no taxes, etc'.

But then the tenor of the letter changed and he continued, 'That poor labourers should have been seduced by promises and hopes of better times, your Royal Highness will not wonder at, when I assure you that they are really in want of everything to make life comfortable. Hunger is a sharp thorn and they are not only in want of food sufficient but of clothes and firing.

'Part of their wants, perhaps, were unavoidable from the dearness of every article of life; but much has arose from the neglect of the Country Gentlemen in not making their farmers raise their wages in some small proportion as the price of necessaries increased. The enclosed paper will give your Royal Highness an idea of the situation.' Nelson attached a table headed, 'An account of the earnings and expenses of a labourer in Norfolk with a wife and three children, supposing that he is not to be one day kept from labour in the whole year.' It was a document that would have been applauded by the corresponding societies he had condemned.

Listing expenditure on necessities – such as clothes, shoes, coal, candles and rent – as £8.13s. 10d. and earnings (including extras from harvesting, gleaning and turnip-hoeing) as £23.1s., he concluded that this left £14.7s. 2d. to buy food for five people throughout the year. 'Not quite twopence a day for each person,' he wrote, 'and to drink nothing but water, for beer our poor labourers never taste, unless they are tempted, which is too often the case, to go to the Alehouse.'

Nelson stressed that he had not exaggerated. 'I have been careful that no Country Gentleman should have it in his power to say I had pointed out the wants of the poor greater than they really are. Their wages have been raised these three weeks, pretty generally, one shilling a week: had it been done some time past, they would not have been discontented, for a want of loyalty is not among their faults; and many of their superiors, in many instances, might have imitated their conduct with advantage.'[30]

Such sentiments aroused a mixed reaction. While the Duke deplored any suggestion of social obligation, as a naval officer, he was aware that men had to be reasonably well fed, clothed and given shelter if they were to remain loyal, healthy and efficient. So he had some sympathy with his friend. But he had no sympathy whatsoever for those who advocated the abolition of slavery in the West Indies – that was, he considered, already an efficient system.

Happening to enter the House of Lords while the proposed abolition of slavery was being discussed, he immediately rose to his feet, apologised for not having prepared a speech and proclaimed, that he 'verily believed the greatest hardship of slavery was in the *word*'. He had been an eye-witness to the treatment of Negro slaves while serving in the West Indies, he said, and considered the slave trade 'of the highest magnitude to the welfare and prosperity of the Kingdom'. Any proposal to abolish it would meet with his 'most serious and unqualified opposition'.[31]

Naturally loquacious, he enjoyed addressing the House of Lords, particularly when the subject was nautical and close to his heart. When Lord Rodney died in 1792, the Duke was on his feet, paying fulsome tribute, but he also demonstrated that he was more than a speechifier by doing what he could for the promotion of the admiral's son, a naval lieutenant whose professional prospects seemed poor.

Naval architecture was another interest and he joined a new society dedicated to 'improve the theories of floating bodies and the resistance of fluids; to procure draughts and models of different vessels, together with calculations of their capacity, centre of gravity, tonnage, etc.'[32] and to conduct experiments to further improvements in the design of ships [later embodied as the Admiralty Board of Naval Architecture].

Such interests and causes for concern were now overwhelmed by news from France. The idealistic euphoria of the Revolution had degenerated into a succession of violent political spasms. When Prussia and Austria tried to restore the *ancien régime* by invading France the preceding summer, they had been routed at Valmy and, in Paris, the royal family was imprisoned and a republic declared. Massacres of real or supposed counter-revolutionaries began within France and, with crusading dynamism, the armies of the French National Convention marched into the Netherlands. This was seen as a direct strategic threat to the British Isles. Finally, in December 1792, King Louis was put on trial for his life and in London the government ordered the mobilisation of the Fleet. For both Nelson and the Duke, this was the moment long awaited and both immediately applied for employment at sea, the Duke applying directly to his father. On 6 January 1793, the King wrote to the First Lord of the Admiralty, 'The Duke of Clarence on Friday morning expressed to me a wish that he might apply to the Admiralty that a ship might be prepared for his hoisting his flag. I told him what Lord Chatham had mentioned on Wednesday that the preparing of ships for Admirals as yet would retard rather than forward the armament. He seems to look forward to being employed in a foreign, not the home, Squadron.'[33]

On the day that the King was writing to the Earl of Chatham about his son's employment, Nelson was at the Admiralty, asking the First Lord about his own. This time he was successful and accepted the first ship he was offered. 'Post *nubila Phoebus* – After clouds comes sunshine', he wrote next day to his wife, waiting in Norfolk. 'The Admiralty so smile upon me that really I am as much surprised as when they frowned. Lord Chatham yesterday made many apologies for not having given me a Ship before this time and said that if I chose to take a Sixty-four* to begin with, I should be appointed to one as soon as she was ready; and, whenever it was in his power, I should be removed into a Seventy-four. Everything indicates War.'[34]

---

* Warships were rated according to the number of guns mounted. First rates were three-deckers of 100 guns or more; second rates mounted 90 to 98; third rates were two-deckers of 64 to 90 guns, most of them 'seventy-fours': fourth rates were also two deckers of 50 to 60 guns. Fifth rates were frigates carrying 30 to 44 guns and sixth rates were small frigates of 28 guns and smaller ships also commanded by a captain. Ships even smaller – sloops, brigs, cutters, and so on – were not rated.

On 21 January, the King of France was beheaded outside his palace in Paris and on 1 February France declared war on Britain. A week later Captain Nelson took command of the *Agamemnon* at Chatham and made his first entry in her log, 'Fresh gales with wind at times. Went on board and put the ship in commission.'[35] In St James's Palace, Rear-Admiral the Duke of Clarence paced the carpet in his stuffy apartment, awaiting the call to arms.

10

A Matter of Scandal and Discomfort

Soon after the Duke of Clarence had dismissed the likelihood of war in his letter to Nelson, Parliament had been reassembled by royal proclamation and warlike preparations were announced in the King's speech. While Whig peers deplored the prospect of conflict with France, the Duke of Clarence enthusiastically supported the government and told the House of Lords that he had offered his professional services, which he thought could be most beneficial to his country.

At last, it seemed, he would return to sea. As operational plans were made, the Duke of York was given command of the expeditionary force bound for the Continent to guard the Scheldt estuary. He himself was advanced from a rear-admiral of the blue squadron to the red squadron, which should qualify him for a more important appointment and he heard that the *London*, a second-rate ship of the line, mounting ninety-eight guns, was being fitted out as his flagship. The Duke was delighted to hear of Nelson's appointment to the *Agamemnon* and claimed that it was in consequence of his own appeals to Lord Chatham. It was now possible that his former commanding officer would come under his command.

Then, on 19 January, while leaving Dora Jordan's town house in Somerset Street, he slipped on the steps (some said he fell, the worse for drink) and broke his arm. The surgeon of the Coldstream Guards was summoned to set the bone and the Duke was taken to Carlton House, bled by another doctor and put to bed. It was a clean break but it was between shoulder and elbow of the left arm, which would have to be held in a sling for some weeks and he was worried that it might interfere with his going to sea. Two hours after the accident, the Prince of Wales wrote to the King on his behalf that he 'hopes, poor fellow, that should there be any service upon which he might be employ'd, that his being obliged to carry his arm in a sling for some time will not be consider'd as a reason to prevent him from exerting that zeal which he feels in common with us all'.[1] The King replied the same day with the assurance that 'this accident cannot affect his being called upon for services when the proper opportunity shall occur.'[2]

Yet it did, as did other factors. There was the expense of fitting his flagship, and he agreed with the Admiralty's estimate of £4000, a sum which gave them the excuse to give priority to more urgent work. But above all was the low opinion in which he was held at the Admiralty, at Westminster and at Court. His over-reaction to disciplinary problems, when a captain, and his haughty manner with the most senior officers had not been forgotten. Byam Martin, now a lieutenant, put it succinctly: 'There was every disposition to give him a lead in the naval service; but (perhaps happily for the nation) he strangled himself as a professional man just when he reached the highest grade of rank.'[3]

His support of the Government was too late. Mr Pitt, while aware that the Duke was no serious politician and lacked cohesive political views, objected both to his siding with the Opposition on most issues – including, initially, the question of making war on France – and to the personal attacks he made on himself and his ministers whenever opportunity offered. The diarist Lord Glenbervie had noted, 'The Duke's idle and indiscreet abuse of the war and of the characters and conduct of his Majesty's Ministers, particularly Mr Pitt, in every promiscuous company, at balls, to women, young officers and boys, is a matter of scandal and discomfort.'[4]

Finally, there was the King's long-standing disappointment in his son. To his disapproval of the sexual adventures and political antagonism had been added recklessness over money; not the usual debts brought on by entertaining and gambling but large amounts he owed as interest on the huge loan he and his elder brothers had raised soon after his return from sea and which was, in his case, assumed to be entirely unnecessary.

On 25 February, the Duke travelled down the south bank of the Thames in a coach and six, past the naval dockyard at Deptford to Greenwich, but it was not to join a ship. He was accompanying his mother and sisters to watch the Duke of York embark with three battalions of the Guards for Flanders. Although dressed, as usual, in his naval uniform, it was the King and the Prince of Wales, attending in generals' uniforms, who seemed more related to the busy scene than he. Even his younger brothers were more favoured: Princes Edward and Ernest were to see active service with the Army in the West Indies and on the Continent respectively.

Thus, the Admiralty considered him unsuitable to command a squadron, or to be second-in-command of a fleet, for which his rank now made him eligible; the Government saw him as a political meddler who should not be given a responsible command, let alone a professional reward; and his father considered he had not measured up to the exacting standards he had set for his children.

In April, while Nelson was making his ship ready for sea, the Duke was in London and Richmond, as impatient for news of employment as his friend had been. He was enjoying his sensual and amusing mistress and calling at the House of Lords to pass the time. He was there on the eleventh of April, when the proposal to abolish the slave trade – the result of the campaign led by William Wilberforce, a Member of Parliament in the House of Commons – was being debated. The Duke again objected to the proposal as 'impolitic and unjust' and also to 'those new-fangled principles of liberty, which have deluged Europe with blood'. Those who promoted abolition were, he declared, 'either fanatics or hypocrites'[5] and Mr Wilberforce was one or the other. 'William made a most *incomparable speech* on the slave trade,' wrote the Prince of Wales to the Duke of York,

'Yet it was in the comprehension *of some people* rather too severe on Wilberforce.'[6]

There was delight, of course, among those with interests in the West Indies and at the British ports engaged in the trade. At Liverpool, where he was to be made a freeman of the city, a fashionable pottery produced an elegant jug, decorated with transfers of an unidentified naval battle and a flattering portrait of the Duke in uniform above the words, 'The Royal British Tar' and the lines: 'He's Royal, he's Noble, he's chosen to be/The Guard of our Island and Prince of the Sea'.

The Duke's occasional outbursts in the House of Lords – and what was worse: the threat of even more disruptive bluster if he continued to be thwarted – became his only political weapon. As week followed week without news that his flagship was ready, he used friends to convey to his family veiled threats of what he might say next if his frustration continued.

One of these, and Irish peer and major-general, the Earl of Moira, who enjoyed political scheming, told the Prince of Wales that the Duke had 'detailed with acute sensibility the continued slights which he had received'. As a result of 'this and similar mortifications', he said, 'The Duke ... retains great asperity towards the Administration'. Then, hinting at the political games he could play – including direct support for Whig politicians and the spreading of hostile rumours – he concluded, 'Finally, H.R.H. said he was ready to serve, could it be put upon terms any way decent, which he explained by saying that the being sent out sixth or seventh in command of the Channel Fleet, or on any mission contrived for the sole purpose of keeping him out of the way, would not be a situation becoming a son of his Majesty's, who had seen a considerable share of actual service.'[7]

However, at this time, his support for a motion in the House of Lords critical of the war seems to have convinced Pitt that he could not consider appointing a politically hostile admiral to any command. 'I am sorry he is not employed,' wrote Nelson to his wife, 'What does it matter to him whether the war is right or wrong? As an officer who I would wish to see rise in the esteem of his country, I wish he were at sea where I am sure he would acquire honour.'⁸

Through this fog of machinations a letter which reached him from Nelson blew like a breeze from the sea. The *Agamemnon* had sailed for the Mediterranean on 11 May and her captain had kept his promise that he would keep William informed of developments there in preparation for the day when he, too, would enjoy an operational command. His letter, written in instalments over three weeks, was a compound of news, unconfirmed reports, comment and anecdote. The fleet, under Lord Hood, had arrived off Toulon, the great naval base, where thirty French sail of the line were thought to lie, and which was believed to be in rebellion against the rule of the Convention in Paris. Nelson told him that they had hailed a Spanish frigate off Alicante and her captain had told them that their fleet was 'sickly, *for they had been* sixty *days at sea*'. He had underlined this and added, 'This speech appeared to us ridiculous; for from the circumstances of having been longer than that time at Sea do we attribute our getting healthy.'

The last entries in the narrative noted that the French fleet in Toulon in fact numbered seventeen of the line and four fitting out, but one of them, the *Commerce de Marseilles* mounted 136 guns and her sides were said to be 'so thick that our shot will not go through them and that she can with ease take the *Victory*'.⁹ Then gall was unconsciously added to these excitements by news that the Duke's younger brother, Prince Augustus, who had been travelling on the Continent, was visiting Hood's ships off the enemy coast before taking passage for England.

The beginning of this correspondence marked a change of course in the friendship between the two men. For the past five years it had been as between patron and supplicant but now it was resumed with warmth, its balance altered and its exchanges more natural. The Duke, although generous by nature, had been conditioned by his upbringing to regard himself as set apart from all except his own family. He was practised at being affable, and even kind, to those he saw as his inferiors, be they sailors or prosperous worthies like the Winnes, but such acquaintance was not an equal exchange and he felt little of the responsibility which friendship demands. When together in the Caribbean as subordinate and superior officers, Nelson had been worth cultivating as well as being an agreeable companion. But during his long unemployment and fall from favour he had been of no value to his royal friend. He had not been cut, of course, and the friendly but spasmodic correspondence he had initiated continued; otherwise he had been relegated to the Duke's memory of past friends.

Now it was Nelson who had been given a command at sea and his new importance warranted increased affability. They might not meet yet awhile, but if the Duke was, as he confidently expected, to command a squadron, letters from sea about strategy, command, manning and conditions afloat would be valuable and these Nelson was invited to write.

Like the Duke, Nelson was a compound of contradictions. He was acutely conscious of human relationships and touchy over real or supposed slights. 'I know myself to be so steady in my friendships that I can't bear the least coolness or inattention in others,'[10] he had said. One reason was his social insecurity, coming from a family which included both land-owning aristocrats and tradesmen; while he was invited once a year to stay with his cousin, Lord Walpole, at Wolterton Hall, two of his sisters had had to work as shop assistants and a brother had failed as a village shopkeeper. Yet this was combined with an underlying self-confidence, perhaps imparted by belonging to a family of clergymen for perhaps he was conscious that, at the last, the richest land-owner, even the King himself, would require their intercession.

Social insecurity had bred vanity and this was flattered by friendship with royalty; there was gratitude, too, for the words of recommendation the Duke had spoken on his behalf at the Admiralty. Nelson, as an instinctive teacher, still hoped to help mould what he saw as a promising but immature young officer into what he could call 'an ornament to the profession'.

Other letters followed, describing the occupation of Toulon by Lord Hood's forces at the invitation of the counter-revolutionaries, then the siege of the city by the army loyal to the Convention and finally its evacuation by sea and its fall. It was some small consolation to the unemployed admiral to be able to read to guests at his dinner-table a letter from the theatre of war, piquant with dramatic details of the last hours at Toulon: 'Such a scene was displayed as would make the hardest heart feel: the mob had risen, was plundering and committing every excess; many – numbers cannot be estimated – were drowned in trying to get off; boats upset.... One family of a wife and five children are just arrived – the husband shot himself. Indeed, Sir, the recital of their miseries is too afflicting to dwell upon.'[11]

In contrast to this, the London crowds at the print-shop windows were laughing at a caricature by Gillray of the Duke as a common sailor, standing with arms folded, pouting and discontented and declaring, 'Damn all Bond Street sailors, I say, a parcel of smell-socks! They'd sooner creep into a Jordan than face the French, damme!' Others would show him, overweight and dressed in a tight-fitting admiral's uniform, wearing the chamber-pot instead of a cocked hat. Yet still he persuaded himself that he would find, as Nelson had said on his return to sea, that 'After clouds comes sunshine'.[12] A glimmer of hope followed in April 1794, when he was promoted vice-admiral but there was still no news of employment.

Professional frustration was eased by personal happiness. In January 1794, Dora bore him a son. He named the infant George after his father Augustus and Frederick after uncles and, since the child was of course illegitimate, gave him the surname FitzClarence after himself. Child-bearing was not to interfere with Dora's theatrical career any more than did her cohabitation with the Duke; indeed, he welcomed her earnings to the point when gossips speculated whether he kept her or she kept him. Her first appearance on stage after the birth was at the newly rebuilt Theatre Royal, Drury Lane, where a benefit performance of one of her favourite plays, *The Country Girl*, was staged to raise money for the dependants of sailors killed in a naval action fought on the first of June that year.

This, the first major sea battle since the outbreak of war with Revolutionary France, became known simply as 'The Glorious First of June'. A French fleet had been covering the passage of a large convoy of grain ships from America to France, when it was intercepted in the North Atlantic by the sixty-eight-year-old Lord Howe with the Channel Fleet. After four days of running battle, six French ships of the line had been taken and one sunk, with no British ship lost, but the convoy reached France so the losses had not been in vain. However, a notable victory was claimed by the English, church bells were rung throughout England and the Duke of Clarence wished he had been present.

Meanwhile events in France – notably the mass executions by guillotine in the reign of terror that year – clarified his view of the war and he finally abandoned his vague, Whig-inspired opposition to it. That, in any case, had been based more upon military arguments against piecemeal involvements on the Continent than any form of pacifism. He declared to the House of Lords that as France had set the example of 'cutting off the heads of their King and Queen, it was not at all improbable that the same system might be adopted in other countries and Europe might exhibit the extraordinary spectacle of thrones without Kings and Kings without heads'. Moreover, England should 'show the regicides that they were not to cut off the heads of Kings and Queens like so many poppies in a garden without meeting with the ... cutting off of *their* heads in return'.

Although this 'wild and extravagant speech' was regarded as one of the most 'inconclusive and unargumentative ever delivered',[13] it at least demonstrated that the Duke was wholeheartedly behind the conduct of the war. Taking advantage of the publicity this was accorded, he wrote to the Board of the Admiralty: 'Conscious that during my naval career I never committed an act which could tarnish the honour of the Flag, I solicit in this hour of peril to my country that employment in her service which every subject is bound to seek, and particularly myself, considering the exalted rank which I hold in the country and the cause which it is my duty to maintain and defend. I regard refusal of that employment as a tacit acknowledgement of my incapacity and which cannot fail to degrade me in the opinion of the public....

'If the rank which I hold in the Navy operates as an impediment to my obtaining command of a ship without that of a squadron being attached to it, I will willingly relinquish that rank, under which I had formerly the command of a ship, and serve as a volunteer on board any ship which it may please your Lordships to appoint me. All I require is active service, and that when my gallant countrymen are fighting the cause of their Country and their Sovereign, I may not have the imputation thrown upon me of living a life of inglorious ease when I ought to be in the front of danger.'[14]

He received no reply so, nine days later, he sent a copy of the letter to the King with the accompanying complaint, 'To neglect they have added insult, inasmuch as they have witheld from me even that courtesy which is due to every individual ... I am emboldened to make this appeal of my Royal Father, soliciting from him that he will be pleased to issue this command which I desire, or publicly to state the grounds on which their refusal is founded.'[15]

This request for a public trial was a curious echo of Lieutenant Schomberg's demand for a court martial in the Caribbean seven years before. It was salt in the wounds that Schomberg – despite having been threatened with another court martial at Madras for brusquely accusing the Governor of insulting him by failing to salute his ship by gun or flag when she arrived – had been promoted to post-captain and had commanded a ship of the line, the *Culloden*, on the 'Glorious First of June'.

He read in the newspapers of the British conquest of Corsica as a base to replace Toulon. Nelson had written him a vivid account of the sieges of Bastia and Calvi, where he had commanded the batteries of naval guns and, at the latter, had been hit in the eye by gravel flung by the impact of a cannon-ball. 'It is now what we call the dog-days, here it is termed the Lion Sun,' Nelson had written from his camp before Calvi in August. 'No person can endure it: we have upwards of one thousand sick out of two thousand and others not much better than so many phantoms. We have lost many men from the season, very few from the Enemy. I am here the reed amongst the oaks: all the prevailing disorders have attacked me but I have not strength for them to fasten upon: I bow before the storm, whilst the sturdy oak is laid low. One plan I pursue, never to employ a Doctor; Nature does all for me, and Providence protects me. Always happy, if my humble but hearty endeavours can serve my King and Country.'[16]

More letters followed, telling of sickness in the ships, the need to refit, the hope of bringing the French to action and praise for his ship's company, 'which had been miserably torn to pieces by, without vanity, I hope I may be allowed to say, as hard service as a Ship's crew ever performed'.[17] The Duke could only read such letters to his friends since he was not welcome at the Admiralty, nor would he have deigned to go there. So he pondered Nelson's words, still confident that they would prove useful when finally he went to sea.

The year 1795 began in a limbo of domesticity at Bushy. Then, in March, Dora bore another son, Henry, and Nelson fought and captured the *Ça Ira*, a French ship of eighty-four guns, off Toulon and wrote a hurried letter to tell the Duke about it. The letters continued as a running commentary on the war in the Mediterranean, with Nelson asking, 'Not having had any signification to the contrary, I still presume to suppose that an account from me of the operations of this Fleet is acceptable to your Royal Highness.'[18] It was indeed.

In France, the terror had ended in July 1794, with the fall and execution of Robespierre, its instigator, but had been followed by an aggressive expansionism. This found expression in the rise of a young artillery officer who had distinguished himself at the siege of Toulon – Napoleon Bonaparte – and in October 1795 he defended the rule of the Directory by putting down an attempted *coup* in Paris.

At home the years had been notable for the marriage of the Prince of Wales to Princess Caroline of Brunswick, despite the fact that he was already secretly married to his early love, Mrs Fitzherbert. The marriage was a disaster – although the couple did manage to conceive a child – for both were wilful and dissolute by nature; after a few months they separated.

The following year began ominously: the armies of the Revolution ranged almost unchecked on the Continent, with General Bonaparte commanding the victorious French in Italy. It was time for the Duke to insist again on active employment and this time he determined to pitch his demands higher so that the expected refusal might bring something modest but acceptable. Earl Spencer, who had been First Lord of the Admiralty since 1794, was ill and in June William suggested to his father that he might succeed him. There was no response, so three months later he applied to the Admiralty for a command. Again, nothing transpired and when, in October, Spain declared war on Britain and the Royal Navy was forced to begin withdrawing from the Mediterranean, he specifically asked for a command there. Only the echo of his pleading came back to him and his humiliation seemed complete. The one consolation was his blissful life at home with Dora, who bore him his first daughter, Sophia, in August that year.

In January 1797, employment was at last offered but it was not at sea. He was appointed Ranger of Bushy Park, a royal estate in Middlesex to the west of London. Under other circumstances and in time of peace it would have been a wholly delightful favour from his father. More than a thousand acres of what had once been a royal hunting park – close to Hampton Court and the Thames and planted with magnificent trees – formed the estate. A noble avenue of chestnuts had been laid out by Sir Christopher Wren, who had sited a large bronze statue of Diana the Huntress at one end and, at the other a fine mansion, Bushy House, where the Duke and his irregular family were to live.

It was the ideal house for them. Comfortable and dignified but not grand and, although small by the standards of other royal residences, it was so designed that entertaining, amorous dalliance and the raising of a family could be kept separate within its red brick walls. A square, paved hall led straight to the drawing-room, dining-room and the ballroom in one of the pavilions joined to each of the four corners of the house by curving corridors. To ensure privacy a door led from the hall to the staircase and the main bedrooms on the first floor and to the nurseries on the second. It was a light, well-proportioned house with a cheerful atmosphere and it became a happy home.

His father also saw to the welfare of faithful servants when his memory was prompted. The Duke's old tutor was comfortably installed as a canon of Windsor but was still ambitious, and the King wrote to the Prime Minister that 'Doctor Majendie, who was preceptor to the Duke of Clarence and attended him with unremitting attention on board the Fleet for four years in the former war, who is certainly one of the best preachers in the Kingdom and a most exemplary Divine, is desirous of exchanging his Stall at Windsor for that of St Paul's ... though I think him unwise in wishing the change.'[19] Majendie duly transferred to the cathedral and, two years later, was appointed Bishop of Chester and later of Bangor.

At the end of February came news that swept away the pessimism induced by the British evacuation of the Mediterranean. On the fourteenth, Admiral Jervis had intercepted and defeated the Spanish fleet in the Atlantic off Cape St Vincent. But what lifted this above news of a distant fleet action was the extraordinary exploit of Captain Nelson. When it had seemed that the British line of battle was slow in turning to cut between two separate Spanish divisions, he hauled his ship, the *Captain*, out of the line without orders and steered straight for the leading ship of the second enemy squadron. Not only did he, heavily outnumbered and out-gunned, fight the enemy to a standstill but he boarded and captured one Spanish ship and then led his men across her deck to board and take another.

The Duke at once wrote to congratulate him and received a short, confident reply: 'Your Royal Highness, who has known me for every hour of sixteen years, will do me justice in saying that at no one period of my life did my zeal and duty to my King and Country abate; and I must rejoice in having gained the good opinion of my Sovereign, which I once was given to understand I had no likelihood of enjoying.'[20] This good opinion was made tangible by immediate promotion to rear-admiral and a knighthood.

Yet the euphoria was short-lived because two months after the great victory came the bitter and almost unbelievable news that the Royal Navy had mutinied. First, the ships' companies at Spithead had refused to obey orders until their grievances over pay and living conditions were met. Lord Howe hurried to Portsmouth and briskly agreed to the most reasonable demands and settled the crisis; the men returned to duty and there were neither floggings nor executions. Then, at the beginning of May, the ships' companies at the Nore mutinied and this was even more serious for they were more militant and effectively organised. It was nearly two months before discipline was restored there, and followed by hangings at the yardarm and floggings.

In April, the Duke had written to Nelson, 'You conclude your last letter by saying you are a *Gallant Fleet.* Gracious God, what a difference in this Country! The Ships at Spithead for a whole week in a perfect state of Mutiny – the Men commanding their Officers and a Parliament consisting of Delegates from each Ship of the Line sitting all that time on board the Queen Charlotte, issuing Orders to his Majesty's Fleet.... The King, with the advice of his Ministers, has very properly pardoned the Seamen and Marines.... But paint to yourself the Fleet at Spithead, during a War, for a whole week, in a complete state of Mutiny and the necessity of the pardon for the whole from the Sovereign!'[21]

The Duke and Nelson differed on the causes and the outcome of the mutinies, the latter having sympathy with the men's complaints. But the Duke wrote sharply to him in July, 'Want of discipline in some of our home squadrons, and the energy of infamous incendiaries, had for many months thrown the whole Fleet into a state of democracy and absolute rebellion.... One word more about what has passed at Spithead, Plymouth and the Nore and I will never mention the disgraceful business again; but I cannot pass over your remark about short weights and measures. Every officer must know that, by the old allowance, the men on board the King's ships had more provisions than they could consume and that they always sold a part; therefore an increase in provisions was not wanted. I will not hurt your mind by relating the horrid particulars of the late events but shall conclude the subject by observing that in your next you will unsay what you have too hastily expressed.... Lenity at first is severity at the last.'[22]

More bad news followed in July. An expedition to seize a Spanish bullion-ship thought to be lying at Santa Cruz, the capital of the island of Tenerife, had been commanded by Admiral Nelson but ended in disaster. The landing-parties had been cut to pieces by strong and alert defences and the admiral himself had been wounded so severely in the right arm that it had had to be amputated. Yet it was seen as a gallant failure and when Nelson returned to England at the beginning of September, he was accorded a hero's welcome.

'His Royal Highness was at Bushy Park ... when the intelligence of the arrival of Nelson drew him away from the improvements which he was superintending,'[23] wrote a contemporary biographer. A few days after Nelson landed at Portsmouth and joined his wife and father at Bath, he wrote to the Duke apologising for not having written immediately, explaining that this was due to 'the not being now a ready writer' as he was learning to write with his left hand. 'I feel confident of your sorrow for my accident,' he continued, 'but I assure your Royal Highness that not a scrap of that ardour with which I have hitherto served our King has been shot away.'[24] They met in London, where 'the interview, after so long an absence, was affecting'.[25] Soon afterwards, the Duke accompanied him to a levée in St James's Palace, where he was presented for the first time to the King, who announced, 'You have lost your right arm!'[26]

In October came better news. Admiral Duncan had been blockading the Dutch fleet, which was allied to the French, in the Texel but was away refitting when they came out. He at once made sail, intercepted and destroyed them at what became known as the Battle of Camperdown, and again the church bells rang in England. But, despite two great victories in the course of the year, the strategic outlook was dark, with the French unchecked on land and in control of the Mediterranean. Underlying this, the British were still shocked by the memory of the mutinies in the Navy, which alone stood between them and their dynamic enemy. Throughout the year, the most eye-catching caricature in the print-shop windows had been Gillray's black humour at its most telling in 'The Promis'd Horrors of the French Invasion', in which 'The Terror' was being re-enacted in St James's Street between White's and Brooks's clubs with the royal dukes amongst the slaughtered.

The Government decided that the opportunity of the presence in London of Admirals Nelson and Duncan must be exploited to enhance the relations between the Royal Navy and the public. So 'the Sovereign wisely resolved to display the importance of the marine service in one view by a naval procession to the metropolitan cathedral.'[27] On 19 December, the procession formed in Whitehall and wound through the City to St Paul's, led by artillery waggons draped with the colours captured from the French, Spanish and Dutch, with lieutenants who had fought in the actions walking beside them. Then, after a detachment of Royal Marines led by their band, came sixteen admirals, including Nelson and Duncan, and it was reported, 'the dignified deportment of the Sons of the Ocean produced a powerful affect upon the beholders.'[28] They were followed by the members of both Houses of Parliament, the Dukes of York, Clarence and Gloucester and finally the King and Queen. Within the cathedral, the admirals filed past the King to lay the captured flags before the altar and the service ended with the anthem which had been sung there when Queen Anne attended a thanksgiving for the Duke of Marlborough's victories at the beginning of the century.

Nelson, nursed by his wife, slowly recovered from the amputation and in March 1798 was received by the King before leaving for Portsmouth to join his new flagship, the *Vanguard*. At Lisbon he rejoined Earl St Vincent – as the enobled Admiral Jervis was now known – and was ordered to make a reconnaissance of the western Mediterranean in force. A large French army had been assembling along the Mediterranean coast between Marseilles and Genoa and it was about to embark in a fleet of transports with General Bonaparte in command. It would be Nelson's task to discover its destination and, if possible, intercept and destroy the convoy at sea.

The Duke of Clarence and Mrs Jordan lived in pastoral bliss at Bushy Park. She was pregnant again (with a second daughter, Mary) but only a brief confinement would keep her from the theatre and the earnings that were so important to her lover and her children. He kept in touch with the news of continuing French triumphs on the Continent but heard nothing of Nelson or Bonaparte beyond the news that, early in June, the French had broken out of Toulon and had disappeared over the horizon. He could only assume that Nelson was in pursuit.

He was, but it was 2 October before news reached London that, after weeks of searching the Mediterranean, he had caught the French fleet off the delta of the Nile in Aboukir Bay on the first of August: there he had destroyed them. Hitherto naval victories had involved the capture of several enemy ships and perhaps a few sunk or burned. But this had been annihilation. Of the thirteen French ships of the line found at anchor in the bay, ten had been captured, the flagship had been blown up and two had escaped, only to be taken later. General Bonaparte and his army were marooned in Egypt; his plans to conquer the Levant and then march on India were in ashes.

The victory had transformed the strategic balance of the war and the British were euphoric. The victor was at once created Baron Nelson of the Nile and Burnham Thorpe, awarded innumerable honours and a handsome pension and was acclaimed a hero as no Englishman had been before. But the Duke of Clarence's initial delight was soured by pique that his friend's courier, Captain Capel, had brought no private letter for himself, which he could read to his friends. So instead of sending his own hearty congratulations, he hesitated and then wrote, 'My dear Lord, on Captain Capel's arrival with the news of your glorious Victory, I was both astonished and hurt at not receiving a line from my old friend.' But, he added, he had now heard that Nelson's personal correspondence had been carried in the *Leander*, which had been captured at sea by one of the fugitives from the battle, so, he continued, 'I take up my pen to congratulate you on your Victory, of which no one thinks more highly than I do. My real friendship for you and my love for the Navy would not allow me to be silent in the House of Lords....'[29]

There he had declared that he joined 'the general exaltation and enthusiasm excited by this extraordinary action ... enhanced, I confess, by a warm affection for the man'. But he admitted that his 'powers, which are inadequate to much smaller tasks' were inadequate 'to exalt, by any possible flight of language, of imagination, or even numbers, this more than epic action'. Yet he tried, saying that it had contributed more to 'the salvation of the rest of the world than perhaps any other single event recorded in history'.

He spoke at length of 'my extraordinary friend', telling the House that 'The world knows that Lord Nelson can fight the battles of his country; but a constant and confidential correspondence with this great man ... has taught me that he is not less capable of providing for its political interests and honour on occasions of great delicacy and embarrassment. In that new capacity I have witnessed a degree of ability, judgement, temper and conciliation not always allied to the sort of spirit which, without an instant's hesitation, can attack on one day the Spanish line with his single ship and, on another, a superior French fleet, moored and fortified within the shoals of an unknown bay.'[30]

The balance of the friendship had changed and it was Nelson who condescended, albeit warmly, to address the Duke. Before receiving the latter's letter of congratulations, Nelson had written again from Naples, saying that he knew his first letter had been lost, so was writing a near-duplicate, but he added, 'I trust you will forgive my not writing so much as my inclination, in truth, prompts me to do; but I find my left hand is fully employed, in not only the business of the Squadron but also in working for the good cause in this Country.'[31] He did not say that he had met Sir William and Lady Hamilton – the British ambassador and his voluptuous wife – and been swept up in a tornado of Mediterranean politics and his own emotions.

Nelson did not receive the Duke's initial reproof until 1 February 1799, when he was in Palermo. After his ecstatic welcome in Naples, the mood had quickly darkened: the French were on the northern frontiers of the kingdom of the Two Sicilies – composed of southern Italy and Sicily itself – and a popular revolution in the city of Naples had been led by the liberal intelligentsia. Nelson had rescued the Bourbon rulers, King Ferdinand IV and Queen Maria Carolina, the sister of the executed Queen Marie Antoinette of France, and taken them and the Hamiltons to exile in Palermo. From there he wrote to the Duke to say that 'it was with real sorrow that I saw, for one moment, you had been displeased with me.' He declared that his attachment to the Duke was 'inferior to none in this world', adding, 'Indeed, Horatio Nelson is the same as your goodness has even known him to be – attached, affectionate and unchangeable; with one hand to a wounded head, and, I may now add, with my heart full and the business of fifteen Sail of the Line, besides my near connexion with the shore.'[32]

The wound was a severe blow on the forehead suffered in the battle, which may possibly have affected the balance of his moral judgement, and his heart was now full of love for Emma Hamilton. He wrote a long letter – another of his commentaries on the war – on 11 April but stressed his other letter-writing commitments, explaining that he had no time to write more because 'besides the business of sixteen Sail of the Line, I have the constant correspondence of Petersburg, Constantinople, Vienna, Venice, Trieste,

Smyrna, Florence, Leghorn, Earl St Vincent, Minorca and Lord Spencer: this must plead my excuse.'[33]

He wrote again in July to say that he expected the Duke had heard of his refusal to obey the orders of his superior, Admiral Lord Keith [formerly Captain the Honourable George Elphinstone] to leave Palermo and join his command for urgent operational reasons. This he had refused to do, deciding instead to concentrate on restoring King Ferdinand to Naples. 'I have been, with God's blessing, the principal means of placing a good Man and faithful Ally of your Royal Father on his throne,' he declared, 'I am well aware of the consequences of disobeying my orders; but, as I have often before risked my life for the good cause ... although a Military tribunal may think me criminal, the world will approve on my conduct.'[34] Soon afterwards he was writing again, saying that the one order he would always obey was 'the great order and object, to *down, down* with the damned French villains. Excuse my wrath but my blood boils at the name of a Frenchman. I hate them all – Royalists and Republicans.'[35]

Nothing could have been in more piquant contrast to this melodrama than the placid surroundings in which the letter was read. Comfortably settled with his mistress and children (a third son, Frederick, was born that year) at Bushy Park, he had become an opulent squire, dabbling in politics but still unwanted in his profession. In the House of Lords he thundered, surprisingly, against adultery: 'a most pernicious crime that strikes at the root of all domestic comfort',[36] and about his two favourite themes: the splendour of the Royal Navy and the need to support the slave trade. He considered himself an authority on both, the latter because he had been 'an attentive observer of the state of the Negroes' and had generally found them 'comparatively in a state of humble happiness'. In July he delivered an unusually long speech on the subject; he announced that at that time the British conducted this trade with '183 vessels measuring 49,065 tons, navigated by 6,276 seamen'. When he urged the Government to 'stretch out your hands to protect, not to destroy',[37] he referred to the trade not the slaves.

Then, early in the summer of the first year of the new century, came a glimmer of hope when he heard that a suitable vacancy was likely to arise when Lord Bridport relinquished command of the Home Fleet. Again he was to be disappointed but he wrote, still optimistic, to his old friend Captain Keats, 'Very extraordinary events indeed have taken place in the Nautical world ... Lord Spencer ... directly contrary to the King's desire to have me appointed Chief in the Home Fleet, has nominated Earl St Vincent ... I believe the situation of *second* in command is to be offered to me, which for every reason I must take if proposed: my present motive therefore is to ask you to accept the office of Captain of the Ship.... From my knowledge of the characters of St Vincent and Spencer, they cannot agree and consequently the Home Fleet will again be shortly vacant and I cannot well be passed over.'[38]

All that the Duke of Clarence was allowed was a visit to Portsmouth, where he went on board a French prize and the frigate that had taken her. On the upper deck of the latter, where the ship's company was drawn up for his inspection, he noticed that she was undermanned because numbers in the divisions of skilled seamen had been made up by obvious recruits, or 'landsmen'. 'I know the jib of a sailor as well as you do!' he laughed and called out the impostors, one by one, to the surprise and admiration of all. 'I see'd he knew a marlin spike from a hand-saw,' said one sailor and another compared him with a celebrated, old-fashioned, tobacco-chewing officer, Captain Rotheram of the *Bellerophon*, saying of the Duke, 'He's as good a craft afloat, I'll be bound, as old Rotheram of the *Bellyruffan*, barring he don't keep a quid in his jaw.' A third remarked, noting the star of the Order of the Garter on his coat, 'I'm blessed if he besn't just like one of our officers but for the piece o' metal on his jacket.'[39]

The Duke was still ashore when Nelson returned to London with the Hamiltons at the end of 1800. There was now a more powerful air of command about Nelson, expressed in the deeper, less humorous lines from nose to the corners of a mouth now touched with sensuality. There had been another reversal in their relationship: a decade before it had been the Duke who was the butt of the caricaturists' mockery; now it was Nelson. His liaison with Lady Hamilton was as familiar an ingredient of gossip in London as in Naples and Palermo and now his rejection of his wife was being enacted in England. The Duke's affair with Dora Jordan had, on the other hand, mellowed into domesticity and in January 1801 she bore him their third daughter, Elizabeth.

Nelson was not to be at home for long because he joined his new flagship at Plymouth in February and in March was appointed second-in-command of a fleet bound for the Baltic. His departure came none too soon because, while in London, he had become neurotically jealous of the Prince of Wales, who, he convinced himself, was determined to seduce Emma Hamilton with the connivance of Sir William. One reason for his frenzy, which he continued to express in letters to her from sea, was that he knew she was pregnant with his child.

In March, the fleet commanded by Admiral Hyde Parker – with Nelson as his restive subordinate – disappeared into the mists of the North Sea and on 2 April destroyed the Danish fleet off Copenhagen. The victory, fought and won by Nelson, while Hyde Parker held himself in reserve, was costly in casualties on both sides and, although it deprived the French of a possible, powerful naval reinforcement, was unpopular in England. So praise for the action from the Duke of Clarence in the House of Lords was welcome and Nelson wrote to thank him with assurances of his friendship.

On his return from the Baltic in July, he was given command of light forces assembled in the North Sea and Channel to counter a sharply increased threat of invasion. In August, he attacked the French flotilla defending Boulogne; it was a disastrous repetition of Tenerife, yet, although Nelson accepted the blame, his heroic reputation was untarnished. For the first time the British people could unreservedly admire, and identify with, an heroic figure, and this hero-worship bound them together in patriotic determination.

So, when the war petered out towards the end of the year and preliminary peace negotiations were begun, Nelson – supported by the Duke of Clarence – was required by the Government to give public support to their policies. On 3 November both agreed to do so in the House of Lords, partly because William Pitt, to whom the Duke had been so antagonistic, had been replaced by Henry Addington and they thought it prudent to support the new Prime Minister.

'The time is however come for making peace,' declared the Duke, 'Each of the powers, from their vast conquests, is placed in that predicament that no blow can be given with effect on either side. France has completely overcome every contending power on the Continent. Great Britain, as far as regards maritime affairs, is in the same state. This is therefore no common peace, but a reconciliation of differences between the two greatest powers in the world!'[40]

If this was seen as out-of-character, it was eclipsed by the apparent contradictions in Nelson's speech. He supported the unpopular peace terms to which Addington had agreed, dismissing the strategic value of Malta, Minorca and the Cape of Good Hope, which Britain stood to lose. His listeners were amazed and he was aware that he had made himself ridiculous. 'You will see my maiden speech,' he wrote to a naval friend, 'Bad enough, but well meant – anything better than ingratitude. I may be a coward and good for nothing but never ungrateful for favours done me.'[41]

He found support in the Duke, who deferred to him by insisting that he second Lord St Vincent's vote of thanks to Rear-Admiral Sir James de Saumarez for his action off Algeciras, and wrote him a letter of thanks: 'At the present moment, when the public have two opinions, the one good, the other disadvantageous, of my Parliamentary conduct, I feel highly obliged to you, as a person qualified to judge, for delivering your sentiments.'[42]

Nelson had learned his lesson and, when he seconded the address of thanks to the King after the speech from the throne at the opening of Parliament in the following year, he said, 'My professional education will plead my excuse for the imperfect manner in which I deliver my sentiments; but I should not have done my duty if I had not, even in this plain, seamanlike manner....[43] By then he had decided to speak on matters he understood, although he did support the Duke in defence of the slave trade and finally wound up his political career by telling the reinstated William Pitt that his were 'sailor's politics'. With relief, he declared, 'I cannot pretend to a nice discrimination between the use and abuse of parties and therefore cannot be expected to range myself under the political banners of any man in or out of place. England's welfare is the sole object of my pursuit ... and I will vote accordingly without regard to other circumstances.'[44] This was remembered by the Duke of Clarence.

Meanwhile Nelson and the Hamiltons had settled at Merton Place, the charming country house he had bought in Surrey, convenient for the road to Portsmouth. When Sir William Hamilton died in April 1803, he, Emma and their daughter Horatia led a blissful, if irregular, family life, like the Duke and Mrs Jordan at Bushy House.

When, on 16 May that year, the fragile peace collapsed and Britain declared war on France, both men re-entered their real and supposed elements. Vice-Admiral Lord Nelson, who had been created a viscount after the Battle of Copenhagen, was appointed Commander-in-Chief in the Mediterranean and hoisted his flag in the *Victory*. The Duke told the House of Lords, 'I wish to see Great Britain chastise France,'[45] and once again applied for employment. Several months before the outbreak of war, he had written to Captain Keats, 'The Ministers themselves consider war inevitable. I have already offered to serve in case of hostilities and have my mind on the command where the most active scene of service can lead our fleet. I consider the Mediterranean will and must be the theatre. I shall again apply when matters are more forward: in case

I am employed I shall hope for the assistance of your abilities as Flag Captain.'[46]

But when war was declared, Nelson was sent to sea while the Duke was given command of the Teddington Corps of Militia, near his home at Bushy, one of the volunteer regiments formed to meet the renewed threat of invasion. He dressed them in elaborate uniform, inspected parades and addressed them: 'My Friends and Neighbours! Wherever our duty calls us, I will go with you, fight in your ranks and never return home without you!'[47] But they were not, of course, going anywhere beyond the local parade-ground and tavern and he knew it. 'As for this rascal Bonaparte, I wish he was at the bottom of the sea,' he wrote to a naval friend. 'All naval officers think invasion impossible and this is clearly my opinion; yet what else can this Corsican scoundrel do against this country?'[48]

So it was particularly frustrating to receive the first of another series of short commentaries from Nelson: 'Having buffeted with a foul wind and nasty sea, we are now entering the Straits and I hope to anchor at Gibraltar before dark....'[49] The letters became shorter and fewer – often giving him news of Keats, who was with him in the Mediterranean, but little more – and the Duke learned most about the long blockade of Toulon from the newspapers. Nelson must have been aware of the consequent frustration for in August 1804, more than a year after he had left England, he wrote, 'If anything the least new was to occur here, your Royal Highness is sure that I would have written to you; but we have a uniform sameness, day after day and month after month – gales of wind for ever.... However, with nursing our ships, we have roughed it out better than could have been expected.'[50]

Spain again declared war on Britain in December 1804, and the renewed maritime alliance made itself felt early the following year when the bulk of the French and Spanish fleets broke out of their ports and disappeared. Nelson, who had been trying to watch Toulon, eventually heard that those which had eluded his frigates had passed Gibraltar, heading west. A long chase began, for, as he deduced, the combined fleets planned to meet in the West Indies before sweeping back across the Atlantic to take control of the English Channel long enough for a French invasion force to cross. This would be the climax of the conquest of Europe by the Emperor Napoleon, who had crowned himself that December; taking the crown from the hands of the Pope, he had placed it on his own head in the cathedral of Nôtre Dame.

Nelson narrowly missed an interception and a climactic battle, but he was so close behind his quarry that they fled to the safety of Spanish ports. 'Your Royal Highness will easily conceive the misery I am feeling at hitherto having missed the French Fleet,' he wrote to the Duke, 'My heart is almost broke.'[57] Thwarted, but still hopeful that the enemy could be brought to action, Nelson, who had not set foot ashore for almost two years, returned to London for consultation with the Government and overdue leave.

The public liaison with Lady Hamilton had offended the King and Queen and he was out of favour at Court and in the higher reaches of polite society. So the friends who visited him at Merton Place tended to be naval officers – among them Captain Keats, to whom he explained the tactics he would employ when he caught the enemy – and a few independent-minded men of originality and consequence. His extended family gathered about him and was present when the head of another such household – to which a fifth son, Augustus, had – followed their fourth daugher, Augusta – drove over from Bushy Park on 22 August.

The Duke of Clarence had come to pay his respects to his friend, who had become more subject to patriotic adoration than any monarch. But he was disappointed to have missed Keats, who was living nearby at Kingston, and, hearing that he had been at Merton recently, sat at his host's desk and wrote him a letter. 'I write from my friend Lord Nelson's, who you may very easily conclude I was anxious to see as I am to shake you by the hand,' he began. 'The Government acknowledges the great conduct of Lord Nelson and I can with safety speak that the nation entertains the highest gratitude of the services of his Fleet. I felt the greatest pleasure in the conversation I have had today with Lord Nelson, relative to you, who speaks of you in the manner that one like me, who has known you for more than six and twenty years, cannot fail to rejoice at.'[52] The two had decided that something must be done to hasten Keats's advancement and, for a start, he would rejoin Nelson's command when he returned to sea.

On 6 September, the Duke returned to Merton to dine with the family, and his host presented his nephews as 'my three props'. One of them, George Matcham, noted that their guest 'talked much', looked 'like the King' and was 'violent against Mr Pitt' and also noticed 'his deference to Lord N.'s opinion'.[53] But the happy and peaceful days at Merton were almost done. Two days before the Duke's second visit, news had reached London that the combined French and Spanish fleets had concentrated at Cadiz and there they could be blockaded or brought to battle. Nelson would have to return to sea for the grand finale.

He went to London for farewell meetings with William Pitt – to whom he finally declared his abdication of all political ambition – and with the Prince of Wales, of whom he had once been so unnecessarily jealous. Then, a week after he and the Duke had parted, he left Merton for Portsmouth to join the *Victory* at Spithead. On 6 November, two weary naval officers arrived at the Admiralty in Whitehall to announce that Lord Nelson had indeed fought and destroyed the enemy fleets, but had himself been killed.

The nation was engulfed by the compound of joy and grief. Both had to find expression, and the consequence was a funereal celebration on a colossal scale. Even tough old Admiral Digby, the Duke's first naval mentor, cut out and kept one of the innumerable odes to Nelson in the newspapers, magazines and broadsheets:

> Oh blest the Hero! how supremely blest!
> Who in the lap of Victory sinks to rest.
> What tho' he fall? His glories still survive,
> And in the Roll of Fame forever live …

The Duke of Clarence was staying at Brighton with the Prince of Wales in the latter's oriental Royal Pavilion. They had been watching bare-knuckled prize-fighting – including 'a great fight' between Henry Pearce ('The Game Chicken') and John Gully up on the Downs because it had been banned by the magistrates in Brighton; firing an air-gun at a target in the drawing-room (one of the ladies shot a fiddler in the next room) and drinking too much. When news of the battle arrived, the Prince of Wales was said to be 'affected most extremely', complaining that 'bad news made him bilious'.[54]

The Duke wrote to his old first lieutenant, now Captain Hargood, 'I wish another brave fellow could have witnessed our celebrations, but he is gone. I mean my friend Nelson ... I did not think it possible, but for one of my dearest relations, to have felt what I have, and what I still do, for poor Nelson.'[55]

For him, his friend's most immediate legacy was a new thoughtfulness. Nelson had told him that he had urged 'the Ministers' to promote Keats and that he had earned a knighthood. Now, on the eve of the funeral, the Duke wrote to their friend, 'You must shortly be a Flag officer and then our naval history will be filled with your exploits: in short, rival Nelson and follow his bright example in everything but his death, glorious as it has been: tomorrow I pay my last mark of love and respect to our friend and a melancholy day it will be.' The royal dukes attended the funeral at St Paul's Cathedral, where they had all taken part in the ceremonial presentation of captured colours seven years before.

On that January morning, George Matcham joined the dead admiral's tremendous funeral procession as it assembled in St James's Park, where he found 'all the Captains and Admirals much confused, not being able to find their carriages'. It moved off and at the Horse Guards was joined by the royal dukes, escorting Nelson's coffin, which was then laid on to a funeral car shaped like his flagship's hull. In the cathedral, which the head of the procession reached before the cortège had left Whitehall, the Duke of Clarence greeted his dead friend's eldest brother William, a pompous clergyman and now the first Earl Nelson, with the banality that comes easily at such times. 'I am come to pay my last duties here,' he said, 'I hope you and I never meet on such a like occasion.'[56] There could, of course, be no other.

Soon afterwards the Duke delivered his elegy to Nelson in the House of Lords by reciting the noble words of the prayer he had written on the day he died: 'May the Great God, whom I worship, grant to my Country and for the benefit of Europe in general a great and glorious victory, and may no misconduct in anyone tarnish it ...'

Nelson's influence did not end there. He had not only been invested with immortality as the nation's hero but had set new standards in his profession. Not only was nothing less than the annihilation of an enemy enough, but he had introduced a new code of attitudes to those in command, particularly in humanity towards those commanded. In the future, more reflective captains and admirals would hope to be liked – even loved – rather than admired or feared. This was not lost on Admiral the Duke of Clarence. Three months later, he was writing to one of Nelson's captains, Sir Edward Berry, about the consequences of the Battle of Trafalgar and he added, 'I cannot forget my friend.'[57]

11

Admiral Tarry Breeks

The Duke of Clarence returned to Merton Place the following year. He was accompanied by the Prince of Wales and by his younger brother the Duke of Sussex, who had stayed with the Hamiltons in Naples while studying music.

For several days they were entertained in the style to which they were accustomed. Emma Hamilton had learned how to amuse and flatter royalty at the Bourbon court and knew that continued expressions of grief would achieve neither. Her aim was to establish some degree of patronage which might help her survive the debt into which she was drifting, although less promising benefactors could hardly have been chosen. In this, Nelson's daughter, Horatia, had to play an important part, and was at her most winsome when performing the 'Attitudes' she had learned from her mother: posing in classical robes while striking attitudes to indicate qualities such as Devotion and Purity.

Indeed, a month before Emma had drawn up her will, which stated, 'I beg his Royal Highness the Prince of Wales, as he dearly loved Nelson, that his Royal Highness will protect his child and be kind to her, for this I beg of him, for there is no one that I so highly regard as his Royal Highness.'[1] The Prince had only had a few formal meetings with Nelson, who had regarded him with the sharpest suspicion and distaste. But she could not involve the Duke of Clarence, who had 'given away' Fanny to Nelson at their wedding on Nevis and had kept in touch with her.

There were parallels and divergences between this household and the Duke's at Bushy. Neither was, nor had been, based upon marriage, although, had he lived, Nelson would probably have married Emma, with whom he had wanted to retire to his estate at Bronte in Sicily. The Duke was prevented from marriage to his extrovert mistress by the Royal Marriage Act, which was unlikely to be relaxed in their case. Yet he and Dora seemed bound by a marriage in all but law. They were exemplary parents and when a fifth daughter, Amelia, was born in 1807 they had ten children, the eldest of whom, George, was to be sent on active service with the Army a year later at the age of fourteen.

But Dora Jordan was now forty-six and no longer the flirtatious gamine he had first known. She was plump and motherly and hoping to retire from the stage, but continued to perform to finance his extravagance as well as their children. She could still throw herself into the task with enthusiasm, writing of an opening night at Manchester, 'The House was prodigiously full. I do not yet know the receipt but you may be able to judge when I tell you there were 1,040 people in the gallery during my final scene. They were so *eager to hear* that they disgraced themselves by their anxiety. However I compleatly *tamed* the *savages* by the end of the play and I never saw an audience more pleased. The applause was deafening. I am now waiting for the money to send.'[2]

To her lover she was as fond as she was understanding and sympathised with his thwarted ambitions. While she would have been happy to see what he had declared to be 'the wish nearest my heart to be the Marine Minister', she realised that an appointment at sea (which he also proclaimed as his most cherished ambition) would have left her in sole charge of their household. 'I sincerely hope you may not be disappointed in your wishes,' she wrote to him when on tour, 'I see and feel as strongly as you do the advantages attending their success ... I was asked at the Theatre if it was true that you were going to hoist your Flag. I had but one answer, that it might be so, but that I knew nothing of it.'[3]

There was no more chance of employment, of course; indeed there was less. William Pitt had died suddenly at the beginning of 1806 and his administration was replaced by a coalition – 'The Ministry of All the Talents' – with the Tory Lord Grenville as Prime Minister and the Whig Charles James Fox as Foreign Secretary – and the Duke might have expected help from his Whig friends. But again he was his own undoing. In that same year, the First Lord of the Admiralty, Lord Melville, was accused of corruption during an earlier spell as Treasurer of the Navy, found guilty of negligence but acquitted. The Duke, however, could not resist denouncing him before the conclusion of the trial, declaring, 'Lord Melville talks of passing the summer off in the Highlands of Scotland but I hope he will pass it in the Tower.'[4] Such talk did not endear him to anybody in authority at the Admiralty, and, after a year, the coalition crumbled and was replaced by another Tory government. A chance had been lost.

At home, he could always count on loyalty and support. However, while his mistress was losing her looks, he had not lost his roving eye and there were occasional rumours of his dalliance elsewhere and of a rift between them. Yet the relationship survived, the Duke once remarking, with pragmatism rather than gallantry, 'Mrs Jordan is a very good creature, very domestic and careful of the children. To be sure she is absurd sometimes and has her humours. But there are such things, more or less, in all families.'[5]

It was his domestic life that offered the only possibility of change. His professional life was blighted by the deliberate neglect of authority; his social life was inhibited by continuing debt; but there was always the possibility of finding a wife, who might be both beautiful and rich, for he felt no permanent tie to Dora. As month succeeded month and warlike activity on the Continent was matched by the Duke's peaceful inactivity at home, he became increasingly restive. Towards the end of 1808, he visited Portsmouth and returned not only 'gratified beyond description at the perfection of our glorious Navy and pleased at the very distinguished and affectionate manner in which I was received by my brother officers', but optimistic. He wrote to a friend, 'I may be absent from England for some time, having applied for the command of the King's Fleet in the Mediterranean. I have so many public and private reasons to wish it, that I am anxious to hoist my Flag ...'[6]

In the same year, his eldest son, George, had accompanied the expeditionary force to the Peninsula and was said to be a promising young officer, showing 'great Quickness, Intelligence and Activity',[7] while his second son, Henry, was going into the Navy. Only his own life was stagnant. In 1809, the French remained supreme within Europe, supported by the Continental System of allies and subject states, defeating the Austrians at Wagram, and a British attempt to help their ally by putting a force ashore at Walcheren was a dismal failure. By the end of the year, the French had taken all they wanted from Austria and only in the Peninsula and at sea were they faced with the serious opposition of the British. In 1810, Napoleon extended his hold in Europe, but the Duke of Wellington fought on in Portugal. Then in 1811 King George III suffered a relapse into insanity and on 5 February the Prince of Wales was declared Regent.

For the Duke, the outlook was transformed. Not only was his brother likely to give him a naval command, but he was unlikely to enforce the Royal Marriage Act should he find a possible wife who might have been less than suitable in his father's eyes. So in June that year, when a pretty young heiress was presented to him during one of the Prince Regent's routs at Carlton House, to which Mrs Jordan had not been invited, more than flirtation came to mind. This was Catherine Tylney-Long, who was vivacious, not particularly intelligent, but was said to enjoy an annual income of at least £40,000 and have some £300,000 in her bank account. The Duke's imagination conjured up a tempting prospect that would transform all but his moribund professional life. Discovering that Miss Tylney-Long was under the guardianship of her aunt, he initiated negotiations with her, through an intermediary, which became extremely frank. During the course of this he was given to understand that the girl could never consent to becoming his mistress and that no other possibility could be discussed while he was living with Mrs Jordan.

That summer Dora was on a provincial tour, conscious that she seldom heard from her lover or their children, but she was stoic and cheerful. At the end of September, when playing in Cheltenham, she was filled with foreboding, believing that lack of money rather than affection was the problem. On the first of October, she wrote to the Duke, telling him that she was tired of the tour: 'I am very fickle ... and always grow tired of the audience before they seem to weary of me,' and then she seemed to cry out, '*Money, money, cruel money*, since my first setting out in the world at the age of 13, at a *moderate calculation*, I have spun *fairly and honestly* out of my own brains above £100,000, and still this cruel *pelf* robs me of even comfort and *happiness*, as I verily believe we have nothing to do with our *own fate*. I may fairly say what a strange one mine has been and *is likely to be*.'[8]

Her letter crossed one from him which left her shocked with grief. He asked her to meet him in Maidenhead at the end of the week to discuss terms for a separation. She replied calmly, agreeing to come, adding that she had to perform again before leaving: 'I must exert myself, play and farce tomorrow night.'[9] She went on stage again in *The Devil to Pay*, in a part calling for her to laugh uncontrollably and for another character to say that she was 'laughing drunk'. But when she began to laugh, she burst into tears and the actor, with a professionalism comparable with her own, changed his words to 'crying drunk'.[10]

She met the Duke at Maidenhead. He was said to have shown some shame but he had been brought up to think of himself as different from lesser mortals and not bound by the same sense of responsibility. The discarded mistress called upon her theatrical skills to present a brave, even noble, bearing. Later, she never blamed her lover, only 'money ... or the want of it',[11] for his abandoning her. Relieved that he had not had to face tantrums, the Duke later declared that she had 'behaved like an angel'.[12]

But the Duke was no longer the bluff and breezy young captain who had courted Sally Winne. He was now forty-six and had thickened in the body; his face was ruddy from claret and port rather than from wind and sun. Instead of his shock of fair hair, he was close-cropped, which showed that his head was (as was said at the time) shaped like a pineapple or coconut. He was still robust but coarse humour was less acceptable from a middle-aged duke than from a hearty young naval officer. Everybody knew that he had been living with an actress for twenty years and had fathered ten bastards. He may have felt much the same man as he had once been, but he was unlikely to appeal to one of the most eligible and sought-after heiresses in the country.

Undaunted, he vigorously pursued what he described as 'the lovely little nice angel' and, after one meeting with her, declared that 'her dear little eyes sparkled with pleasure at many things I said'.[13] However, he had a rival in an archetypical Regency rake, William Wellesley-Pole, who was twenty-four, handsome, witty and related to the Duke of Wellington. The gossips were delighted up the piquancy of the contest and the caricaturists, who had become bored by the Duke, except as a background figure in their mockery of the Prince Regent, promoted him to principal butt of their jokes.

Meanwhile a settlement had been reached with Mrs Jordan, under which she would receive a total annual income of £4,400 and she appeared satisfied, saying that the arrangement 'did high honour to the Duke of Clarence'.[14] Yet, in the event, it was not enough, for her first child – the daughter by the theatrical manager, who had seduced her in Ireland – had an extravagant and rapacious husband who made increasing demands upon her, while the husband of one of her daughters by Richard Ford was to embezzle more of her money; nor did she receive the support she might have expected from the rest of her children.

She moved from Bushy House to Cadogan Place in Chelsea and had soon begun the same steep decline in circumstances, health and spirits as Nelson's former mistress. Public opinion supported her and there was a spate of encouraging verse, mostly addressed to the Duke:

> Return to Mistress Jordan's arms,
> Soothe her and quieten her alarms;
> Your present differences o'er,
> Be wise and play the fool no more.

But he was too excited by the chase of Miss Tylney-Long, and assumed from Dora's gratitude for the financial arrangements that all would be well with her. He did not try to emulate Nelson's self-deceiving attempts to justify his abandonment of his wife for Emma Hamilton. But, like Emma, Dora was caught in a downward spiral of unhappiness – even a return to the stage was a failure – and eventually escaped her creditors, but not her desolation, by choosing exile in France.

By the end of the year, Catherine Tylney-Long had announced her engagement to Mr Wellesley-Pole, but the Duke's blood was up and he quickly followed other scents, of which the principal ingredients were money, social suitability and looks in that order. Matrimonial ambitions had temporarily taken precedence over his hopes of employment, but he still kept in close touch with his naval friends. Admiral Lord Collingwood had succeeded his friend Lord Nelson both in command of the Mediterranean Fleet and in correspondence with the Duke: 'With me, it is enough to have been the friend of Nelson to possess my estimation,' the latter wrote. When the admiral had confided that his health was failing and that he had hopes of recall, the Duke had immediately applied for his command, but cannot have been surprised to be disappointed once again. Collingwood died on board his flagship in May 1810 and, although the Duke of Clarence was not even considered as his successor, he was promoted a year later to be an admiral of the fleet.

To have reached the highest rank in the Royal Navy without having been to sea for twenty-one years was gratifying for the Duke and a relief to the Admiralty, for he was now too senior to expect any operational, seagoing command and could be considered simply a ceremonial figure. He was preoccupied with looking for a wife to keep him company at Bushy House. He first proposed marriage to, and was rejected by, another heiress, Margaret Mercer Elphinstone (the daughter of Admiral Lord Keith), then by Lady Charlotte Lindsay; there were overtures to two widows, Lady Downshire and the Countess of Berkeley, and these were only the first of a dozen.

After the first year of the Regency and there being no hope of the King's recovery, the Prince Regent was able to exercise more executive power and eventually wondered what he could offer his younger brother by way of diversion. The current of war now favoured the allies for, after the victory at Trafalgar, Napoleon had concentrated on land warfare and, in 1812, invaded Russia and lost his army in the winter retreat from Moscow. In the following summer, the Duke of Wellington routed the French at Vitoria in Spain and by the end of the year had crossed the Pyrenees into France.

It was then that the Prince Regent decided that William could take a look at the war before it ended. So, when the Duke once again asked for active service, the Prime Minister, Lord Liverpool, agreed. The most convenient scene of action was in the Netherlands and Flanders, where a British expeditionary force was engaged, and a visit was authorised. The Duke implied to his family and friends that he was embarking on some important and possibly dangerous mission but deceived nobody, his sister Charlotte noting that he was 'quite ridiculously *consequential* and close about his journey.... The real truth is he goes for his own amusement, but does not allow of that and thinks proper to make importance.'[16]

The only secret aspect of his jaunt was the hope of meeting, and perhaps wooing, the Grand Duchess Catherine of Oldenburg, sister of Tsar Alexander, the Emperor of Russia. Of the outcome of this he was supremely confident; even before leaving Bushy House, he had written to a friend, 'Nothing that is human is certain: but from the favourable state of affairs in Russia and the good understanding between the Prince Regent and the Emperor Alexander, there is every probability of my marriage taking place.'[17]

But first he had to visit the war and was provided with a frigate, the *Jason*, for the purpose. So in January 1814 he hoisted his flag for the first time and set sail to sniggers in the clubs of St James's and the wardrooms of the Fleet. These were also set out in verse:

> Dear brother, I own I am delighted,
> To find myself kindly invited,
> To take the command
> Of a squadron well mann'd,
> At a time when I thought myself slighted.
>
> You know I am gallant and clever,
> And ready to do my endeavour,
> For eating and fighting,
> Since both I delight in,
> And would fain be meddling for ever.
>
> Too long have my amorous capers,
> Been a dish for the saucy newspapers,
> Those vile scandal breeders,
> To serve to their readers,
> To chase hypochondriac vapours....
>
> I'll make war on the coasters I meet,
> And compel all the boats to retreat;
> To the wave and the gale,
> Not a smack shall set sail,
> Through the terror of me and my fleet....

> May I hope the Grand Duchess will deign,
> To approve the exploits of her swain;
> And sweetly to bless
> Him with nuptial caress,
> When he comes back from scouring the main.

Once ashore at The Hague, the Duke was conducted to the scene of action and watched the bombardments of Bergen-op-Zoom and Antwerp. He came under fire and was said to have been bruised by the explosion of a shell, which, however, 'did not impede his exertions'.[18] From the British headquarters outside Antwerp, he composed his despatch to the Prime Minister about a relatively quiet spell of warfare, telling him that 'two entire days and part of a third were dedicated to the most perfect and unmolested practice of our artillery against the ships and buildings. We ought to have been crowned with success, for every exertion was made and all ranks tried who could most do their duty.... Being, therefore, perfectly satisfied with the Commander-in-Chief and his gallant officers and men, I remain with the British Army on the march and shall continue with them at least four-and-twenty hours....'[19]

He continued to Brussels, where he heard that peace negotiations had begun, and wrote to London, 'If the news this day arrived is true, the game is over, thank God, with Bonaparte: at least tomorrow the Duke of Saxe-Weimar, Bülow [General von Bülow] and myself go to hear *Te Deum* sung in honour of the event: we shall once more see the Bourbons in France and ... order restored to Europe: how happy must the Prince Regent feel.'[20]

The Duke found the singing of the *Te Deum* 'beautiful and imposing',[21] then returned to The Hague to meet the Grand Duchess Catherine and escort her to England. Their meeting was inauspicious for she was in a towering rage. Instead of a British ship of the line waiting to carry her and her suite of thirty-seven (and four carriages) across the North Sea, there was no ship. When one did arrive to collect her, it was a little cutter, a single-masted vessel no bigger than a fishing-boat. The Duke was appalled by 'this unintentional but *real* insult offered to the Grand Duchess' and at once reported the position to London, pointing out that King George I had sent his whole fleet to meet her ancestor Peter the Great 'and *now a cutter* is sent for the Grand Duchess ... I hope yet to see this elegant and fascinating lady landed on our shore in a suitable manner.'

So he had his own ship converted to take her party and their baggage and reported that she was now 'in high health and spirits ... and has quite forgot her ill humour and dissatisfaction'.[22] It was not enough to win her affections, however; after her arrival in London, she complained about his 'vulgar familiarity and of his want of delicacy'.[23] But before he had time to learn of another disappointment, he was back at sea. At the end of March the allies had entered Paris and a Bourbon had been installed on the throne of France. The war was over and the Duke was allowed to resume his naval career, if only temporarily. He was given command of a ship of the line, the *Impregnable*, and the task of collecting the monarchs of the victorious alliance – and the newly-enthroned King Louis XVIII of France – to carry them across the Channel for the victory celebrations in London.

The King of France was ferried first, then the Duke returned for the Tsar of Russia, the Emperor of Austria and the King of Prussia. For this purpose he had the *Impregnable* as his flagship and two royal yachts, the *Royal Sovereign* and the *Royal Charlotte*, and several Russian warships under his command. But embarrassment was only just avoided when the Admiralty failed to deliver fifty beds the Duke had ordered for his ships and to avoid having to sling his guests in hammocks, he had to send a cutter to collect them from Deal. At first it was planned to take his passengers there, but it was thought too dangerous to put them ashore in boats, which would have to brave the surf to land them on the beach. Instead, they would go to Dover, where their carriages could wait on the quay and the Tsar's escort of Cossacks could be stabled at the Life Guards' barracks.

The ferrying was finally completed early in June and the three sovereigns drove to London in open carriages through a thunderstorm. After a week of splendid celebrations conducted by the Prince Regent, the royal visitors set out for Portsmouth to see 'a naval exhibition' prepared by the Duke of Clarence. This was to be more celebrations and inspections with a review of ships of the Royal Navy as its climax. But there was more responsibility involved than assembling the ships and ensuring that they were smart. Shortly before he arrived at Portsmouth, the Duke had received a secret memorandum from the First Lord of the Admiralty with a warning. 'On the conclusion of the wars in 1783 and 1802,' this began, 'serious disturbances broke out in the Fleet and, though there is every reason to believe that no unpleasant feeling exists at the present time in the minds of the Seamen, the Board of Admiralty have been careful, as a measure of precaution (without it appearing to be the effect of design) to avoid as much as possible a considerable assemblage of ships at any one Port....

'The present state of affairs at the close of a long war with France and the discharge of only a portion of the Seamen, when a great number are still retained on account of the American War [the Anglo-American War, 1812 – 15], is the most likely thing that can well be imagined to excite uneasy feelings ...'[24] Therefore he had to be alert for signs of another mutiny and keep the numbers of ships in any one concentration to a minimum.

Yet he was to command a large assembly, brought together for the great celebrations. Fourteen ships of the line and thirty frigates were anchored at Spithead in a single line seven miles long, and, as the flotilla of royal barges approached and departed, each ship fired a salute of forty-two guns, hiding their hulls in smoke. The ships' companies were too busy to brood on injustices and mutiny and, swept up in the excitement, cheered the potentates, who had defeated the heirs to the French Revolution which earlier mutineers had hoped to emulate. All agreed that the naval review was a spectacular success. In a social sense it was the Duke of Clarence's Trafalgar.

The Grand Duchess Catherine, it was said, 'bore the shock of firing with much fortitude'. The monarchs were conducted around the flagship and given tots of rum, which the Tsar was reported to have said 'in very intelligible English, "you call grog and I think is very good" '. When it was explained that it was diluted with six parts of water to one part of rum, 'a Tar observed that it would be no worse for being stronger'.[25]

Also on board the *Impregnable* was Rear-Admiral Sir Thomas Byam Martin, who now watched his former captain with concealed amusement. 'The yards of the *Impregnable* were manned,' he remembered, 'and something real, or imaginary, struck the Admiral of the Fleet as wrong, or careless, by one of the men on the fore topgallant yard; whereupon his Royal Highness, who had been pretty vehement in the use of speaking-trumpet, sent forth at the unfortunate man the most tremendous volley of oaths I have ever heard; it quite made one shudder to hear such blasphemy. But it was taken in a very different light by the Prince Regent, who turned at the sound of these oaths to Lord Melville, the First Lord of the Admiralty, and said, "What an excellent officer William is!" '[26]

He also remarked, while his royal guests watched a squadron of frigates manoeuvre under sail for their entertainment, 'I hope you two will not be jealous of my Navy.'[27] The Duke of Clarence had earned his brother's gratitude by his management of the spectacle and it was reported in *The Gentleman's Magazine* that, 'The Prince Regent can never feel himself more truly the Sovereign of the greatest maritime power that ever existed than when he thus beheld his Country's greatness witnessed by Foreign Monarchs on his Country's own element. He evidently felt his high destiny and declared it to be the grandest sight he ever saw.'[28]

Even the cynical Admiral Martin was impressed by the size of the crowds which packed hundreds of pleasure-craft, thronging the Solent and lying in a tight ring six hundred feet wide around the flagship. 'On going ashore,' he said, 'no part of the soil could be seen … it was a mass of human heads, rending the very skies with their cheers.'

It was, he thought, 'such a scene as was never witnessed before, or probably ever will be again'.[29]

Surprisingly, the officers of the ships at Spithead had been impressed by the Duke after an unexpected stroke of Nelsonian magnanimity. When he hoisted his flag in the *Impregnable* he would have been within his rights to replace at least some of her officers with his own friends. He did not do so and his predecessor's officers remained on board. Even if this was primarily due to his long absence from active service having limited the number of lieutenants known to him personally, it was taken as a generous gesture.

The Duke now prepared for escorting of the monarchs back to the Continent with his own anthem set to the tune of 'God Save the King' and to be sung on appropriate occasions:

> Thanks to Royal Clarence,
> Who guides our King to France,
> Thanks to Clarence.
> He maintains the glory
> Of the British Navy,
> Oh God, make him happy,
> God save Clarence!

Whether or not important guests were on board, he was literally in his element, delighting in the routine he had almost forgotten. 'I get up at six and till dinner-time the pen is hardly ever out of my hand,' he wrote to his son George, 'In short, an Admiral is a slave, but the King's service *must* be carried on and I am the last man not to do his duty.'[30]

His present duty was made clear by orders from the Admiralty: to strike his flag and come ashore. Distraught at losing his new-found authority and the splendour of his command, he could not accept that he had to give up his flagship and return to Bushy House. So he wrote an anguished letter to the First Lord of the Admiralty and another to the Prince Regent's private secretary, Colonel McMahon, and sent them to London with a trusted servant so that they arrived the same day.

He complained that having carried out his important duties, he, 'the *Admiral of the Fleet* and *the brother of the Prince Regent*, am ordered to haul my Flag down: I *must* and *do* feel this *unmerited indignity*.' He told them 'how very *deeply* and *keenly* I feel this cruel treatment, which I really do not deserve'.[31] Lord Melville's reply, which reached him next day, was bland but firm. Of course, the Duke would be invited to hoist his flag again should their royal visitors return to Portsmouth or, indeed, any British port. But, he added, 'I have had no intimation from the Prince Regent that your Royal Highness was to carry on the port Duties ... at Portsmouth, or to command any portion, or the whole of his Majesty's Ships in the Channel or any other Station ... I should object at any time to a person holding the high situation of Admiral of the Fleet being employed on any subordinate duties.'[32] So he had to come ashore; he might be allowed to command ships again but only if – as was courteously implied – he obeyed orders now.

Back at Bushy House and lonely, he again set about searching for a bride. He considered his cousin, Princess Sophia, daughter of the Duke of Gloucester – 'Silly Billy' – but, at forty-two, she was thought too old for child-bearing and he needed a legitimate heir. He again made advances to Miss Elphinstone without success and then turned his attention to the aristocracy and minor royalty of the continent; initially the daughters of the Landgrave of Hesse, the Prince of Hesse-Cassel and, finally, the King of Denmark. Nothing came of his advances.

When the visiting monarchs had gone, the celebrations continued with a service of thanksgiving at St Paul's and a depiction of the Battle of the Nile by model ships on the Serpentine in Hyde Park. In November, the Congress of Vienna began to discuss the future of Europe. Then in March 1815 Napoleon escaped from exile on Elba, landed in France and King Louis fled Paris. The 'Hundred Days' of political and military melodrama had begun and on 18 June ended on the battle-field of Waterloo.

There were no special victory celebrations this time and no need for the Duke to hoist his flag again. The following year, while he continued his search for a rich wife, his niece, Princess Charlotte, the only child of the Prince Regent and his estranged wife, the former Princess Caroline of Brunswick, married Prince Leopold of Saxe-Coburg. This seemed likely to remove him even further from the line of succession to the throne, for their children would take precedence over the Duke of York and he, married for twenty-five years to the daughter of the King of Prussia, had had no children. So it seemed that William would remain the squire of Bushy and a beached admiral for the rest of his life.

Now that the war really was over and he was not missing any battles, the Duke was more content. He would be more so when married because, while he had hopes of betrothal to the Danish princess, Lord Liverpool, the Prime Minister, proposed more than doubling his grant to £40,000 and writing off £17,000 of debt. In the excitement of anticipation, the news of the death of Dora Jordan came as a sad echo from the past. In exile from her creditors at St Cloud on the outskirts of Paris, she had rapidly sunk into depression and illness and – a year after her companion in adversity, Emma Hamilton, had died in Calais – she died there, alone, on 5 July 1816.

The Duke had not been directly in touch with her for seven years, had doubtless assumed that her allowance was adequate and that she was being cared for by her fourteen children. But he did feel duty-bound to provide for her children, and not only those he had fathered, continuing to pay allowances to two of her children by Richard Ford. He also felt a nostalgic affection for her memory and bought portraits of her whenever they came on to the market.

But he did not slacken his pursuit of a bride. The next to catch his eye was a Miss Wyckham, the heiress to an estate in Oxfordshire and an annual income of £16,000. He was enthusiastic but the Prince

Regent and the Cabinet were not, for she was considered unstable and unsuitable and had to be dropped.

Then, in November 1817, came a disaster which added a new dimension to his quest. Princess Charlotte, the second in succession to the throne, died in childbirth. Her place would be taken by the Duke of York, but he was in poor health, so, the Duke of Clarence was faced with the possibility of eventually becoming King. It was therefore essential that he find a suitable wife and, if possible, father a legitimate heir. Again he raked through the candidates on the Continent until he came to the unmarried daughter of the Bavarian Duke of Saxe-Meiningen, aged twenty-five. She was Princess Amelia Adelaide Louisa Thérèsa Caroline and was said to be amiable but not beautiful. Diplomatic enquiries were begun and, when there was a favourable response, miniature portraits were exchanged.

It was to be an arranged marriage with the couple consenting for reasons other than love, or even liking. 'Both public and private duty conspired to make me see the absolute necessity of marrying a Princess,'[33] the Duke told his eldest son, George, now home from the war, 'I believe I shall have virtue and innocence – at least, misery will not attend me.'[34] There was no pretence that the arrangement was anything more, even in public, and in the House of Commons a senior member of the government, George Canning, said, 'The Duke of Clarence would not have thought of contracting this marriage, it never would have entered into his contemplation to engage in this alliance, if it had not been pressed upon him as an act of public duty.... He contracted this alliance not for his own private gratification but because he had been advised to do so for the political purpose of providing for the succession to the throne.'[35]

As neither of his elder brothers now had heirs, he could at least look forward to his child becoming monarch and there was even a remote possibility that he might do so himself. It was almost a matter of bloodstock breeding and the idea of it did not dismay the House of Hanover, which had itself mostly been bred in this way. Yet, once the pair who were to be mated were brought together, the niceties of etiquette were, of course, observed.

Princess Adelaide arrived in London with her mother on 4 July 1818, and was met at her hotel by the Prince Regent. 'The First Gentleman of Europe', as he liked to be known, was charming but his handsome, petulant face and, indeed, his whole body was obscured by fat. He looked as dissolute as he was, and it was common knowledge that he enjoyed a series of mistresses while still officially married to Princess Caroline.

Adelaide's future father-in-law was incarcerated at Windsor, demented; the Queen was ill with dropsy: a sense of doom and decadence seemed to hang over their whole family. So when, while the Prince Regent was still with her, the Duke of Clarence arrived, his breezy presence came as a relief. He was, as she knew, nearly fifty-three and she could see that he was thick-bodied and red faced. Yet there was something wholesome about him, when seen with his brother, and he greeted her with elaborate gallantry.

He could see that she was not pretty – her nose was too long and sharp for that – but she had charm and elegance, ladylike manners and she could speak English. After seven years of public humiliation from those he had courted, he was delighted to think that this porcelain-like creature had already agreed to be his. As his past sexual encounters rose in his memory, he guiltily wrote to George FitzClarence, 'She is doomed, *poor dear innocent young* creature, to be my wife.'[36]

Before the wedding, Princess Adelaide was received by the Queen, who told her that she would be expected to put the Duke's finances in order, stop him drinking too much and polish his manners. She had heard that Adelaide was willing to treat the FitzClarence children as her own, but it was much more important that she should provide an heir to her husband; for that child 'it was made clear' his other children would be unsuitable company. Privately, the Queen was delighted with the young woman, who seemed sensible and dignified enough for the task ahead.

The marriage took place on 11 July at Kew, the scene of the bridegroom's early childhood. It was a double wedding with a younger brother, the Duke of Kent – who had seen service with the Army throughout the war, becoming Commander-in-Chief in North America and Governor of Gibraltar – also marrying a German, the widow of Prince Ernst of Leiningen.

To the surprise of those who knew the Duke by reputation, but not to those who understood the simple satisfactions he needed, the marriage was an immediate success. Only two days later, the Prince Regent reported seeing the couple 'sitting by the fire exactly like Darby and Joan'.[37] She treated him with understanding and respect, not as a buffoon or a roué. But the Duke's allowance had not been increased by Parliament to what he considered a fitting sum for a married life and they decided to move, temporarily, to Hanover. There, in November, the Duke was told that his wife was pregnant. A few months later, she fell ill with pleurisy, resulting in a premature birth and the baby – a daughter whom they named Charlotte – died a few hours later.

The Duchess became pregnant again a few months later but on their return journey to England suffered a miscarriage. They decided that they could afford to live at Bushy House, and the Duchess was at last introduced to the stratified maze of English society. But her mingled bewilderment and pleasure at the Regency *haute monde* of smart, often rakish, sometimes clever, courtiers, aristocrats, politicians and fashionable bohemians did not last long.

At the beginning of 1820, the Duke of Kent died and was followed by his father a fortnight later. The death of King George III came as a shock, despite his long isolation with his doctors and keepers at Windsor, for it ended the long reign and the heroic times which had taken the country from the creation of its empire in the Seven Years' War to final victory over its great French rival. The old King had seen titanic changes in the world, when the dominating motive forces were trade, revolution and war. Now King George IV had succeeded him and the motive forces would be different: trade and the growth of industry would give the nation its power. Whatever his faults, the new King was cultured and a patron of the arts and the nation could expect even more from his passionate interest in architecture which was beginning to reflect post-war self-confidence. But there was the dark side, and this soon took the portly shape of Queen Caroline, who had been living abroad in what was said to be gross dissipation worthy of her husband. She could have remained on the Continent, enjoying her substantial allowance, but she chose to return with the intention of taking her place as Queen. So, before the coronation, she had to be removed – preferably by divorce – and the bizarre circumstances were examined by the House of Lords.

Despite the Queen's reputation, she became a popular figure, or at least a plump heroine to set against her extravagant and unpopular husband. Factions for and against both of them exchanged salacious accusations and the Duke stoutly defended his brother. He now saw himself as a robust, land-owning duke, with a wife who was worthy of him, and also, of course, as a retired naval officer. But in the public mind he was still the tough old rake and the flogging captain. So when he denounced Queen Caroline for what she undoubtedly was, he drew a counter-attack from a balladeer signing himself 'Ben Backstay' in the subversive magazine *The Black Dwarf*, which saw him as much of the nation still did:

> Admiral Tarry Breeks, a Royal Duke,
> The moral brother of a moral King,
> Is anxious 'mongst the Lords to look
> A sapient, nautical and moral thing.
> But 'ere he points at Britain's Queen a shaft,
> Or steps (the ship that chases her) aboard on;
> He should remember, memory looks aloft,
> And read his morals in the hapless Jordan.

12

The Eloquence of Our Guns

The coronation of King George IV on 19 July 1821 was more pantomime than religious ceremony, yet its magnificent theatricality silenced some who might have laughed.

No expense had been spared in staging the pageantry in the Abbey and in Westminster Hall, where the coronation banquet was to be held. Any tradition which would add colour to the spectacle was revived, including the King's Herb-Woman and her attendants who strewed his path with scented flowers and herbs; the King's Champion, who rode on horseback, clad in armour, into Westminster Hall to throw down a gauntlet in symbolic challenge to the sovereign's enemies; and a troupe of flower-girls, who cast rose-petals before him.

All eyes sought the new King and he ensured that he was impossible to miss. The painter Benjamin Haydon, who saw him arrive for the banquet described how, 'Something rustles and a being buried in satin, feathers and diamonds rolls gracefully into his seat. The room rises in a sort of feathered, silken thunder. Plumes wave, eyes sparkle, glasses are out, mouths smile and one man becomes the prime object of attention to thousands. The way in which the King bowed was really royal. As he looked towards the peeresses and foreign ambassadors, he showed like some gorgeous bird of the East.'[1]

In pantomime there had to be a Demon King but on this occasion it was the Queen. Saved from the humiliation of divorce, she nevertheless came to claim her throne alongside his. The King had feared she might present herself at the Abbey and demand admittance, and she did. She was, of course, refused entry and drove away through excited crowds. There was only one defiant gesture she could now make: only twenty days later, burned out like some elaborate firework, she died and her body was sent back to Brunswick.

Throughout the performance, the Duke and Duchess of Clarence played prominent supporting roles and it was noticed that his manners had greatly improved. He was said to be 'even gentlemanlike' and an acquaintance was surprised that he 'did not say a single indecent or improper thing'.[2] The credit was given to the Duchess, and one peer remarked, 'You would be surprised at the Duke of Clarence if you were to see him, for his wife, it is said, has entirely reformed him.'[3] She had done so with charm and by example. Indeed, they had become a devoted couple and were seen to be mutually supportive when her pregnancies ended with bereavement: in 1820, another daughter, Elizabeth, had died after four months; two years later, the Duchess was pregnant with twins but suffered another miscarriage. They now gave up hope of providing an heir to the throne.

His children by Dorothy Jordan were now at marriageable age and finding husbands and wives to match their social ambitions, for their illegitimacy had given them a sharp awareness of their royal blood and irregular origins. George, for example, had covered both aspects by marrying the illegitimate daughter of Lord Egremont and prudently named their first daughter Adelaide after his stepmother. But the Duke was particularly fond of the child born to his sister-in-law, the Duchess of Kent, in 1819, shortly before the death of her husband, and named Victoria.

The Duke now accepted a reduced allowance offered by Parliament on his marriage, which he had then spurned; the increase of £6,000 was backdated to the year of the offer and he was also given the rank (and pay) of General of Marines. This enabled them to live a comfortable but quiet life at Bushy House and to travel to her home in Bavaria whenever inclined. He bore his disappointments stoically and seemed a reasonably contented man.

One pleasure was that on his visits to the continent he was entitled to make the sea-crossing in a royal yacht and in 1825 the command of the most elaborate of these, the *Royal Sovereign*, was given to Captain Sir William Hoste. Their particular bond was that the captain had been Lord Nelson's favourite protégé. Also the son of a Norfolk parson, Hoste had gone to sea in the *Agamemnon* in 1793 and had been with Nelson in every action until he was given his own command after the Battle of the Nile. Towards the end of 'the Great War' he had fought the French in the Adriatic, capturing both Catarro and Ragusa [now Kotor and Dubrovnik] after bombarding the fortress-cities with naval guns hauled to the summits of commanding mountains; he had also won his own Trafalgar in miniature, fought between squadrons of frigates off Lissa in 1811. Hoste was now consumptive but, as a special honour, had been given command of the yacht, a three-masted ship decorated with gilded carvings of cupids and cabin-ports shaped like oval picture-frames.

The Duke and Duchess also crossed from Woolwich to Calais in the new steam-packet *Comet* and he and Hoste discussed the future of steam as a ship-propellant, for they were living in times of change. Naval officers who had brooded on future technology during long wartime watches at sea were now, in retirement, suggesting all sorts of exciting and alarming innovations in ship-design and weaponry. The Royal Navy was cautious, for it remained supreme and unchallenged with its existing ships and weapons. When William Pitt had shown interest in the development of the torpedo by the American marine inventor Robert Fulton, Earl St Vincent had remarked that he was 'the greatest fool that ever existed, to encourage a mode of war, which they who commanded the seas did not want, and which, if successful, would deprive them of it'.[4] But St Vincent had died in 1823 and attitudes might be changing.

The Duke did his best to keep up with such debate, but most of his contemporaries had retired, or were dead. Of those still active, Admiral Sir Richard Keats was Governor of Greenwich Hospital and out of close touch, while the most powerful naval member of the Board of Admiralty was Vice-Admiral Sir George Cockburn, an officer he disliked as much as the First Lord himself, Lord Melville. So he talked to cronies in the clubs, read naval history, looked at his paintings of naval battles – and at a section of the *Victory's* main mast mounted in Bushy House – and regarded his past career as a naval officer with deep nostalgia.

The life of the Duke of Clarence was changed by two deaths. The first was that of the Duke of York on 5 January 1827, so that he became first in succession to the throne. As chief mourner at this brother's funeral, he chatted to the congregation and was heard asking one about the game he had killed on his country estate. Parliament was asked to increase his official annual income and finally did so, giving him an extra £3000 (less than half the sum asked) but £6000 (half as much again as asked) to the Duchess, for his reputation still did not stand high. But he was grateful, sending the King 'the warmest and sincerest thanks'.[5]

However, his elder brother was said to have remarked to Princess Lieven – a particularly sharp-eyed, sharp-tongued observer of the London scene – when watching the Duke at dinner, 'The Duke of Clarence will be a fine King! Look at that idiot! They will remember me, if ever he is in my place.'[6] But he was fond of him, and wanted to give him some mark of honour.

The following month, the Prime Minister, Lord Liverpool, died and a new administration was formed by the former foreign secretary, George Canning. In the political upheaval this brought, one of those who refused to serve in the Cabinet was Lord Melville and a replacement as First Lord of the Admiralty had to be found. Canning and the King, casting about for a successor, seemed to have passed over the long-standing claim of the Duke of Clarence on the grounds that he was not suitable as a Cabinet minister. Then they had second thoughts. An idea struck them, which Canning knew would appeal to the King's love of mock-historical pageantry and the Duke's longing for recognition, and would also dispose of any attempted return to office by Melville. The archaic and extinct title of Lord High Admiral could be revived. It had once been held by King James II when Duke of York and after his accession, and then by Prince George of Denmark, consort of Queen Anne, and finally by the Earl of Pembroke, before being replaced by the title of First Lord of the Admiralty in 1709.

The Duke of Clarence could be given this title and nominal charge of the Royal Navy. This would delight him and give the Canning administration the cachet of royal involvement. However, he would not be a member of the Cabinet – unlike a First Lord of the Admiralty – and, while the Board would be replaced by a Council which, he would be told, was to advise him, he could take no executive decision without their concurrence.

So, soon after Canning formed his government on 11 April 1827, the Duke was approached and offered the appointment. He was as overjoyed as had been expected. It was explained that, although decisions would be announced as being those of the Lord High Admiral, they would be reached – and certainly ratified – by the Council, and when he was at sea, he would have to be accompanied by a member of the Council to confirm his orders. These restraints did not worry the Duke, for his inspiration had been Nelson, who had disobeyed Lord Keith's orders in the Mediterranean and disregarded his superior officer's signal to disengage at Copenhagen. If necessary, he would do likewise because, as he saw his task, it was quite simply and without qualification, 'the care and control of the Naval Power of the United Kingdom'.[7]

Nor was this the only potential problem. Three of the six members of his Council were regarded as his personal enemies and they included both the naval members. The first was Vice-Admiral Sir William Hope, who as Lieutenant Hope had supported Lieutenant Schomberg in his quarrel with Prince William in the *Pegasus* forty years before. But both men had matured and now that the Duke no longer felt the baleful eye of his father upon him, he allowed his natural generosity to prevail. They had shaken hands some years later, but the Duke now decided to make formal peace.

'I ask it as a favour of you to stay here,' he wrote to Hope, on accepting his new office. 'You may remember that when you were a lieutenant in the ship I commanded, we had a violent quarrel and that you quitted the ship; and that our quarrel was not made up for ten years; but the world at large, who know of the quarrel, may not have known of our reconciliation; and I wish that, by your staying now, they may become fully acquainted with it. Moreover you cannot know that, after you left my ship, I thought you in the right and *myself in the wrong*, and that is another reason, so you must stay and be of my Council.'[8]

But Vice-Admiral Sir George Cockburn was a different matter. He was a tough professional, who had served under Nelson and come into the public eye when commanding the British expeditionary force in America which sacked Washington and burned the White House in 1813. Two years later, he had commanded the squadron escorting Napoleon to exile on St Helena. Regarded as 'a very highly educated gentleman, gifted by Nature with a powerful intellect', who could 'pen a despatch like a secretary of State', he had 'a haughty and dictatorial bearing' and 'considered that he could carry everything by brute force'. One of his staff considered him 'the most uncompromising representative of things as they were.... It often surprised me that a man of his powerful intellect could not be brought to see that this world did not stand still.' Like the former First Lord of the Admiralty, Lord Melville, Cockburn had been opposed to the introduction of steam, if only because 'since the introduction of steam-vessels, he had never seen a clean deck or a captain … who did not look like a sweep.'[9]

The Duke had not liked him for years. 'He was never fit to be at the Admiralty any more than my old Grandmother,'[10] he told one friend, and another that he was 'self-conceited',[11] but he was determined to start a new and positive relationship with him at the Admiralty. There was a problem in achieving this because the First Secretary, John

Croker, was Cockburn's friend and no friend of the Duke's. A suave, quick-witted Irishman, a former Member of Parliament and temporarily Chief Secretary for Ireland, he had some literary skill, but little direct knowledge of the Navy, owing his position to his friendship with Canning. He and the Duke had been guests of the King at Brighton and, after the usual elaborate meal at the Royal Pavilion, had been arguing some point, at which the latter had remarked, 'Croker, were I King, I'd be my own First Lord of the Admiralty and you should *not* be my secretary.' Croker had asked him when a monarch had last presided over the Admiralty; the Duke had not known; so Croker had been able to tell him that it had been King James II. At this, the King, hearing raised voices, had asked, 'What, Croker, what is that? One of your good things, I suppose.' Croker had replied, 'No, and please your Majesty, nothing. But your royal brother is saying what he will do when you are no longer King.'[12] King George turned and walked away.

So, in late April, on the day before he first attended the Admiralty, the Duke summoned the Second Secretary, John Barrow, a cultivated man who had served at sea and had worked at the Admiralty since the time of Nelson, and asked to be briefed. He told Barrow that Hope and he were 'old friends and shipmates' and that he 'knew Sir George Cockburn well'. In turn, Barrow told him that he would find 'the whole of his Council intelligent officers and agreeable gentlemen' and that, as it was peacetime, there should be little work except 'numerous pressing demands from old officers'.

Next day he arrived at the Admiralty and was escorted up to the magnificent Board Room, decorated by Grinling Gibbons, where the pointer of the dial on the wall showed the direction of the wind blowing the vane on the roof. Taking his place at the head of the table, where so much dramatic news had been announced and so many critical decisions taken, he greeted Cockburn, Hope and the two civil members, Keith Douglas and John Denison – both Members of Parliament – and the two secretaries with becoming modesty. As Barrow reported, he told them, 'how little professional knowledge could be expected from *him* and how much he had to look to from *them*'.

After a short meeting, he asked Barrow to show him the adjoining Admiralty House, which would be his official residence. In the dining-room, he enquired how many could be seated at table; Barrow thought about thirty, although he had never seen more than twenty. Had many First Lords entertained, the Duke wanted to know, and had Lord Spencer often given dinner parties there? Barrow replied that a week had rarely passed without Lord Spencer giving two or three large dinner parties. 'That's quite right,' said the Duke, 'I delight in hospitality and mean to practise it here.'

Not only did he begin to plan dinner parties but also levées, which he decided would eventually be attended by every commissioned officer in the Navy. Another interest he could now indulge was the Hanoverian passion for uniforms, and he began to tinker with the design of the classic naval officers' uniforms of blue, white and gold. He instituted high collars, coloured blue instead of white; abolished full-dress uniform and instructed that knee-breeches were to be worn only on formal social occasions ashore.

During his long unemployment, he had heard much about the causes of discontent in the Navy, and he set about finding remedies. One cause was the poor prospects for lieutenants in peacetime, when those who had served as first lieutenants of ships of the line again found themselves just ordinary lieutenants. So now the Lord High Admiral planned, with the agreement of his Council, to establish the rank of commander. Hitherto, this rank, like that of commodore, had been only temporary but now it was to be another step in promotion and an incentive. He also encouraged the revision of schemes for retirement and pensions, which had become more relevant as the officers who had come ashore on demobilisation after 1815 advanced into middle and old age.

Nor was his interest confined to officers. Realising that ratings had no comparable hierarchy, or prospects of promotion – able seamen could be made 'boatswain's mates' and returned to their former rating at an officer's whim – he initiated the substantive rank of petty officer with a badge of rank to be worn on the sleeve. Aware that discipline could be imposed by an inadequate captain by the fear of flogging – and perhaps remembering his own excessive use of the cat-o'-nine-tails – he asked for quarterly returns of punishments in ships, with a view to reducing the offences for which flogging could be the sentence to a few serious crimes, including mutiny. He even showed interest in education on board ship, discussing it with Barrow and initiating the ideas which later produced the Seamen's Library to encourage reading.

As soon as he had started the process of these reforms, he decided to leave for a tour of inspection, sailing to Plymouth and Portsmouth in the *Royal Sovereign*, commanded by Captain Hoste, while the Duchess, who hated the sea, followed overland. The royal yacht was to be accompanied by a brig to repeat signals to and from shore and by the steamer Comet, in case either ship needed to be towed. None of his Council was to accompany him except Barrow, whom he ordered to stock the yacht with good wine. He also asked the King if he could borrow some of the royal silver, but this was refused.

Once aboard the *Royal Sovereign* and flying the flag of the Lord High Admiral, the Duke was, at last, supremely happy and confident. On 9 July 1827, he arrived off Plymouth to see its green hills thick with welcoming crowds. Mr and Mrs Winne and the lovely Sally were dead, so echoes of Foxhole Quay and dances at the Long Room did not intrude into the royal pageantry which now began.

Inspections and parades followed in succession. He inspected the ships in the harbour, parades of the Royal Marines, and the new breakwater being built across the Sound; when the engineer, John Rennie, showed him drawings for the lighthouse planned for it, he remarked that a lighted buoy would be cheaper. He toured the dockyard and the storehouses and the barracks. Finally he gave a ball on board the royal yacht, with the *Lightning* – the first steamer to be commissioned by the Royal Navy – lying alongside, both decorated with 'the flags of all nations intermixed with flowers and flowering shrubs', while the flagship *Britannia* 'exhibited in her port-holes splendid blue lights for the entertainment of the party … the whole arrangement,' as John Barrow declared, 'presented one of the prettiest sights I ever remember to have seen.' Mindful of possible accusations of extravagance, the Duke told Barrow to charge the entertainment to his own account, which was already overdrawn.

He was joined at Plymouth by the Duchess, who, as she drew near, was terrified that the welcoming crowds would take the horses from their traces and themselves drag the carriage through the streets; her companion, who ordered them to desist, was Admiral Sir Byam Martin, now Controller of the Navy.

After a regatta in the Sound, the couple left – he by sea, she by land – for Milford Haven and Pembroke Dock, where they saw a first-rate ship of the line named after him, the *Royal William*, building on the stocks. At the end of July, they departed for Portsmouth, the Duke in the royal yacht, towed by the *Lightning*, but he was gratified when, as Barrow recorded, 'it began to blow so strong that the steamer was cast off. The Wolf Rock roared tremendously, between which and the coast of Cornwall the yacht went beautifully, and rounded Land's End without our seeing anything more of the steamer.'[13]

On arrival at Portsmouth another round of inspections, parades, receptions and dinners began. What was particularly pleasing to the Duke was that the dinners presented frequent occasions for speech-making, of which he took full advantage. At one, he was even able to look back with affection to his father, telling a banqueting-hall filled with naval officers and Portsmouth worthies that, 'when it pleased the Sovereign of this happy nation, distinguished above all others for its maritime superiority, to decide upon my joining the Navy, it was determined that … I should be skilled as a seaman and that I should not command until I had been well taught how to obey. This, Gentlemen, has been my pride and my glory…. As a midshipman, I trudged his

Majesty's quarterdeck. Much may be said, Gentlemen, concerning the advantages of education, and I do not undervalue any school, but ... there is no education to equal that ... afforded by the quarterdeck of a British man-of-war.'

Warming to his oratory, he continued, 'Gentlemen, look upon the globe and compare this little island of Great Britain, a mere speck in the ocean, with the great nations of the world and then consider in how many parts of the world our flag is, for various purposes, unfurled – by how many myriads of its inhabitants our language is spoken – and then let anyone ask how those great ends and that vast importance has been obtained? I will answer – by the Navy!'

Such speeches always resulted in rounds of toasts to his hosts, to himself and to anybody connected with the Navy, Portsmouth or the royal family. He was particularly gratified when the health of his wife was proposed and he responded. Admitting that royalty were 'from state reasons ... prevented from exercising their own judgement, and placing their affections on an object of their own choice' but had to marry 'without having once seen the person intended to be their future companion for life', he declared that, in the case of his own wife, 'every day of my life since my union with her, every leisure hour that I could spare from my official duties, has brought some addition to my domestic comforts and happiness.'[14]

The patriotic jamboree was to end with a naval review at Spithead, which was to include a squadron commanded by Admiral Sir Thomas Hardy – Nelson's flag captain at Trafalgar – and a visiting Russian fleet, combined with a military review on Southsea Common overlooking the anchorage. The Duke had presented some regimental colours and was watching the troops drilling when the shutters of the semaphore signalling stations linking London with Portsmouth began to clatter. Soon after, a staff officer handed a message to Admiral Stopford, the Commander-in-Chief. But it was in code and he had no cypher book, so the Duke called Barrow, who had one with him, and said, 'What is it? Quick, quick.' Barrow rapidly decoded the message and said, 'Sir, it is brief but painfully distressing. Mr Canning is dead.'[15]

The loss of the Duke's political patron was a blow, and he was relieved that the inspections were almost over and that, after a quick review of the assembled warships, he could leave for London, where Lord Goderich had been appointed to succeed Canning as Prime Minister. Resuming his place at the head of his Council, the Duke now found himself occupied with, and stimulated by, a crisis in the eastern Mediterranean and the Balkans. As he read despatches from the Mediterranean Fleet, an old ambition stirred. He had reviewed fleets, inspected dockyards and was instituting reforms, but he had not yet fought and won a great naval victory.

There had been no such opportunity for twelve years, of course, but now mutually hostile fleets, one of them British, were again eyeing each other in the Mediterranean. The cause which had engaged British attention was the Greek struggle for freedom from Turkish rule. Few British had been to Greece, but the ruling class had been educated in the classics and Greek civilisation had been vividly illustrated by the arrival in London a decade before of the marble statuary acquired by Lord Elgin from the Parthenon in Athens. The Greeks were seen as European Christians enslaved by cruel Islamic conquerors, and among those drawn to fight on their behalf was the romantic poet Lord Byron, who had died there of fever in 1824. So while the policy of the government was to avoid a direct collision with Turkey, which dominated the Middle East and the overland trade-routes with India and the Far East, the sympathies of the British were with the Greeks.

In the strategic alliance, which seemed an echo of the Crusades, the British, French and Russian governments had sent squadrons to the eastern Mediterranean to try to prevent continued massacres of the rebellious Greeks by the Turks and to lend oblique support to the cause of their freedom. On 6 July 1827, the three had signed an agreement calling upon the two sides to observe an armistice, which would clearly favour the Greeks, who agreed to comply. However, in

September the Egyptian fleet landed fresh troops to support the Turks in southern Greece in defiance of the European demands, bringing about a political crisis and the risk of direct confrontation.

The senior officer of three allied squadrons was British and an old friend of the Duke's. Vice-Admiral Sir Edward Codrington, who had commanded the Orion at Trafalgar, had become one of Nelson's successors in command of the Mediterranean Station at the beginning of the year. An active and ambitious officer – lean and bald with a sharp predatory nose – he too venerated Nelson. Indeed, when stricken by the news of the latter's death, his wife had written to him, 'I know with what devotion you would have attended your most admired hero and example.... Let us not continue to lament a death so fine and well-timed for *himself*; but rather turn with hope and reanimating confidence to our future Nelsons, who, perhaps, want opportunity alone to equal him. Need I say that amongst these my fond enthusiasm sees *you*, my good man, not least worthy of inspiring that dear hope? Heaven grant your career as brilliant as his.'[16]

Now he was the senior officer of a combined fleet in the sea Nelson had once made his own. Moreover, he was supported at the Admiralty by one of Nelson's friends; now that the Duke was sixty-two and held the highest rank in the Navy, he no longer expected any sea command, seeing himself instead as the wise, strong disposer of events. On Codrington's arrival at Malta in June he had heard of the Duke's appointment as Lord High Admiral and wrote to congratulate him. Saying that he would shortly report to him 'some details of the horrors' in Greece, he added, 'The mild forbearance of the English law is not applicable to the circumstances of the war carrying on here and I contemplate being called upon to act with a rigour, which nothing but a strong sense of the absolute necessity of it would induce me to adopt.'[17]

This was an attitude which appealed to the Duke, but he reflected the Government's view when he replied that 'prudence and moderation will be your best guides.'[18] The British ambassador at Constantinople, Stratford Canning (a cousin of the late Prime Minister) put his instructions succinctly: 'You are not to take part with either of the Belligerents, but you are to interpose your forces between them and to keep the peace with your speaking-trumpet if possible; but in case of necessity, with that which is used for the maintenance of a blockade against friends as well as foes – I mean *force*.'[19]

Ashore, Turkish repression continued, and in July Codrington reported to London, 'a dreadful massacre of thirty thousand Greeks, including women and children, which has stained with still deeper dye the bloody name of Turk!'[20] Both the French and Russian admirals felt as vengeful as he did, and they were supported by their governments. But the British attitude remained pacific, and the Lord High Admiral's letters reflected this policy, although at the beginning of October he added a more characteristic touch: 'I cannot too often urge the necessity and propriety of constant practice at the guns.'[21]

Meanwhile the combined Turkish and Egyptian fleets had concentrated at Navarino [the modern Pylos], a magnificent natural harbour with a narrow entrance at the south-westerly tip of the Peloponnese peninsula. It soon became apparent that they were to use the anchorage as a base for further operations against the Greeks so on his own initiative, Codrington told the Turkish admiral, Ibrahim Pasha, that his orders were to enforce an armistice and that he must insist that his fleet either remain within the bay or withdraw from Greek waters.

It was agreed that revised orders could be sought from Constantinople. But while these were awaited the Greeks, often under British officers – including the brilliant maverick, Lord Cochrane, a former captain in the Royal Navy – took advantage of Turkish inactivity and went on to the offensive. Deciding that, as the armistice had been breached by the Greeks, he was no longer bound by any agreement with Codrington, Ibrahim ordered some of his ships to sail and take action against them. All were intercepted by the British at sea and forced to return to Navarino, where they were again concentrated by mid-October.

Then reports reached Codrington of new Turkish atrocities in the Peloponnese. He was in a dilemma: he could not continue the blockade of Navarino throughout the winter, when his ships would be blown off-station, and Ibrahim, while still awaiting orders from Constantinople, showed no signs of complying with his demands. The one positive action open to him was to enter the bay and anchor alongside the Turkish and Egyptian fleets so that they could not move without a fight. In that event, the Europeans would be heavily outnumbered; themselves mustering twenty-seven fighting ships – including four ships of the line from each of the three allies – mounting thirteen hundred guns and manned by 17,500 men. Their opponents had sixty-five fighting ships – including seven ships of the line and seventeen heavy frigates – mounting more than two thousand guns and manned by almost 22,000 men. Supported by shore batteries, these ships had been anchored in a crescent formation devised by an experienced French officer, with the opening in their line facing the entrance to the bay so that fire could be concentrated upon it.

The risk of a battle provoked by entering the anchorage was considerable, but all three European admirals agreed it had to be taken and only the British Government was urging caution. Codrington was well aware of what Nelson would have done and may have had more than an informed opinion of what the Lord High Admiral would order were he present.

Later there were to be several claims that, enclosed with the orders from the Admiralty which reached Codrington off Navarino, was one of the slips of paper on which short memoranda from the Council were written. On this was written – so it was said – in the spiky handwriting of the Lord High Admiral, 'Go in, my dear Ned, and smash these damned Turks!'[22] Whether or not such a note was sent, it was wholly in character. None was found in Codrington's papers and he later denied having received it, but veterans of the Great War were accustomed to secret orders and to treating them as such. There were also diplomatic reports on the Continent – notably Austrian – that Codrington *had* received secret orders from the Lord High Admiral.

Whatever the spur – and it certainly included Codrington's own enthusiasm, the belligerence of the French and Russian admirals and, at least, the supposed inclinations of the Duke of Clarence – the allied fleet prepared for action. On the morning of 20 October 1827 (the eve of the anniversary of the Battle of Trafalgar) the ships were cleared for action. Then, at one o'clock that afternoon, the ships formed line of battle, the British leading, followed by the French and the Russians, with all sails set, port-lids open and guns run out, and steered for the harbour mouth.

It was an extraordinary spectacle. The fleet was not sailing towards another under sail on the open sea, but waiting at anchor as Nelson's enemies had in Aboukir Bay and off Copenhagen. Beyond their bare masts and yards – standing thick as a leafless plantation of trees – rose hills which sheltered the anchorage from the wind. In any case, the battle, if there was to be one, would be fought at point-blank range, gun-muzzle to gun-muzzle.

At two o'clock, the leading British ship – Codrington's flagship, the *Asia* – glided into the harbour, within pistol-shot of the batteries commanding the entrance. But no gun was fired; the Turkish gunners watching from ramparts and earthworks. It began to look as though there might not be a battle after all. Then, at twenty-five minutes past two, a Turkish boat pulled past the British frigate *Dartmouth*, as she was anchoring, its crew climbed aboard a moored fireship loaded with combustibles, and began to prepare a powder-train for ignition. The first lieutenant of the British ship was sent to warn them to stop but as his boat drew alongside the Turks opened fire, killing and wounding its crew. The Turks then lit the train and the fireship began to burn and drift towards the British frigate. A moment later, an Egyptian corvette fired a gun, hitting the French flagship. One by one, the opposing ships opened fire until the whole array of ships in the bay was hidden by smoke stabbed with gun-flashes.

The Battle of Navarino, as it came to be called, was fought for three and a half hours. When darkness fell, burning wrecks lit a panorama of destruction not seen since the Battle of the Nile. 'Night threw her sable mantle over the bloody scene and served as a pall to hundreds of dead and dying victims,' ran one account. 'The wind had totally sunk and left a perfect calm and not a sound was heard save that of a few random shots fired at intervals from the guns of the forts and which rather added to than diminished the solemnity of the scene. The harbour, which but a few hours before had presented the most animated picture imaginable, was now covered with darkness and filled with desolation, rendered occasionally visible by the momentary bursts of light from the burning of exploding vessels.... The magnificence of the picture it produced is not to be described.'[23]

More than sixty Turkish and Egyptian ships had been destroyed, the survivors burning, run aground or abandoned; their losses were thought to be more than six thousand killed and four thousand wounded. The Europeans had not lost a single ship and their casualties amounted to less than two hundred killed and five hundred wounded, with the British suffering marginally more than the others. It was victory by annihilation, such as Nelson had established as the conclusion to be desired.

When the news reached London three weeks later, the Lord High Admiral showed his true colours, telling his friend Lord Mayo that he 'must feel pleased at the result of the event at Navarino ... I believe the Turk never before felt the eloquence of our Guns.'[24] He sent Codrington a ceremonial sword 'as a small token of my admiration of your conduct in Navarino Bay';[25] then, having recently been appointed Acting Grand Master of the Order of the Bath, he recommended that the King award him the Grand Cross and make all his captains and commanders Companions of the Order. The King, whose immediate reaction had been that 'his old English heart bounded again and again with delight',[26] complied. But, as the political and diplomatic complaints began to arrive, he changed his tone, saying of Codrington's honour, 'I have sent him a riband but it ought to have been a halter.'[27] This was the first gust of the storm.

As Lord High Admiral, the Duke wrote an official and ominously-worded letter to Codrington beginning, 'In the first place, I am to congratulate you on the splendid victory you have obtained ... I admire your perfect conduct on the day of battle and most highly appreciate the exertions of all ranks under your orders.' He then warned the admiral that the Cabinet planned to 'obtain a complete and satisfactory explanation ... respecting the cause of your going into Navarin* Bay and the commencement of the firing'.[28]

This was the first of many indications to Codrington that his victory had not been acclaimed as another Battle of the Nile. The Lord High Admiral might crow with triumph and promote all the commanders and senior lieutenants in the British squadron, but the British Government was appalled. It was seen as a gratuitous massacre, which would harm British commercial interests in the Levant and risk igniting a war between Turkey and Russia; this could result in Russia taking control of the Dardanelles and becoming an even more powerful force in the Mediterranean. At the Admiralty, the Council reflected this political view and the Lord High Admiral had to argue with them for the confirmation of the promotions he had ordered. 'Ministers would gladly shelter themselves ... by throwing the blame on Codrington,' he commented, 'but he has done nobly.'[29]

Yet he knew how weak his position was when, having won honours and promotion for the victors of Navarino, he could do nothing more to help them. Instead of more laurels, Codrington received from the Government a demeaning 'List of Queries' as to the necessity of the action. There was also an unexpected accusation that, after the battle, when he had let the surviving enemy ships depart, they had taken with them several hundred Greek women and children to sell as slaves in Alexandria. He bridled at what both he and the Duke saw

---

* Naval officers often referred to 'Navarin' rather than 'Navarino'.

as insults, the most hurtful of which were still to come. Those who had fought were not offered compensation for clothes and belongings lost during the battle, and the admiral was asked to pay the cost of his Grand Cross of the Order of the Bath. He refused. On his return, he met a country gentleman of his acquaintance, who enquired, 'How are you, Codrington? Have you had any good shooting lately?' He shrugged and replied, 'Why, yes, I *have* had some rather remarkable shooting.'[30]

In the King's Speech at the Opening of Parliament on 20 January 1828, the great victory was dismissed with the words, 'Notwithstanding the valour displayed by the combined fleet, His Majesty laments that this conflict should have occurred with the naval force of an ancient ally, but he still entertains the confident hope that this untoward event will not be followed by further hostilities....'[31] But it was: in April, Russia declared war on Turkey.

Even so, the Duke was determined that Codrington should bask in some Nelsonian glory, and a month later wrote to him, 'You ought, with your friends, to be most perfectly satisfied; and *I* once more repeat you *were fully* authorised by your instructions to strike the blow you did in Navarin Bay and the *whole of Europe* has *amply* and *honourably* done you justice.'[32]

The Lord High Admiral drew some satisfaction from analysing the performance of the squadron in action. He was dismayed to learn of the poor standard of gunnery, which had been effective because of the point-blank range but had almost emptied the ships' magazines. He was aware that gunnery, which had combined to such effect with Nelson's tactics in winning his great victories, had been neglected. Here was something he understood and could achieve. It would also offer some political satisfaction because in the War of 1812 his disliked predecessor, Lord Melville, had allowed under-gunned British frigates to go into action against the big, new American frigates, which were virtually ships of the line in weaponry with the speed of frigates. It was not only more powerful guns that were needed but gun-drill which matched Nelson's standards. He was dismayed to discover that one sloop had just completed a three-year commission without firing a single shot in practice, let alone anger. Guardships anchored in the main naval ports seldom exercised their guns – one reason being that it tended to tarnish brasswork and dirty the scrubbed decks – and he determined to put a stop to that.

Guardships offered comfortable berths to lazy officers, but the Lord High Admiral was deciding that this had to change. Every ship in commission, including the guardships, would have to submit quarterly returns of gunnery exercises and the ammunition expended. He also discussed with Admiral Sir Thomas Byam Martin the possibility of using a guardship at Portsmouth as a gunnery training ship for two or three hundred seamen.* He himself delighted in watching gunnery trials, such as those of new types of carronade, devised by Nelson's former flag-captain, Admiral Hardy, and Sir William Congreve, the inventor, which were test-fired at Woolwich Arsenal before the Admiralty decided which to put into production.

In trying to improve the capabilities of the Navy, he was confident that he would have the support of the Government which took office in January. Goderich had been unable to hold his bickering administration together and had been replaced as Prime Minister by the Duke of Wellington, albeit with reluctance, and with Sir Robert Peel as Home Secretary. Here, the Lord High Admiral believed was a practical leader, who understood the realities of power better than anybody. 'I augur *well* of the *new* Government,' he told a friend, 'I know the *greatness of mind of the Duke*.'[33] Now aged fifty-eight, the handsome, laconic aristocrat with the high-bridged Roman nose which had stamped his image on the public imagination as surely as had Nelson's missing right arm, he seemed the man to give the nation self-confidence. The grotesque old King might sometimes pretend that he had fought at Waterloo, but Wellington had not only won that climactic victory but

---

* From this idea developed the gunnery training ship HMS *Excellent* and, later, the shore establishment at Whale Island.

all the others from the Tagus to Toulouse. With his cool assurance, he now looked to future achievement rather than past glory.

The Duke now looked at the new technology which was beginning to affect ships as well as factories. The most important was the introduction of steam propulsion. By 1815, at the end of the war, there had been a number of small paddle-steamers carrying passengers in English coastal waters and a year later a steam-sloop, the *Congo*, ordered by the Admiralty for the exploration of African rivers, had been launched. But steamers, it seemed, were unsuitable as warships: their paddle-wheels inhibited the mounting of broadside guns and were themselves vulnerable to gunfire; they quickly burned their stocks of coal and, as they did so, rose higher, lifting their paddles clear of the water. They clearly had their uses as tugs to take sailing warships in tow when the wind dropped, as the Lord High Admiral's tour of the naval ports had demonstrated.

However, there was another, more profound reason for distrust by conservatives, prominent among whom was Admiral Cockburn, the dominant member of the Council at the Admiralty. This was that the propulsion of ships by wind harnessed to machinery of canvas, hemp, wood and human muscle was supremely efficient and would remain so as long as all potential opponents were constricted by the same forces of wind and tide. The successful development of steam would change that and the most powerful maritime nations would suffer the most.

Despite this, the Lord High Admiral was determined that the Royal Navy had to investigate the possibilities, particularly as the American inventor, Robert Fulton, who had worked on naval projects in both England and France, had developed in the United States a steamer capable, it was said, of eight knots. The Admiralty had, in fact, commissioned a steam packet, the *Regent*, designed by the versatile engineer Marc Isambard Brunel in 1817 and, a few years later, brought two steam-tugs, the *Monkey* and the *Comet*, into service. The Duke now ordered that, whenever possible, steamers would be used to carry members of his Council on tours of inspection, particularly up and down the Thames, where steam had the advantage over sail.

As a practical seaman, the Duke saw that even if steamships could not yet take their place in the line of battle they might have a role as warships, perhaps towing the big ships in – or out – of such actions as Navarino when they could not manoeuvre under sail. He determined that their capabilities should be evaluated and asked Captain Hoste, 'the favourite *élève* of his lamented friend Lord Nelson',[34] to do so. So Hoste put to sea in the *Royal Sovereign*, in company with three steamers: the *Lightning, Meteor* and *Echo*, for trials in the Channel.

He was asked to be 'particularly attentive to the relative properties of the several steam-vessels and report which of them you consider best adapted for sea service to carry a gun in the event of war'.[35] Off the North Foreland, the experimental flotilla was struck by a gale in which the royal yacht performed gracefully under sail while the little steamers wallowed in troughs or lurched over crests, paddles thrashing in air. Then the weather moderated and it was the steamers' turn to excel, churning across to Calais in a trial of speed. Later, Hoste reported that the *Lightning* proved 'infinitely preferable ... both as to stability and speed'.[36] As a result, the Lord High Admiral decided, with the concurrence of his Council, that she should be commissioned as HMS *Lightning*, the first steam warship.

Among naval officers interested in plans for 'perfecting steam vessels for action in time of war',[37] was a Lieutenant William Innes Pocock, a son of Nicholas Pocock, the fashionable marine artist. Like Hoste, he had seen action in the Adriatic, which had given scope to officers of originality and daring. An inventive young man, he had attracted attention during the war by publishing a proposal for replacing wooden casks for the storage of liquids on board ship with fixed metal tanks, which had been approved in principle by the Admiralty.

One advantage of Pocock's tanks was that, when empty and sealed, they gave a ship added buoyancy. Also, of course, when flooded with sea-water they would lower or sink a floating ship. If they could be flooded and pumped dry at will, they could turn the marine inventors' dream of a submersible warship, or submarine, into reality. For at least three centuries, ship designers had been sketching plans for submarines, but, until recently, they had been no more than technological *capriccios*. That they might actually be built, go to sea and submerge had been demonstrated by Robert Fulton, the pioneer of steamships, whose crude torpedoes had been used to attack French ships off Boulogne during the threatened invasion of England two decades before.

Fulton's first submarine, the *Nautilus*, had been built in France and undergone trials on the Seine. Twenty-one feet long and built of copper plating over an iron frame, she was propelled by sail on the surface and by a hand-worked propeller when submerged; her armament was a mine to be fixed to the bottom of the ship under attack. But the French, while recognising its potential, flinched from developing what they saw as an inhuman weapon which broke the accepted rules of warfare. Moving to London in 1804, Fulton had again aroused interest and a commission – including Lords Melville and St Vincent from the Admiralty; Sir Joseph Banks, the President of the Royal Society; John Rennie, the civil engineer; and Sir William Congreve, the military inventor – was formed to study its potential. St Vincent dismissed the submarine and the torpedo as too great a risk to established naval powers, and the commission agreed that it would not be prudent to support so revolutionary a concept. So, after two years, Fulton had returned to America to continue his work.

The submarine Pocock planned was five times the size of the *Nautilus*, her hull surrounded by ballast-tanks and propelled by paddle-wheels, steam-powered on the surface and hand-cranked when dived. But there was another designer ahead of the field, and his were the plans which now appeared on the desk of the Lord High Admiral. Captain Tom Johnstone was neither a naval officer nor an engineer; he was a smuggler and a spy. A Hampshire man, Johnstone had originally been a Channel pilot but had taken to smuggling and running intelligence agents to and from France. During his melodramatic career, he had been involved in the attacks on Boulogne at the beginning of the century and there he had met Fulton and become involved in his submarine and torpedo operations.

When the American departed, Johnstone remained convinced of its possibilities. But the Admiralty was no more ready to let so dangerous a genie out of its bottle than was the French Ministry of Marine. Finally, in 1813, Johnstone managed to interest the Duke of York, Commander-in-Chief of the Army, who had been fascinated by Fulton's experiments and was able to persuade the Admiralty to sanction the building of a submarine, financed by Secret Service funds. Johnstone estimated that the cost would be £100,000 should he 'prove the practicability of so dreadful a power'.[38]

With written assurance from Lord Sidmouth, the Home Secretary, [the former Prime Minister, Henry Addington], that he was 'now employed on his Majesty's Secret Service on submarine and other useful experiments',[39] Johnstone supervised the building of his submarine at Southbury Castle on the banks of the Thames in Oxfordshire. It was complete and ready for trials in 1815, but the war ended and, with it, official interest, although Johnstone was eventually paid £4,735.11s.6d. Trials were carried out on the Thames, but the Admiralty maintained its indifference.

Others did not and, in 1820, after Johnstone had been paid, Bonapartists were said to have offered him £40,000, with a promise of more to come, if his submarine could be used in an attempt to rescue the exiled Emperor Napoleon from St Helena. There is evidence that Johnstone took the submarine down the Thames and tried to reach the sea, possibly for this enterprise. The Chelsea waterman and artist, Walter Greaves, recorded in autobiographical notes, 'My Father said that there was a mysterious boat that was intended to go under-water ... for the purpose of getting Napoleon off the island of St Helena. So on one dark night in November, she proceeded down the river (not being able to sink as the water not being deep enough). Anyhow, she managed to get below London Bridge. The Officers boarding her, Capn. Johnson in the meantime threatening to shoot them. But they payed no attention to his threats, seized her and, taking her to Blackwall, destroyed her.'[40] Six months later, Napoleon died in exile.

Even then, Johnstone did not abandon hope of making a fortune from the submarine and on 19 April 1828 the minutes of a meeting of the Council at the Admiralty recorded, 'Mr. Thos. Johnson formerly employed in constructing a vessel for Submarine Navigation, having called on one of the Members of the Lord High Admiral's Council to inform him whether it is the wish of the Government to communicate further with him on that subject, or whether Government leaves him at liberty to offer ... his Plan to any Foreign Government, of which he states that two have made overtures to which his Poverty compels him to listen, unless this Government is disposed to treat with him.'[41]

The Duke was showing an interest in steam-propulsion for warships, but he, like St Vincent, thought submarine warfare a dangerous and unethical invention. He remembered hearing from Admiral Digby of an unsuccessful attack on the *Ramillies*, which he had once commanded, by a crude submarine torpedo off the American coast, which had seemed particularly dishonourable and sly. It could threaten the very existence of those great sailing-ships to which he was so devoted. Therefore, the response was recorded: 'It is proposed that he be informed that His Royal Highness cannot recommend the Government to treat further with him on the subject.' Beneath was added, 'A very proper answer to give him'[42] and initialled by Admiral Cockburn. It was one of the last occasions on which the two of them were in agreement.

Strains within the Council had become increasingly apparent. It was not just that the Lord High Admiral had taken a very different view of Navarino from the government but that he disliked both Cockburn and the First Secretary, Croker, while remaining friends with Admiral Hope and the Second Secretary, Barrow. The differences were professional as well as personal. Despite his love of the Navy's traditions, the Duke could cast an eye forward and under his chairmanship the Council agreed to consider Major Congreve's plan for 'a shot-proof steam-vessel' and another for 'propelling boats by machinery'. But in the Lord High Admiral's absence, the more rigidly conservative Cockburn rejected an unspecified 'plan by which an enemy's ship may be sunk in action by the smallest armed vessel',[43] which recalled Fulton's unethical torpedo.

The Duke had taken to spending more time at Bushy and Windsor and less at St James's Palace and the Admiralty, conducting much of his official business through Barrow while consulting his Council less and less. He saw himself as having full and direct control of the Royal Navy and seemed to be challenging the Council to disagree.

In the early summer of 1828, he planned another tour of inspection to the dockyard at Sheerness, the anchorage of the Downs off Deal, Portsmouth and Plymouth. Before departing he supervised a Venetian regatta on the Thames to celebrate the anniversary of the Battle of Waterloo with a procession of City barges and the Duke of Wellington himself in a cutter rowed by young noblemen. Then, accompanied by Barrow, he sailed in the *Royal Sovereign*, which was commanded by Captain the Honourable Charles Spencer, his private secretary, since Captain Hoste was ill. He had taken the Duchess of Clarence to collect her mother from Calais and his tuberculosis had suddenly worsened, causing the Duchess to write to his wife, 'I am truly sorry ... to learn that Sir William Hoste is so unwell and hope it is not in consequence of our travels by sea.'[44] It was and, although the Hostes took a house at Petersham, near the scene of the Duke's early days with Dorothy Jordan, and he seemed to recover a little but died in the following December.*

Accompanied by the faithful Barrow, the Duke busied himself enjoyably. At Sheerness, he planned a new naval hospital, but recommended that steamers should not be used for bringing the sick and wounded ashore 'as the very concussion of the engine would be

---

* His widow later became a lady-in-waiting to Queen Adelaide.

distressing'.[45] At Deal, he agreed in principle to the eventual building of a breakwater to shelter the anchorage. On his way to Portsmouth, he decided that the Committee on Gunnery, which he had set up at the Admiralty, should meet him there on 14 July. There was no sanction from the Council for this and he worded his order brusquely, as if to challenge Cockburn and Croker, stating that 'it is my directions' that the Committee 'should wait upon me' and 'be prepared to remain at Portsmouth if I think proper'.[46]

As he might have expected, Cockburn rose to the bait and replied, albeit at length and in flowery language, that such orders from him were 'neither in accordance with the spirit of the Act of Parliament regulating the appointment of the Council, nor consistent with the real nature of the high office your Royal Highness has condescended to accept'. Moreover, he pointed out, 'the office of Lord High Admiral, as at present established, is that of a high and important department of the State, rather than that of the first Flag Officer of the sea service; a capacity in which I humbly submit your Royal Highness cannot properly appear without the special order of the King.'[47]

The Duke replied that Cockburn's letter 'does not give me *displeasure* but *concern* to see *one* I had *kept* when appointed to this situation of Lord High Admiral *constantly* opposing what I consider *good* for the King's service. In this free country every one has a *right* to have *his* opinion, and *I* have therefore to have *mine*, which *differs* totally from *yours*.'[48] Cockburn apologised with convoluted flourishes for appearing to upset the Duke but confirmed his initial criticism.

So the Duke wrote to Wellington demanding that Cockburn be removed from his Council because of '*continued* and *serious* differences of opinion'[49] and be replaced by his friend Rear-Admiral Sir Charles Paget. The Prime Minister immediately sent this letter to the King with a covering letter saying that Cockburn – 'an honest counsellor' – could not be removed 'without causing public discussion and doing his Royal Highness the utmost injury'.[50] But the Duke had already written to Cockburn, telling him that he had applied for his dismissal.

As soon as he heard that Wellington was not supporting his complaint, he wrote to him that Cockburn had been so disrespectful and impertinent 'that it is *totally* out of my Power to carry on His Majesty's Naval concerns with Sir George Cockburn as a member of *my* Council and I must therefore desire Your Grace to ask the King *to remove* from *my* Council Sir George Cockburn....'[51] He was angered when Wellington wrote telling him flatly that he must be aware that 'your Royal Highness cannot hoist the flag of the Lord High Admiral for the purpose of exercising a military command and power.'[52]

While the correspondence continued, the Duke arrived at Portsmouth to see Rennie's plans for improvement to the harbour and for new depots, one of which was to be called Clarence Yard. But it was there that he received a letter from the King, which Barrow noted, without knowing the contents, 'appeared to annoy him greatly'.[53] Telling his brother that Wellington had shown him their correspondence, the King told the Duke, 'It is with feelings of the deepest regret that I observe the embarrassing situation in which you have placed yourself. You are in error from the beginning to the end.

'This is not a matter of opinion, but a positive fact.... Let me ask you how Sir George Cockburn could have acted otherwise? Let me remind you, my dear William, that Sir George Cockburn is the King's Privy Councillor, and so made by the King to advise the Lord High Admiral. What becomes of Sir George Cockburn's oath towards me, his Sovereign, if he fails to offer such advice as he may think necessary to the Lord High Admiral? Am I, then, to be called upon to dismiss the most useful and perhaps the most important naval officer in my service for conscientiously acting up to the letter and spirit of his oath and duty? The thing is impossible.

'I love you *most truly*, as you know, and no one would do more, or go further, to protect and meet your feelings; but on the present occasion I have no alternative; you must give way and listen to the affection of your best friend and brother.'[54]

The Duke replied that he would come to London to present his case against Cockburn who, he declared, '*cannot* be the *most useful* and the most *important* officer in your Majesty's service, who *never* had the ships *he* commanded in *proper* fighting order'.[55] He then left for the capital, leaving Barrow and Spencer to wonder what it was all about and guess that 'we shall lose him ere long'.[56] In London, he saw Wellington, then sent a note to the King, telling him that he would leave to continue his inspections and then 'exercise for a few days with the three-deckers'.[57] He returned to Portsmouth, boarded the *Royal Sovereign* and sailed for Plymouth in what Barrow described with surprise as 'the most calm, mild and tranquil state of mind'. The Duke confided that in London he had threatened to resign over differences of opinion, but the King had 'implored him with tears in his eyes to remain' while Wellington had promised to make 'any new arrangement of the office he held that could constitutionally be given'[58] if he would remain.

This time it was not to be just another tour of inspection, because the Duke had arranged a special treat for himself. One of Nelson's most trusted captains, now Vice-Admiral Sir Henry Blackwood – who had commanded the inshore squadron off Cadiz and the frigates at Trafalgar – was Commander-in-Chief at the Nore and was to meet the Lord High Admiral off Plymouth with a 'squadron of manoeuvre'. When the Duke arrived, another reminder of the past awaited him: a letter from Admiral Sir Sidney Smith, whom Nelson had disliked, although (or perhaps because) they shared an heroic theatricality. He was hoping to become Commander-in-Chief at Plymouth but was sent a short reply, ending brusquely, 'I *cannot* and *will not* make any promises.'[59] Blackwood was still awaited, although most of the ships were there.

This did not matter because two first-rate ships of the line, the huge *Britannia*, mounting one hundred and twenty guns, and Blackwood's flagship, the *Prince Regent*, of ninety guns, were at anchor, together with three sloops. Having already announced that he expected this squadron to join him in a 'summer cruise', the Duke had given orders that their ships' companies be brought up to strength and that their magazines be filled with 'as much powder as they can store'.[60] On 30 July, after a levée on board the royal yacht, he formally took command and gave orders to get under way. Admiral Blackwood returned to Plymouth and arrived on board the *Prince Regent* just in time to see the rest of his ships, led by the *Royal Sovereign*, flying the flag of the Lord High Admiral, standing out to sea.

For the next five days, the Duke of Clarence played with his ships. He entertained their captains to dinner in the royal yacht and, off the Lizard, he watched gunnery practice with the *Britannia* and the sloops shooting at a floating cask. Then a gale blew up and, while the squadron sheltered in Torbay, they were joined by Admiral Blackwood, who had been searching for his missing ships in his flagship, because the Lord High Admiral had neglected to tell him, or anybody else, where he had gone.

On 4 August, the whole squadron was back in Plymouth Sound, the escapade at an end. But now there was another excitement, for the Duke had ordered that the two paddle-steamers, HMS *Lightning* and the *Meteor* should join him there. They were required to tow the royal yacht on her return voyage to Spithead and the Thames. On the eighth, the *Royal Sovereign* berthed at Deptford and the Lord High Admiral went ashore and returned to London, ready for the worst. He arrived at the Admiralty on 9 August to find a long letter from the Prime Minister awaiting him. Saying that he knew that the squadron had been at sea 'under the personal command of your Royal Highness, acting under the military flag of the Lord High Admiral', he reminded him that 'neither the constitution of this country, nor that of your Royal Highness's office allow of your taking such measures without the assistance of your Council' and that the King had 'expressed the greatest concern and surprise'[61] at the news.

In another flurry of correspondence, the Duke claimed that he had taken command only because Admiral Blackwood had not arrived in time for the exercises, and that there was no need for his Council to have been involved in his decision because they were only to advise him on financial affairs. This was not accepted and the King, who supported Wellington, told him, 'I love my brother William, I always have done so to my heart's core; and I will leave him the example of what the inherent duty of a King of this country really is. The Lord High Admiral shall strictly obey the laws enacted by Parliament ... or I desire immediately to receive his resignation.'[62]

So the Duke wrote to the Prime Minister and, with royal self-importance, asked him to call at the Admiralty. When he did so, on 11 August, the Duke told him that he wished to resign; when asked for his resignation in writing, he rang a bell for Captain Spencer. 'Sit down,' he told his private secretary, 'and write that "I this day resign my commission as Lord High Admiral of England into the hands of his Grace the Duke of Wellington." ' He signed the paper and gave it to Wellington, who put it into his pocket. At the door, the Duke of Clarence held out his hand and said, 'Though the Lord High Admiral and the Prime Minister may differ in matters of policy, the Duke of Clarence and the Duke of Wellington must ever be friends. God bless you.'[63]

The Duke was determined to go gracefully. He wrote to the King, saying that he left 'without the least feeling of any anger or disappointment'.[64] On the fourteenth, he presided over his last meeting of the Council. He told them that he was taking the chair only because no replacement had yet been chosen and that 'in his military character he could only say that he had resigned and would give no reason for it'.[65] At first, Croker noted that he treated Admiral Cockburn with 'marked displeasure', then became 'more civil' and 'charged Sir George with some communications with the different departments'.[66] He later called Croker into his room and to his surprise thanked him, albeit briefly, for his work. Barrow, who thought that the Duke's behaviour had been brought about by others expecting him to have unlimited power, was given an especially warm farewell and a silver ink-stand engraved with 'a small testimonial of his esteem and regard'. With that, he was gone.

There were many regrets at the departure of one so ebullient and positive. Barrow could have been expected to declare that he had 'never met with a more kind-hearted man, more benevolent, or more desirous of relieving distress'.[67] Cockburn felt that he was seen as primarily responsible for what had happened and passed a mes-sage to the Duke, via Captain Spencer, that others, including Croker, had shared his views. At that the Duke summoned the admiral and thanked him, adding that 'he had no longer any enmity against *him* and begged to shake hands with him'. He then invited Cockburn to dine with him at Bushy House on his birthday, together with his other critics, excepting Croker, who confided to Wellington, 'I am to become his *bête noir* for he *must* have one; a result, however, as to which I for-tunately am quite indifferent.'[68] The Duke had accepted Cockburn and the others as professional critics, whereas Croker was, in his view, a functionary who should not have taken sides.

A brave face was supported by brave words and Croker reported, again to Wellington, that the Duke had said that 'he was delighted to be out of office … that he looked upon the character of a *Flag Officer* of the Fleet as a much higher one than that of *Lord High Admiral*. This, your Grace will see, was still harping on the pretensions to *independ-ent military authority*. His Royal Highness gives his conduct as many colours as the rainbow, but *independent power* was his real object.'[69]

The title of Lord High Admiral was abolished forthwith and that of First Lord of the Admiralty restored. To general surprise, the Duke of Wellington decided to re-appoint Lord Melville with Admiral Cockburn as the senior naval member of the reconstituted Board of Admiralty. At once, the two of them set about undoing the Duke of Clarence's most cherished reforms: the improvement of naval gunnery and the introduction of steam-propulsion. When it was proposed that every gun should be fitted with sights for aiming, instead of each alternate gun, Cockburn replied, 'You have gone gunnery mad, for they are little more or less than damned gimcracks.'[70] Nor did he favour techniques for concentrating gunfire, preferring the old-fashioned broadside. He and Melville saw steam as useful propulsion for tugs and tenders but full of dangerous possibilities if developed further, and they announced from the Admiralty, 'Their Lordships feel it their bounden duty to discourage to the utmost of their ability the employment of steam vessels as they consider that the introduction of steam is calculated to strike a fatal blow at the naval supremcy of the Empire.'[71]

Yet all was not lost. The secured ranks of commander and petty officer remained, flogging continued to be restrained and there was a new and more humane emphasis on conditions of service. The Duke had earned the gratitude of all but his own Council, not only as a reformer but as an honest man. He had, it became known, run up bills of £23,000 for entertaining while Lord High Admiral, but he admitted this and many had enjoyed his hospitality. He would not countenance corruption, or even the hint of bribery with little gifts, writing on one occasion, 'I hate presents and shall send back the truffles to Captain Rich as I have the cask of cape Wine to Commodore Christian.'[72]

After ten months of the naval glory he had craved so long, he was at the age of sixty-three again unemployed and unwanted, although still an admiral of the fleet. Towards the end of the crisis he had been under great strain. 'His family are afraid the fatigue will kill him,' a friend had written. 'He is now and then mad – or very nearly so.'[73] But at Bushy House he could be soothed by his Duchess and the pastoral surroundings. Yet this might not be the end of the ambition that had driven him. The King was now sixty-six, a gross recluse at Windsor; still sharp-witted but a physical ruin, surprising his doctors that he had lasted so long. William, Duke of Clarence, was still robust and in November that year an enquirer after his health was told by one of his sons that he was '*perfectly* well and in good spirits'. He was of course, also the heir to the throne.

13

Happy as a King

At six o'clock on the morning of 26 June 1830, the Duke and Duchess of Clarence were woken by a servant at Bushy House and told that two gentlemen, named Sir Henry Halford and Sir Wathen Waller, had arrived and wished to see them.

'Ah! Then we knew at once the reason for their coming and had a presentiment of our loss,' wrote the Duchess in her diary later that day, 'God helped us to master the shock of that moment.'

The two men were the King's doctors and their visit at that hour could only mean that he was dead. A few days before, when the couple had called to see him at Windsor, the Duchess had noted, 'The King is in a coma through opium…. He is not able to live or to die.'[1] Now they were told that, three hours before, the King had felt faint, taken hold of Waller's hand, then tightened his grasp, looked at him 'with an eager eye' and exclaimed, 'My dear boy! This is death!'[2] With that, King George IV had died. Soon afterwards the Duke of Wellington arrived at Bushy House and then, the former Duchess of Clarence recorded, 'The King drove into town and we spent a sorrowful day there.'[3] Her husband had become King William IV.

The news of his brother's death and his accession to the throne had long been expected but, until this moment, his predominant emotion had been sadness. Now his feelings were conflicting currents of joy and grief, as when he had heard the news of Trafalgar and the death of Nelson, and soon the former prevailed. As he drove first to

Windsor and then to London, he wore, as mourning, 'a bit of crape on a white hat' and was 'grinning and nodding at everybody as he whirled along'.[4]

He changed into naval uniform for the meeting of the Privy Council, which assembled at noon, and was said to be 'like an ordinary levée'. The King spoke of his dead brother in a suitably hushed voice but as the Councillors were sworn to allegiance to 'King George IV' and this was hastily corrected, there was laughter, and when the new King was given a pen to sign his declaration of accession, he remarked, 'This is a damn bad pen you have given me.'[5] Afterwards, he escaped from the ceremonial and wandered up St James's Street, where he was soon surrounded by a cheerful crowd and was kissed on the cheek by an Irish trollop. Seeing the commotion, members of White's Club sallied into the street and escorted him inside to await an escort from the palace. When it arrived, he was unperturbed, remarking of his excursion, 'Oh, never mind all this: when I have walked about a few times they will get used to it and will take no notice.'[6] They did, of course, and the Prime Minister had to ask Queen Adelaide to stop him wandering about his capital.

At the late King's funeral at Windsor a fortnight later, the mood of suppressed merriment continued. 'A gayer company I never beheld,' noted Charles Greville, the political diarist. 'They were all as merry as grigs. The King was chief mourner and, to my astonishment, as he entered the chapel directly behind the body, he darted up to Strathaven ... shook him heartily by the hand and then went on nodding to the right and left.'[7]

But the crowds had been amused and touched by what they saw: 'A little old, red-nosed, weather-beaten, jolly-looking person with an ungraceful air and carriage',[8] with 'an easy and natural way of wiping his nose with the back of his forefinger'[9] and 'a Wapping air'.[10] To them this was a delightful contrast to the perfumed and corseted voluptuary who, growing ever more gross, had ruled them as Prince Regent and King for so long. Instead of a sluggish recluse, they had a monarch who not only threw open the royal parks of London but allowed them to visit Bushy House and even wander on the terraces of Windsor Castle. When he saw them scratching their names on his marble statuary, he complained but did not exclude them. After dismissing his brother's German band and French chefs he sent the wild animals and exotic birds of his private menagerie at Windsor to the new Zoological Gardens in Regent's Park. He realised that, although racing did not interest him any more than hunting or shooting, he had to keep the royal stud in being; but when asked which horse to enter for a particular race replied that it would be best to 'send down the whole squadron'.

Reflecting this, the caricaturists presented him as a jolly Jack Tar breezing through the effete halls of power. One drew him as an elderly but robust coastguard with pistols in his belt – 'The New Preventive Man' – come ashore from his cutter to clear out corruption. His long-past indiscretions were remembered with nostalgia as endearing and acceptable Georgian and Regency excesses. 'Our Citizen King',[11] he was thought to be by one startled lady of refinement, and another, Princess Lieven, remarked, 'The King, for whom the proverb "Happy as a King" seems certainly to have been invented by anticipation, imparts to all about him this extraordinary animation. He shows by his manner, his good nature and cordiality a sense of gratified pleasure which is quite contagious.'[12]

He at once began to indulge his enjoyment of entertaining, shaking men firmly by the hand with a brisk 'How d'ye do?' and kissing women on the cheek, or on both if they were pretty. One of his first banquets was a dinner for two hundred Windsor worthies at the castle and another, on the same day, for three thousand of the less affluent, among whom he spent at least half the evening, enjoying a feast of roast beef, ham, veal and plum pudding. When he met an old naval acquaintance in the street and invited him to dinner and was told that his guest had no suitable clothes for such an occasion, he replied, 'Come along directly, do not bother about clothes.'[13] Conviviality was what mattered: in one year of his reign thirty-six thousand bottles of wine were drunk at St James's Palace alone.

His social gaffes became the delight of sophisticated society, as when, in a speech praising the wide spread of social rank among Army officers, he said of one general at table, 'You, my Lord, are descended from the Plantaganets', then turning to another – a veteran of the Peninsular campaigns, who had had no social advantages – added, 'And you are descended from the very dregs of the people'.[14] When a guest looked tired and the King's suggestion that he went to bed was refused on the grounds that it was improper to leave before the sovereign, the King replied, 'Oh, damn it, I'll smuggle you out!'[15]

As host, the King's conversation might be confined to 'Exactly so', and, when annoyed, 'Damn'd stuff', or he might launch into a long discourse on naval strategy or tell an improper joke. Once at dinner, after the ladies had withdrawn, he decided to make a speech in French in honour of a guest, Prince Talleyrand, the French ambassador, and proposed the indelicate toast to *'Les yeux qui tuent, les fesses qui remuent, et le cul qui danse, honi soit qui mal y pense.'* Questioned by a neighbour's raised eyebrow, Talleyrand muttered, *'C'est bien remarquable'.*[16] Yet he could also show touches of charm, as when he and the Queen retired early from one of their dinner parties: 'Now ladies and gentlemen, I wish you a good night. I shall not detain you any longer from your amusements and I shall go to my own, which is to go to bed. So come along, my Queen.'[17]

Planning of the coronation was begun although it was not to take place for another year. At first the King declared that he did not want one and, like Napoleon, could put the crown on his own head. In any case he did not like the prospect of having to kiss the bishops during the ceremony. Then a memory of the last occasion stirred and he asked whether it would be in order for him to hold a coronation banquet; when told that it would, he replied that he would have two. So he told the Earl Marshal to make the necessary arrangements, but with the uncharacteristic instruction to keep the cost to a minimum.

The sweet moment for revenge had arrived, should he wish to take advantage of it. Through straightforward political power he could exercise in the dissolution and formation of governments and patronage through the award of honours, the King could destroy the careers of his old enemies: notably Cockburn, Croker and, indeed, the Duke of Wellington, who had brought him down from the plinth of Lord High Admiral.

But the King was not now a vindictive man and the instinctive generosity which in the past had sometimes been distorted and buried by the weight of contradictions in his upbringing had come to the forefront of his character. The example he seemed to be trying to emulate in magnanimity was Horatio Nelson's. So when Cockburn was succeeded at the Admiralty by Nelson's last flag-captain, now Vice-Admiral Sir Thomas Hardy, the King saw to it that Cockburn was given one of the most highly-prized naval appointments as Commander-in-Chief of the North America and West Indies Station. It was the same with Cockburn's henchman, John Croker, to whom he was pointedly friendly and when he welcomed him as a Privy Councillor. Even before his accession, he had made a point of shaking hands with the Duke of Wellington and now went out of his way to treat the Prime Minister with what the latter described as 'the greatest tenderness, condescension, confidence and favour that so long as I live I never can forget'.[18]

The King – now squat and red-faced, his wide mouth grinning, like a genial toad – radiated good humour. This prevailing mood was, however, in contrast to that of his immediate family: the Queen, demure and a little dull, was a foil to his boisterous unpredictability, but one of his brothers, his sister-in-law and his children were less passive; envy and ambition were their spurs.

The Duke of Cumberland, whose reputation as a libertine was far more sinister than his brothers' and who dressed like a Hanoverian hussar, had been a powerful influence on the late King. He began to assert himself again, particularly in reorganising the Household

Cavalry, which he commanded, by trying to weaken its responsibility to the sovereign. A squabble ensued, with the King employing his most decisive quarterdeck manner, which ended by the Duke departing to sulk in Hanover. The Duchess of Kent, the widow of another brother, was a different matter, because her daughter, Princess Victoria, had now become first in succession to the throne. The King and Queen were fond of the child but her mother – like other members of the royal family and aristocracy – affected to despise them and showed it, while accepting the courtesies shown her. The danger was, as he saw it, that he might die before the princess came of age so that the duchess would become her all-powerful regent. That was something he determined to avoid if he could.

But by far the most painful difficulties were with his children by Dora Jordan. All five girls had married, three of them into the peerage, but the sons were a different matter. Within a few months of their father's accession, the FitzClarences jointly demanded honours and allowances far more vehemently than he had at their ages. This was perhaps understandable as their standing, or lack of it, as bastards was now more obvious than ever.

'We are well aware of the cruel position in which we are placed as natural children,' they wrote to the King, 'and feel too acutely that in the eyes of the Law we are at present nameless and devoid of many rights and advantages of our Fellow Subjects.' So they demanded 'that reasonable rank in society which we may expect'.[19] The Duke of Wellington was consulted and decided that it would never do for them 'to be all made Dukes and Duchesses'.[20] Thwarted, the FitzClarences ostracised their father; George threatened suicide and Frederick to become a disruptive Member of Parliament, as his father once had. Finally the King agreed to give George one of his own titles, Earl of Munster, the others the rank of children of a marquess, and Hanoverian knighthoods to three of his sons-in-law. 'I had to make him a Guelphic Knight,' he said of one to an old naval friend, who replied, '*And serve him right*, your Majesty.'[21]

Even then the Earl of Munster was dissatisfied, asking for a bigger allowance and the Order of the Garter in recompense for the part he expected to play in the coming coronation. 'Let me carry your crown at the Coronation,' he asked, 'Who is more fit than your own *flesh and blood?*'[22] This angered the King, who was determined that this occasion should reflect his own style. When some Tory peers, piqued by the plans for a relatively simple ceremony, hinted that they might not attend, he expressed his satisfaction; their absence would give 'greater convenience of room and less heat'.[23]

The King was crowned a year after his accession at a ceremony costing an eighth of his elder brother's extravaganza. 'What a changement *de décoration*,' the diarist Charles Greville commented. 'No longer George IV, capricious, luxurious and misanthropic, liking nothing but the company of listeners and flatterers ... but a plain, vulgar, hospitable gentleman, opening his doors to all the world, with a numerous family and suite, with a frightful Queen and a posse of bastards....'[24]

He had no time for his brother's artistic taste as displayed in the collections at Windsor and Brighton: 'Aye, it seems pretty – I daresay it is,' he remarked of one picture. 'My brother was very fond of this sort of nicknackery.'[25] His taste ran more to paintings of naval battles and pretty girls. When he inaugurated the new London Bridge he decided against the *avant garde* artist Turner to paint the official picture of the ceremony, choosing instead Clarkson Stanfield, who had served in the Navy. This artist, who had also been a scene-painter in the theatre, specialised in pictures of stormy seas; that was what had caught the eye of the King, who also commissioned a view of Portsmouth.

Among the people of England, he was seen as a nautical John Bull, lovable, sometimes absurd and unpredictable, except in terms of a peppery retired admiral. All might seem set for a placid reign by an elderly monarch, except for the groundswell of unrest, which had been gathering for more than half a century into a tidal surge. The wars with Revolutionary and Napoleonic France had occupied the thoughts and energies of the nation – more particularly of its Government – for half that time, but profound changes elsewhere had found their echoes and responses. The American struggle for independence and the Revolution in France had found admirers, and sometimes partisans, in all social classes.

Even King William, in his younger days when he had vaguely emulated his brothers in support of the Whigs as a gesture of rebellion against their father, had been critical of the Tories' implacable opposition to libertarian change. Some Whiggish sentiments remained and he was still convinced that the loss of the American colonies had been as unnecessary as it was tragic. Once at Brighton he was entertaining the ambassador of the United States to dinner and, as another guest put it, the King was 'seized with his fatal habit of making a speech' but then said that 'it was always a matter of serious regret to him that he had not been born a free, independent American and considered Washington the greatest man that ever lived.'[26]

He remembered how Nelson had sent him his protest against the living conditions of Norfolk farm labourers and accusations against the landowners and, a decade later, had boldly given evidence at the trial of the revolutionary and intending regicide, Colonel Despard, whom he had known twenty years before, declaring that he had been a fine man. William now felt an increasing affinity with Nelson's distrust of politicians after he had flirted with both Tories and Whigs and finally been exploited by the Tories in defence of the unpopular peace terms. The King's own view was much like his friend's decision to follow only 'sailor's politics', which, as he had told William Pitt before leaving London for the last time, was simply fidelity to 'King and Country' and the constitution.

Violence in support of political change continued elsewhere and, even as William acceded to the throne, another revolution in France overthrew the Bourbon monarchy, stirring memories of the convulsions four decades before. In Britain, stability had been maintained by a large and growing middle class of which their present King seemed an example. But there were political aspirations which found their focus in the need for the reform of representation in Parliament. Throughout the wars, a revolutionary movement compounded of 'clubs' and 'corresponding societies' had sprung up across the country but they were fragmented, disorganised and easily isolated, and broken up when they became too assertive. But the majority of the people were united in the demand for a wider political franchise and this became the principal appeal of the perennial party of opposition, the Whigs. The cause they espoused was called simply 'Reform'.

For most citizens, Great Britain was not a democratic country. Since the accession of King George III in 1760, the population had more than doubled but its representation in Parliament remained the same. The huge influx from the country into the new industrial towns had not been reflected in the House of Commons and some could not elect a single Member of Parliament. There was no secret ballot and often the choice and election of a candidate was in the hands of a local plutocrat.

The issue began to come to a head at the general election which had to be held on the accession of a new sovereign. In this, the Tory government lost fifty seats and was left with a precarious hold on power. At the end of the year it lost its grasp through a curious incident. In November, the new King was to be entertained by the Lord Mayor of London at the Guildhall. There had been demonstrations demanding reform throughout the country and, two days before the banquet, his host wrote to the Duke of Wellington with the warning that something of the kind might attend the King's visit to the City and that he should arrive under heavy escort. The Prime Minister thereupon cancelled the function without reference to the King who was furious. The Duke's decision made him appear cowardly and, in any case, he felt an affinity with the London crowds and had no fear of them. So when, a few days later, the Government was defeated on a vote in the House of Commons, the King exercised his right to dissolve Parliament, sent for the Leader of the Opposition, Lord Grey, and invited him to form a new administration.

Now began nearly two years of intense political warfare as it became clear that the new Whig Government was dedicated to reform. Those who considered the King a conservative were amazed by the public support he gave to his new Prime Minister, Lord Grey, creating him a supernumerary member of the Order of the Garter and surrounding himself with Whigs at Court. In the summer of 1831, his apparent enthusiasm for reform gave an added edge of celebration to the coronation and confirmed his reputation as a populist King.

Although he did not approve of political reform on principle, seeing it as weakening the established order and so the monarchy, the King was dutiful in his support of the new government. When its Reform Bill, which widened the franchise, abolished long-redundant constituencies and gave hope for further change, had been presented to the House of Commons in the spring, it was passed by only a single vote and he had again dissolved Parliament. Early in the summer after the Whigs had been returned in a general election, the Bill was passed by the House of Commons, then, in the autumn, it was rejected by the House of Lords.

There was an immediate eruption of protest throughout the country. Marches and mass meetings broke up in violence, the worst of which was at Bristol where, at the end of October, three days of rioting engulfed the city, streets were plundered and burned, hundreds injured and some killed. It seemed that revolution might be about to tear the British apart, as it had the French forty years before.

The King, although identified with the idea of reform, was jeered in the streets. (The nickname 'Silly Billy' was transferred to him from his cousin the Duke of Gloucester, who had originally earned it, to replace 'Coconut', inspired by the shape of his head.) There seemed to be no way of overcoming the opposition of the conservative peers, other than by a drastic change in the constitution, or by creating new peers favourable to reform, who would out-vote them. Only the King could do this and he was appalled at the prospect of what he described as 'the dreaded alternative'.[27] One woman guest at his table recorded,

'The poor King looked worried to death.... When one looks at him with his good-humoured, silly countenance, it does strike one that Fate made a cruel mistake in placing him where he has to ride the whirlwind and direct the storm.'[28]

He retired to his brother's Royal Pavilion at Brighton and brooded on the future in the oriental nightmare of its exotic halls, which threw his simple, sailor-like character into piquant relief, as when, during a country dance at his New Year's Eve party, he suddenly seized as his partner the sixty-one-year-old Admiral Lord Amelius Beauclerk, with whom he had once acted in midshipmen's theatricals on board the *Prince George*. Here Lord Grey explained to him that only the creation of some sixty new peers could ensure that the will of the people, as expressed by the House of Commons, was made law. Not only was he reluctant to agree but the Queen, his family, the court and most of the establishment of the state were against the creation of peers for a purely political end.

Finally, in January 1832, he capitulated to Lord Grey and agreed. But there was the condition that, so as to avoid a permanent distortion of the House of Lords, the new creations would only be among the heirs of Whig peers, who would eventually become legislators in any case, and by giving seats in the House to selected Scottish and Irish peers.

There was an upsurge in his popularity but it was not to last. Again the Reform Bill passed the House of Commons but again, despite the Government's reinforcements, it was defeated in the House of Lords. Grey returned to the King to say that only the unlimited creation of peers willing to support the Bill would be enough to ensure its safe passage and, if he would not agree, he, the Prime Minister, would have to resign. It was one thing to advance the heirs of peers and to give seats in the House to those already peers in rank, but quite another to use the ancient institution – the foundations of the monarchy, it seemed – for political manipulation. To the King, such blatant gerrymandering was unthinkable, so he refused and sadly accepted Lord Grey's resignation.

Ironically, the blame for the failure of the Reform Bill to become law fell not so much upon the stubborn peers but upon the King, who was trying to do his duty as he saw it. 'Our beloved Billy cuts a damnable figure,'[29] wrote the diarist Thomas Creevey, and he was booed as his carriage swept through the streets, prudently escorted by cavalry.

He invited the Tories to form a new Government. But they felt he had betrayed them by his original agreement to create peers just as the Whigs felt betrayed by his refusal to create more. So strong was the tide running for reform, and so volatile had political passions become, that even the Duke of Wellington was unable to form an administration which could survive. The dreaded alternative now was not the creation of peers but the possibility of revolution: the King had become the scapegoat and as unpopular as he had once been popular; mass meetings were being held throughout the country and there were fears that the Army might not be willing to put down civil disorder. So the King had to recall Lord Grey and, as the price of his returning to power, agree to create as many peers as necessary to win the vote in the House of Lords.

In the event, he did not have to do so, for his agreement achieved the end. When the Reform Bill again passed the House of Commons, enough peers abstained to enable it to pass the House of Lords. On 7 June, it was given the Royal Assent and became law at last.

Although a great advance in political development, the passage of the Reform Bill to become the Reform Act had shaken the foundations of the nation: the electorate, the Houses of Parliament, the establishment and the aristocracy and monarchy. The King, knowing that he had been dragged from his pedestal into the political brawling below, was disillusioned and bitter, feeling that it was he who had been betrayed. Now he suspected both Whigs and Tories with the naval officer's traditional distrust of politicians.

The gleam of greatness the King had shown during the crisis had nothing to do with political dexterity but with a Nelsonian touch of selflessness which surprised those who had known him when he was young. He disliked most of the policies that Parliament was to implement but, understanding the over-riding priority of constitutional government, was determined that he would do his duty and see that the national will prevailed. He advocated consensus politics and could not understand why his ministers would not consider a coalition.

He himself maintained that Lord Bolingbroke's essay, *The Idea of a Patriot King*, had a profound effect upon him: 'the duty of a prince seems to require that he should render by his influence' the conduct of government and 'the warmth and hurry and rashness of party conduct … more orderly and more deliberate'. But there was no need to invoke political theorists; the real model for his simple 'sailor's politics' had been Lord Nelson.

No gathering storm was likely to match the one he had just weathered, but there were patches of rough weather ahead. Ireland, as was its wont, again became a political issue in England. Just before he had come to the throne, the King had voted in the House of Lords, for Irish emancipation motivated by sentiment rather than conviction, it seemed. Discussing the issue at Lord Ellenborough's dinner-table, his host recorded, 'He got into a long story about Lord St Vincent and I know not how many other admirals, with little episodes attached to each, and supposed them all to put up their heads and express delight at seeing the Irish sailors, who had fought the lower-deck guns, emancipated.'[30]

But emancipation, which in 1829 had made Irishmen eligible for all but the highest offices of state, had led to further aspirations, although no public demands for independence from Great Britain were made. Legislation at Westminster resulting from this involved both the reform of the Church of Ireland, through which the Protestant minority had dominated the Catholic majority throughout the country, and the tightening of the Coercion Act, which would increase a form of martial law. It was disagreement within the Cabinet over the implementation of this which led to the resignation of Lord Grey in the spring of 1834 and his replacement as Prime Minister by Lord Melbourne.

By now the King not only distrusted politicians but was looking for an opportunity to assert himself. It came in the autumn of that year when Melbourne announced that he was appointing Lord John Russell, whom the King disliked intensely, to be Leader of the House of Commons. When Melbourne persisted, the King turned on him like a baited bull and exercised his constitutional rights to dismiss the Government. The result was immediate chaos. Sir Robert Peel, who had to succeed Melbourne as Prime Minister, was abroad and the Duke of Wellington again had to take temporary command. The new government was defeated a few months later, resigned and was replaced by the Whigs, with the hated Russell as Leader of the House of Commons.

'The greatest piece of folly ever committed',[31] was how one prominent Whig described the King's high-handed action. The King realised that these governmental somersaults had to stop, telling an old naval friend, 'I will have no more of these sudden changes; the country shan't be disturbed in this way, to make my reign tumble about like a topsail sheet-block in a breeze.'[32] He found comfort in the company of such cronies and talk about ships and the sea, but even among them he could be short-tempered.

He publicly insulted Admiral Lord de Saumarez, the only one of Nelson's captains, other than Cockburn, he had never liked, for failing to take his place as a pallbearer at the funeral of their friend, Admiral Keats, reminding de Saumarez of a battle thirty years before when he had failed to come to Keats's assistance. But the King no longer harboured grudges and when de Saumarez called the following day to explain and apologise for his absence from the funeral, he was 'quite delighted with the manner in which he was received'.[33]

Surprisingly, he gave rough treatment to Captain Frederick Marryat, a man of his own humour, with whom he had never served because his conventional naval career had been ended sixteen years before Marryat had gone to sea. While he himself had introduced social reforms when Lord High Admiral, he was suspicious of officers with similar ideas; in Marryat's case it was his opposition to the use of the press-gang for forcible recruiting. So when the King was asked to give him permission to wear the order of the *Légion d'Honneur* in recognition of his advice to the French on a new signal code, he first replied, 'You best know his services; give him what you please.' Then he remembered, and exclaimed, 'Marryat! Marryat! Bye the bye, is not that the man who wrote a book against the impressment of seamen?'* 'The same, your Majesty.' 'Then he shan't wear the order; he shall have nothing.'[34]

He kept an eye on two particular naval interests: uniforms and steam. Naval officers' uniforms were again altered to his design (this time with military red instead of white facings, giving them a Hanoverian look); he reintroduced the wearing of full-dress uniform and began designing the first uniform for naval engineers, who would be rated as warrant officers. Writing to his Foreign Secretary, Lord Palmerston, about the strategic importance of Egypt he pointed out that 'communications by Canal and by Steam Vessels might be established from Cairo to Suez and the Red Sea.'[35] Although a canal had been suggested before, sails would be impracticable for its passage and he saw the importance of steam-propulsion for the Empire trade and troopships.

It was galling and ironical that the only battles fought by the Royal Navy during his reign were in the suppression of the slave trade, of which he had been so energetic an advocate. The shipping of slaves to British colonies had been stopped in 1807 – although it was not until 1833 that all existing slaves were freed by law – so the Navy maintained patrols of small ships off the coast of West Africa to intercept slavers, and these fought a succession of gallant little actions. But as much as the King might admire them, he liked to hark back to the great days of lines of battle and rolling broadsides. It had briefly seemed possible that these might return in 1832 when two crises in

---

* *The Naval Officer, or Scenes and Adventures in the Life of Frank Mildmay*, his novel published in 1829.

foreign affairs, which disrupted British trade, required the threat of naval intervention. During civil war in Portugal, a British fleet – led by Codrington's old flagship, the *Asia* – cruised off the Tagus and, as a result of a dispute between France and Holland over the future of Belgium, an Anglo-French fleet blockaded the Dutch ports. But no broadsides rolled.

Not even women were spared the King's recollections and dissertations. On the anniversary of the Battle of Camperdown in 1835, a dinner was held at Greenwich. John Barrow, who was still Second Secretary to the Admiralty, although made a baronet that year, recalled, 'The Queen was about to retire but the King desired that the ladies would stay as he had something to say on this occasion that would bring to the recollection of the naval officers then present the battles that their predecessors and brother officers had fought and won....

'All being attentive, his Majesty began with noticing the first invasion of Britain by Julius Caesar, which, he said, must have proved to the natives the necessity of a naval force to prevent and repel foreign invasion. From that period he passed on rapidly to the landing of the Danes and northern nations on our coasts till he came down to more recent times, when the Navy of Great Britain had become *great* and victorious ... and it was remarked by the officers present how correctly he gave the details of the great actions fought in the course of the last and present centuries. I believe, however, that the Queen and the ladies were not displeased to be released....

But the King was worried and asked the Second Secretary, 'Barrow, I think – nay, I'm sure – I omitted one general action; and you must know it.' The dazed Barrow was sure he had omitted nothing but the King continued, 'I fear I forgot to mention the name of Anson and the action he fought off Cape Finisterre: I am not sure I know the details correctly; pray send me an account of it tomorrow.'[36]

The boredom induced by such occasions, even when set against his good humour and usual generosity, tried even those closest to him. The Queen reacted to life with her husband, who tended to tell seafaring or indelicate stories, or fall asleep after dinner, by enjoying the company of the Lord Chamberlain of her household to the point where it was rumoured they were lovers. Certainly nobody could have been in more marked contrast to the King: half his age, Earl Howe – the first of a new creation and not descended from the admiral – was foppish and amusing. He was also a Tory and schemed against the Whigs when they were in power. When Lord Grey persuaded the King to dismiss him, it put a strain on the marriage.

On the day of the dismissal, the Queen wrote in her diary, 'I would not believe it, for I had trusted in, and built firmly on, the King's love for me … I had a hard struggle before I appeared at table after this blow, which I felt deeply as an insult, which filled me with "Indignation". I felt myself deeply wounded both as wife and Queen and I cannot conquer the feeling. It was for me a distressing evening, which I shall never forget,' and next day she felt her 'loss more and more'.[37] It was certainly a romantic attachment, although a love affair seems unlikely, and it proved one more problem for the King because Howe continued to influence the Queen with Tory ideas.

Nor were his children of help. Although he had been generous in provision for his sons – one of whom, Henry, had died in 1817 while serving in India – with titles and employment in the Army, the Navy (Adolphus commanded the royal yacht) and the Church of England. But they wanted more. He longed for their company as confidants and so gave them much of what they asked. The most rapacious was still the eldest, George, who showed affection for a while after his father had appointed him his aide-de-camp with the rank of colonel, Deputy Adjutant-General, Privy Councillor, Lieutenant Governor of the Tower of London, then Governor and Constable of Windsor Castle and deluged him with other honours – but was soon making further demands with scorn rather than gratitude.

William did not respond, as did his own father, with reproof and banishment, for the memory of the loving family he had raised with

Dora Jordan was still with him. Indeed, one of his first acts on accession was to summon the sculptor, Francis Chantrey, whom he later
knighted, and commission a statue of his dead mistress. This showed
her as a girl with two small children, her skimpy classical robe slipping
to reveal a soft shoulder. His request to have it set up in St Paul's
Cathedral, close to Nelson's tomb, was refused by the Dean and
Chapter because of the irregularity of the relationship and, no doubt,
because of its eroticism, understated as that was.

Yet he delighted in the presence of his growing horde of grand-
children as, to her credit, did the Queen. He continued to be particularly fond of his niece, Princess Victoria, and his affection was
returned despite the hostility of her mother. The Duchess of Kent was
fiercely resentful of the elderly monarch for staying alive and keeping
her daughter from the throne and herself from the regency, which she
would assume if Victoria succeeded before the age of eighteen, and
time was running out. As with the FitzClarences, the King's kindness
was rebuffed with resentment and more demands. She snubbed him
whenever opportunity arose, tried to keep her daughter away from
his Court and even took over a suite of rooms he himself planned to
occupy in Kensington Palace.

But again there was a limit to his patience. In the summer of 1836,
a few days after pointedly ignoring the Queen's birthday, she attended
a banquet at Windsor Castle. Until now, the King had kept his temper
under control; but Princess Victoria was nearly 18, he was 71 and
the race with her mother's regency might be close-run. At the end of
dinner, after his health had been drunk, he rose, looked directly at the
Duchess of Kent, then at her daughter, and addressed the company,
who immediately froze with embarrassment.

'I trust in God,' he announced, 'that my life may be spared for nine
months longer, after which period, in the event, no Regency would
take place. I should then have the satisfaction of leaving the royal
authority to the personal exercise of that young lady ... and not in the
hands of the person now near me, who is surrounded by evil advisers

and who is herself incompetent to act with propriety in the station in which she would be placed. I have no hesitation in saying that I have been insulted – grossly and continually insulted – by that person, but I am determined to endure no longer a course of behaviour so disrespectful to me. Amongst many other things, I have particularly to complain of the manner in which the young lady has been kept away from my Court ... I would have her know that I am King.'[38]

Princess Victoria sobbed quietly while her mother, stiff with shock, left the room as soon as she could. But his outburst cleared the air and relations with the duchess assumed a cold formality, which allowed him to see more of her daughter. Indeed, Victoria presented to him a handsome young man, who was paying attention to her, Prince Albert of Saxe-Coburg-Gotha [who married Queen Victoria in 1840 and became Prince Consort], and the two men took to each other.

Tranquillity now descended on the court. There always had been an underlying solidity in the reign and it was that which had helped the King weather the storm of the Reform Bill and lesser squalls. His dislike of politicians was muffled by the tact and efficiency of his private secretary, Sir Herbert Taylor, and he was sometimes able to show his old affability, once asking his ministers to dine with him 'and drink two bottles of wine a man'.[39] There were political and diplomatic problems in Ireland, Canada, Spain and France, which he still saw as the traditional enemy. But these seemed distant now and he was confident that, as he put it, 'The country ... was never more prosperous or more contented.'[40]

This was reflected in the character of the period. It was a sociable time, in which the family drawing-room and the club assumed greater importance than the *salon* or gaming-room. Even new designs for household furniture managed to add stolidity to Regency elegance. Within the family, the influence of the cosy, even stuffy, values of Queen Adelaide's household were coming into fashion, including the Germanic Christmas with a decorated conifer as an, originally pagan, centrepiece.

It was a time of expansion and not only of the new industrial towns. Social intercourse and knowledge were popularised. In London, the convivial gentlemen's clubs spread across the West End with the founding of the Carlton, Reform, Garrick, Oxford and Cambridge, the Army and Navy and the building of a noble *palazzo* for the Travellers' in Pall Mall. Books – particularly the popular novel – were becoming shared entertainment for a vast readership, and Charles Dickens had begun to write. Patronage of the arts was being offered to the masses by the new Art Union and fostered by new artistic and literary societies. Steam locomotives were going into service on the first passenger lines and the end of the stagecoach was forecast in a comic drawing by George Cruikshank of horses looking aghast at a steam-powered coach puffing past and one watching mongrel saying to another, 'I say, Wagtail, what do you think of the new invention?' The other, cocking an eye at the startled horses, replies, 'Why, I think we shall have meat cheap enough.'

As a nation, Great Britain was still living on the credit of Trafalgar and Waterloo. The framework of the British Empire was already established with Canada and the West Indies, the Cape of Good Hope, India and Australia as its pillars, although settlement in the English-speaking colonies were still sparse. Ireland was a constant political and sociological problem, but it always had been. In looking to the future, the greatest asset of the British was self-confidence.

His health was failing but his thoughts lingered on past naval glories, in which he had played so small a part. In May 1837, on the hundred and forty-fifth anniversary of the battle of Barfleur, he gave a dinner party for retired and serving officers and let his fancies have free rein. 'In the course of the evening,' it was recorded, 'the King detailed with great minuteness the causes, the progress and consequences of the different naval wars ... during the past and present century and gave, perhaps, greater proof on that than any occasion of the extraordinary accuracy of his memory.... His Majesty's voice, with the exception of one or two moments of oppression of breathing, was very strong and clear but no one present could fail to entertain apprehensions as to the effects of this exertion.'

On 24 May 1837, Princess Victoria came of age and the possibility of her mother's regency came to an end. She had only known her uncle as a testy, comic old man, beset with problems, thinking of him as 'very odd and singular'.[41] But he was comforted to know that he would be succeeded by this self-possessed young woman, for he realised that this could not be much longer delayed. Shortly before the Princess's birthday, the King had suffered a severe bout of asthma, which compounded with circulation and liver trouble,[*] left him weak and breathless. He sent her a present of a grand piano, but was unable to attend the ball celebrating the occasion at St James's Palace. Three days later he arrived in a wheeled chair to preside over a meeting of the Privy Council at Windsor and the Queen went to the races at Ascot alone.

The twenty-second anniversary of Waterloo was imminent, and the King said to one of his doctors, 'I know I am going but I should like to see another anniversary of the Battle of Waterloo. Try if you cannot tinker me up to last out that day.' They did, and on the eighteenth of June, he sighed, 'Let me but live over this memorable day. I shall never see another sunset.' 'I hope your Majesty will see many,' replied the courtly doctor. At this, his chaplain noted, the King 'replied in a fashion he commonly employed but the peculiar force of which those only who had the honour of being frequently admitted into his Majesty's society can fully appreciate. "Oh! That is quite another thing!" It was usually employed by his Majesty to express his dissent or incredulity....'

It was a Sunday and the King received the Sacrament from the Archbishop of Canterbury. Then the captured French standard, which was presented to him each year by the Duke of Wellington, arrived with the news that the anniversary dinner, due to be held next day,

---

[*] He was suffering from arterio-sclerosis and enlargement and hardening of the liver.

was to be cancelled because of the King's illness. Stroking the silk and touching the gilded eagle, he said, 'Tell the Duke of Wellington I hope the dinner may take place tomorrow. I hope it will be an agreeable one.'[43] He would have loved to attend but was resigned to the inevitable. 'The King dies like an old lion,'[44] wrote Benjamin Disraeli, the literary Member of Parliament, reflecting the feelings of those around him.

The Queen, who had not been to bed for ten days and was exhausted, began to weep and he told her, 'Bear up! Bear up!' Next morning, recorded the chaplain, 'On awaking, he observed to the Queen, "I shall get up once more to do the business of the country." ' On being wheeled in his chair from his bedroom to his dressing-room, he 'turned round and, looking with a benign and gracious smile at the Queen's attendants, said, "God bless you!" ' He then asked why he had not been given the state papers he expected and was told, 'It is Monday, Sire.' 'Ah, true. I had forgot.'

That evening, as he sat propped in an upright leather chair to ease his laboured breathing, three of his sons arrived, the eldest, Lord Munster, being notable by his absence in his customary state of self-pity.* His thoughts turned to religion and at around midnight he muttered, 'Believe me, I am a religious man.' He then whispered the name of his valet – the last word he spoke.

At twenty minutes past two on the morning of Tuesday, 20 June 1837, his life ended in the room where King George IV had also died; the chaplain recorded that 'His Majesty expired without a struggle and without a groan, the Queen kneeling at his bedside and still holding his hand, the comfortable warmth of which rendered her unwilling to believe the reality of the sad event.'[45]

The accession of the young Queen was an invigorating as that of the old King had been seven years before, but his funeral on 8 July was as lacking in grief and reverence as his brother's had been. He

---

* The Earl of Munster was never able to adjust to his circumstances and committed suicide five years later.

belonged to the past: to the eighteenth century, the Great War with France and to the Regency; throughout his short reign he had seemed to stumble from one crisis to another. The nation was looking eagerly to the future which the eighteen-year-old girl seemed to symbolise. That they did so was due in large measure to King William IV.

One of the first to appreciate his worth was his contemporary, Robert Huish, whose biography of him was published in the year of his death. 'His Majesty was constitutionally open and candid,' he concluded, 'Utterly free from pride, and with a perfect contempt for the arts of the courtier … he carried with him to the throne none of those assumptions, which are put on to elevate the monarch above the man but that really produce the opposite effect. The neglect he experienced on the part of successive ministers and from the King his father … who scarcely seemed to recollect that a bluff, thorough-bred seaman existed in the royal family … had the effect of flinging the Duke of Clarence back upon himself, causing reflections and making him more independent of the will of those who surrounded the Court.… A good part of the nobility never liked the Duke.… His Majesty's great desire was to govern in unison with public opinion.'[46]

He had cleared the air for the monarchy, opening the windows of the increasingly musty Hanoverian and Regency Courts to a fresh, salty breeze from the sea. Lacking in sophistication, and even taste, he may have been, but he made a clean break with the past and particularly with the reign of his deeply disliked brother. He brought a basic decency to the throne and, above all, a simple sense of duty.

It stayed with him to the end. Shortly before he died, the Queen asked, 'Shall I not pray to the Almighty that you may have a good day?'; he replied, 'Oh, do! I wish I could live ten years for the sake of the country. I feel it my duty to keep well as long as I can.'[47]

But it was more than duty; there was humanity and generosity too. There had always been such elements in him but, as a young man, they had been distorted and buried by the pressures of his upbringing and the anomalies of being a royal demi-god. Alternately spoiled, hectored, flattered, lectured and fawned upon, it was not surprising that he had ful-filled his father's apprehensions. That he had overcome negative traits and that his most pleasant characteristics came to the fore was due in considerable part to two people from other backgrounds, to whose influ-ence he had been subjected: Horatio Nelson and Dorothy Jordan.

Nelson had shown him, by example, that humanity and discipline were compatible, indeed complementary. He had demonstrated the value of original ideas so that, when Lord High Admiral, William had encour-aged the development of steam warships, although he had believed the submarine to be unfeasible and improper. Nelson had taught him the value of sheer efficiency as in the gun-drill which had been decisive in the 'pell-mell' battles he had brought about, so he had concentrated on that when in power at the Admiralty. He had also shown that, however patriotic one might be, it was important to recognise reasons for discon-tent and look for remedies. Above all, he had done his duty, as they both had known it to be, putting constitutional duty before personal inclination.

Dorothy Jordan had also demonstrated responsibility, both to her family and to her profession. She had to earn money, of course, but her determination to continue acting, even at the expense of her life at home, would have made her, in theatrical slang, 'a real trouper'. No wonder that when the political contortions of statesmen and courtiers exasperated the King, he found comfort in memories of her presence in her portraits on his walls.

Together, the parson's son and the actress had set an example which offset that of tutors and courtiers, promotion-hungry admirals and place-seeking politicians, and royal parents determined to force their son to be something he was not.

In the event, he had not been an inspired monarch but he had been good-hearted and dutiful. He had made mistakes but the worst of them – dismissing the government in 1834 – had taught a lesson not only to him but to his successors and it was never contemplated again. After him, the way ahead for Queen Victoria was clear and shone with promise.

On the day of his death, *The Times* had received the news in time to print an extra edition, edged with black. As usual, there were advertisements on the front page and those for shipping companies were an unintended memorial to one of the achievements of the late King's enthusiasms. Travel by steamship was now the fashion and one advertisement after another proclaimed: 'Steam to Ipswich', 'Steam to Hull', 'Steam to Aberdeen', 'Steam to Plymouth', 'Steam to Dublin', 'Dover Steam Packets'.

Its formal obituary was in striking contrast to its condemnation of King George IV on his death seven years before, which had declared, 'There was never an individual less regretted by his fellow-creatures than this deceased King.'[48] But now *The Times* mourned 'the most excellent, the most patriotic and the most British Monarch that ever sat on the imperial throne of these realms ... William IV, the Sailor King ... William IV, the Reformer ... who taught this populous and intelligent community the necessity and value of obedience to the law by his own implicit and deliberate obedience to it as a subject ... William IV, the good, the kind, the affable, the companion and commander of his people....'[49]

He would not always have earned such praise. His most notable success had not been over the nation's enemies, nor his own, nor over its conspiring politicians, but over himself. The ship of state sailed on without him, but its timbers were sound, its rigging taut and the wind was fair.

The Children of King George III and Queen Charlotte

1 George, Prince of Wales, Prince Regent, then King George IV, 1762–1830
2 Frederick, Duke of York, 1763–1827
3 William, Duke of Clarence, then King William IV, 1765–1837
4 Charlotte, Queen of Württemberg, 1766–1828
5 Edward, Duke of Kent, 1767–1820
6 Augusta, 1768–1840
7 Elizabeth, 1770–1840
8 Ernest, Duke of Cumberland and King of Hanover, 1771–1851
9 Augustus, Duke of Sussex, 1773–1843
10 Adolphus, Duke of Cambridge, 1774–1850
11 Mary, 1776–1857
12 Sophia, 1777–1848
13 Octavius, 1779–1783
14 Alfred, 1780–1782
15 Amelia, 1782–1810

Children of King William IV and Queen Adelaide

1 Charlotte, b. and d. 1819
2 Elizabeth, 1820–1

Children of Duke of Clarence by Dorothy Jordan

1 George (m. illegitimate daughter of Lord Egremont), 1794–1842
2 Henry, 1795–1817
3 Sophia (m. Lord de L'Isle and Dudley), 1796–1837
4 Mary (m. illegitimate son of Lord Holland), 1798–1864

5 Frederick (m. daughter of Lord Glasgow), 1799–1854

6 Elizabeth (m. Lord Erroll), 1801–56

7 Adolphus, 1802–56

8 Augusta (m. (1) son of Lord Ailsa; (2) Lord Frederick Gordon), 1802–65

9 Augustus (m. daughter of Lord Henry Gordon), 1805–54

10 Amelia (m. Lord Falkland), 1807–58

Manuscript Sources

The most important collections covering the life of King William IV are in Royal Archives at Windsor Castle, although most of the official correspondence of his reign was destroyed after the death of his secretary, Sir Herbert Taylor. Much of his naval correspondence – notably with Nelson, Hood, Keats and Codrington – is at the National Maritime Museum, Greenwich, as are his midshipman's log-books. His logs kept when he was a captain are at the Public Record Office, Kew.

Among relevant manuscripts in private hands are the papers of Admiral Robert Digby in Lord Digby's archives at Minterne, Dorset. George Winne's 'Memorandums' book and other Winne family papers are in the keeping of Commander Humphrey Jenkins. An account of early submarine development is in the appendix to the thesis, *British Submarine Policy, 1835–1918*, by Michael Dash at the Department of War Studies, King's College, University of London, and Lieutenant William Innes Pocock's plans for a submarine are in the author's possession.

SOURCE NOTES

Details of a book are given only if it is not listed in the bibliography.

Abbreviations:
RA – Royal Archives
RA Add. – Royal Archives, Additional Manuscripts
Add. Mss. – British Museum, Additional Manuscripts
Later Corresp. – Later Correspondence of King George III

NMM – National Maritime Museum
PRO – Public Record Office
PW – Prince William
DC – Duke of Clarence
KW IV – King William IV
KG III – King George III
P of W – Prince of Wales
PR – Prince Regent
KG IV – King George IV

Prologue

1 Byam Martin, Vol. 1, p. 2.
2 Papers of KG III, No. 2324.

1 The Young Sailor

1 KG III to Hood, 16 April 1783. RA 16346.
2 Watkins, p. 15.
3 D'Arblay, *Diary and Letters of Madame*, London 1854, Vol. 3, p. 31.
4 RA 44598A.
5 Papers of KG III. To Lord North, 5 May 1778. No. 2325.
6 Ibid., 8 May 1778. No. 2330.
7 Naval Miscellany, Vol. 1, p. 225. KG III to Hood, 27 May 1778.
8 Hood to KG III, 15 July 1778. RA 16147.
9 *Naval Miscellany*, Vol. 1, p. 226. KG III to Hood, 27 May 1779.
10 KG III to Budé, 11 June 1779. RA 16156–7.
11 RA 44598A.
12 KG III to Budé, 11 June 1779. RA 16156–7.
13 *Naval Miscellany*, Vol. 1, p. 226.
14 KG III to Digby. RA Add. 15/461.
15 Ibid., RA 16154.
16 KG III to PW, 13 June 1779. RA 16158–9.

2 The Intrepid Boy

1 PW's log, NMM.
2 Ziegler, p. 29.
3 Ibid.
4 Cook's menu book, NMM.
5 PW's log, NMM.
6 PW to KG III, 11 July 1779. RA 44600–1.
7 PW to KG III, 3 September 1779. RA 44602–3.
8 Wright, Vol. 1, p. 32.
9 PW to KG III, 18 October 1779. RA 44604–5.
10 Ibid., RA 44606–7.
11 PW's log, NMM.
12 RW to KG III, RA 44609–10.
13 PW's log, 10 January 1780. NMM.
14 Ibid., 17 January 1780. NMM.
15 Watkins, p. 40.
16 Huish, p. 57.
17 PW to KG III, 26 January 1780. RA 44611.
18 PW's log, 16–17 January 1780.
19 Ibid., 18 January 1780.
20 Ibid., 19 January 1780.
21 PW to KG III, 8 February 1780.
22 Wright, p. 47
23 Huish, p. 62.
24 Ibid., p. 65.
25 PW's log, 23–24 February 1780, NMM.
26 PW to KG III, undated. RA 44615–6.
27 Laird Clowes, *The Royal Navy*, p. 450.
28 KG III to PW, 2 March 1780. RA Add. 4/123.
29 PW's log, 16 March 1780. NMM.
30 Digby Papers.
31 Huish, pp. 76–7.

32 PW to KG III, 16 June 1780. RA 44619–20.

33 PW to KG III, 29 September 1780. RA 44622.

34 Huish, p. 80.

35 Ibid., p. 85.

36 Ibid., p. 89.

37 Ibid., p. 96.

38 Prince Frederick to PW, RA 43402.

39 PW to KG III. RA 44625.

40 Byam Martin, Vol. 1, pp. 7–11.

41 PW to KG III, 21 August 1781. RA 44628–9.

3 *Welcome to this Western Shore!*

 1 PW to KG III. RA 44630–1.

 2 Huish, p. 101.

 3 Ibid., p. 103.

 4 PW to KG III, 28 September 1781. RA 44632.

 5 Ibid., 27 September 1781. RA 44630.

 6 E. Stuart Wortley, *A Prime Minister and His Son*, p. 174.

 7 PW to KG III, 3 March 1782. RA 44638.

 8 Ibid., 28 September 1781. RA 44632.

 9 Christopher Hibbert, *Redcoats and Rebels*, p. 324.

10 Hood to Admiralty, October 1781. Hood Papers 6, NMM.

11 Hibbert, p. 325.

12 PW's log, NMM.

13 PW to KG III, 10 November 1781. RA 44633–4.

14 Huish, p. 103.

15 Ibid., pp. 103–8.

16 KG III to PW, 5 February 1782. RA Add. 4/123.

17 Prince Frederick to PW, 4 January 1782. RA Add. 4/15.

18 KG III to PW, 4 September 1782. RA Add. 4/16.

19 Queen Charlotte to PW, 4 September 1782. RA Add. 4/17.

20 KG III to Hood, 6 August 1782. Hood Papers 1/115, NMM.

21 KG III to PW, 4 September 1782. RA Add. 4/16.

22 Digby to KG III, 25 October 1782. RA Add. 15/719.

23 Ibid., Digby Papers.

24 PW to KG III. RA 44640.

25 Digby Papers.

26 Majendie to PW, 4 February 1783. RA Add. 4/19.

27 PW to KG III. RA 44640.

28 Majendie to PW, 4 February 1782. RA Add. 4/19.

29 Digby to KG III, 25 October 1782. RA Add. 15/719.

30 Digby to Hood. Digby Papers.

31 Hood to KG III, 30 October 1782. Hood Papers 1/115, NMM.

32 PW to KG III. RA 44640.

33 Digby Papers.

34 Hood to Lady Hood, 14 November 1782. Hood papers 1/120, NMM.

35 Hood to Digby, 13 November 1782. Hood Papers 6, NMM.

36 Hood to Lady Hood, 14 November 1782. Hood Papers 1/120, NMM.

37 Hood to KG III, 14 November 1782. Hodd Papers 1/121, NMM.

38 PW's log, NMM.

39 Clarke and M'Arthur, *The Life of Horatio Viscount Nelson*, Chaper 2.

40 Sir Harris Nicolas (ed.), *The Dispatches and Letters of Vice Admiral Viscount Nelson*, Vol. 1, p. 67. Nelson to his father, 19 October 1782.

41 Clarke and M'Arthur, op. cit., Chapter 2.

42 Nelson to Lieutenant Pilford, 13 November 1782. Sir Anthony Stamer's collection.

4 An Ornament to our Service

1 Digby to Hood, 18 November 1782. Hood Papers 6, NMM.

2 PW's log, 21 November 1782.

3 Hood to Digby, 27 November 1782. Hood Papers 6, NMM.

4 Digby to Admiral Pigot, 22 January 1783. Hood Papers 6, NMM.

5 Hood to Budé, 20 March 1783. RA Add. 15/749.

6 Hood to Pigot, 18 February 1783. HP 6, NMM.

7 Nicolas, op. cit., Vol. 1, p. 72. Nelson to Captain Locker, 25 February 1783.

8 Hood to Philip Stephens, 9 April 1783. HP 6, NMM.

9 Hood to Budé, 20 March 1783. RA Add. 15/749.

10 Aspinall (ed.), *The Correspondence of the Prince of Wales*, Vol. 1, p. 102, fn. PW to KG III, April, 1783.

11 Hood to KG III, 5 February 1783. RA 16334–5.

12 Ibid.

13 *Naval Miscellany*, Vol. 1, p. 227. KG III to Hood, 16 April 1783.

14 Budé to Hood, 16 April 1783. RA Add. 1/127.

15 Aspinall (ed.), *Corresp. of P of W*, Vol. 1, p. 124, fn. KG III to PW.

16 Hood Papers 6, NMM.

17 Hood to Pigot, 21 April 1783. Hood Papers 6, NMM.

18 Huish, p. 120.

19 Ibid., p. 121.

20 Hood to Unegara, 14 March 1783. Hood Papers 6, NMM.

21 Clarke and M'Arthur, op. cit., Chap. 1. Nelson to R. W. Spencer, 1801.

22 Nicolas, op. cit., Vol. 1, p. 72. Nelson to Locker, 25 February 1783.

23 Huish, pp. 125–6.

24 Ibid., p. 141.

25 Ibid., pp. 154–6.

26 Digby Papers.

27 Huish, p. 146.

28 Horace Walpole, *Letters Addressed to the Countess of Ossory*, Vol. 2, p. 157.

29 Nicolas, op. cit., Vol. 1, p. 77. Nelson to Locker, 12 July 1783.

30 Huish, pp. 185–6.

31 Ibid., p. 169.

5 This Unallowable Passion

1 Huish, p. 204.

2 PW to P of W, 23 July 1784. RA 44664.

3 Ibid., 1 April 1785. RA 44674–5.

4 Ibid., 23 July 1784. RA 44664.

5 Aspinall, *Later Corresp. KG III*, Vol. 1, p. 124.

6 Hood to PW, 19 September 1783. RA Add. 4/21.

7 Ibid., 28 November 1783. RA Add. 4/23.

8 Aspinall, *Later Corresp. KG III*, Vol. 1, p. 107. KG III to PW, 28 October 1784.

9 Ibid., p. 77. KG III to PW, August 1784.

10 PW to KG III, 20 August 1784. RA 44668–9.

11 Aspinall, *Corresp. of P of W*, Vol. 1, p. 153. PW to P of W, 23 July 1784.

12 Ibid., Vol. 1, p. 155, 12 August 1784.

13 Aspinall, *Later Corrresp. KG III*, Vol. 1, p. 120. Duke of York to KG III, 1 April 1785.

14 Ibid., p. 152. PW to KG III, 1 April 1785.

15 Ibid., pp. 157–8. KG III to PW, 6 May 1785.

16 PW to KG III, 13 May 1785. RA 44676.

17 Huish, p. 247.

18 Ziegler, p. 54.

19 PW to KG III, 6 November 1785. RA 44685–6.

20 Huish, p. 247.

21 PW to P of W, 14 July 1785. RA 44676.

22 Ibid.

23 Aspinall, *Later Corresp. KG III*, Vol. 1, p. 175. PW to KG III, 4 August 1785.

24 Ibid.

15 Huish, p. 254.

26 Aspinall, *Later Corresp. KG III*, Vol. 1, pp. 175–6. Queen Charlotte to PW, August 1785.

27 PW to P of W, 25 November 1785. RA 44690–1.

28 Hamilton, *Byam Martin*, Vol. 1, p. 20.

29 Ibid., p. 42.

30 Ibid., p. 205.

31 Aspinall, *Later Corresp. KG III*, Vol. 1, pp. 185–6.

32 PW to P of W, 25 November 1785. RA 44698–9.

33 Aspinall, *Corresp. of P of W*, Vol. 1, p. 219. PW to P of W, 10 February 1786.

34 Roger Fulford, *The Royal Dukes*, p. 90.

35 Aspinall, *Later Corresp. KG III*, Vol. 1, pp. 211–12. Queen Charlotte to PW, 3 March 1786.

36 Aspinall, *Corresp. of P of W*, Vol. 1, p. 219. PW to P of W, 10 February 1786.

37 Hamilton, Vol. 1, pp. 206–7.

38 Aspinall, *Corresp. of P of W*, Vol. 1, p. 222. PW to P of W, 1 March 1786.

39 Hamilton, Vol. 1, p. 209.

40 Ibid., p. 208.

41 Ibid., p. 213.

42 Aspinall, *Corresp. of P of W*, Vol. 1, pp. 219–21. PW to PW, 10–22 February 1786.

43 Aspinall, *Later Corresp. KG III*, Vol. 1, p. 218. PW to KG III, 19 April 1786.

44 PW's log, NMM.

45 Aspinall, *Later Corresp. KG III*, Vol. 1, p. 218. PW to KG III, 19 April 1786.

46 Huish, p. 254.

47 Aspinall, *Corresp. of P of W*, Vol. 1, p. 264. PW to P of W, 20 May 1786.

48 Ibid., p. 264, 1 December 1786.

49 Hamilton, Vol. 1, p. 29.

6 Farewell Discipline

1 Hamilton, Vol. 1, p. 28.

2 Ibid., p. 32.

3 Aspinall, *Corresp. of P of W*, Vol. 1, p. 230. PW to P of W, 2 July 1786.

4 Aspinall, *Later Corresp. KG III*, Vol. 1, p. 249. PW to KG III, 21 September 1786.

5 Hamilton, Vol. 1, p. 36.

6 Aspinall, *Later Corresp. KG III*, Vol. 1, p. 247. PW to KG III, 21 September 1786.

7 Aspinall, *Corresp. of P of W*, Vol. 1, p. 247. PW to P of W, 1 December 1786.

8 Hamilton, Vol. 1, p. 56.

9 Ibid., p. 57.

10 Aspinall, *Later Corresp. KG III*, Vol. 1, p. 291. PW to KG III, 20 May 1787.

11 Hamilton, Vol. 1, pp. 62–4.

12 Naish, G. P. B., *Nelson's Letters to His Wife*, p. 37.

13 Nicolas, Vol. 1, p. 203.

14 Naish, op. cit., p. 38.

15 Ibid., p. 39.

16 Ibid.

17 Ibid., p. 40.

18 Log of HMS *Pegasus*, PRO, ADM 51/676.

19 Watkins, pp. 148–9. KW to Clarke and M'Arthur.

20 Naish, op. cit., p. 40.

21 *The Naval Miscellany*, Vol. 4, Navy Records Society, Prince William and Lieutenant Schomberg. PW to Hood, 9 February 1787.

22 Ziegler, p. 62.

23 Nicolas, Vol. 1, p. 204.

24 Ibid., p. 205.

25 Aspinall, *Later Corresp. KG III*, Vol. 1, p. 251, fn.

26 Ibid., pp. 273–4, fn. Princess Augusta to Prince Augustus, April 1787.

27 Hamilton, Vol. 1, p. 67.

28 Aspinall, *Later Corresp. KG III*, Vol. 1, p. 268, fn. PW to Lord Elphinstone, 3 January 1787.

29 PW to P of W, 20 May 1787. RA 44769.

30 Copy of Order Book, HMS *Pegasus*, RA 44771–80.

31 Order Book, HMS *Pegasus*, NMM, WQB 40.

32 *Naval Miscellany*, Vol. 4, Prince William and Lieutenant Schomberg, p. 278.

33 PW to Schomberg, 12 January 1787. RA 44738–51.

34 *Naval Miscellany*, PW and Schomberg, pp. 274–81.

35 Nicolas, Vol. 1, pp. 208–9. Nelson to PW, 23 January 1787.

36 Ibid., pp. 210–11. Nelson's order, 28 January 1787.

37 Ibid., pp. 215–16. Nelson to Locker, 9 February 1787.

38 Naish, op. cit., p. 41. Nelson to Fanny Nisbet, 13 January 1787.

39 Ibid., p. 50, 6 March 1787.

40 Oliver Warner, *A Portrait of Lord Nelson*, p. 64.

41 Clarke and M'Arthur, op. cit., Chapter 3.

42 *Naval Miscellany*, PW and Lieutenant Schomberg, p. 282. PW to Hood, 15 March 1787.

43 Nicolas, Vol. 1, pp. 237–9. Nelson to Gardner, 13 May 1787.

7 Those Damned Women

1 Hamilton, Vol. 1, p. 69.

2 Aspinall, *Corresp. of P of W*, Vol. 1, p. 316. PW to P of W, 10 June 1787.

3 Ibid., p. 318. PW to P of W, 4 July 1787.

4 Ibid., p. 320, 19 August 1787.

5 *Naval Miscellany*, Nelson and Lieutenant Schomberg, p. 288. PW to Hood, 5 October 1787.

6 Aspinall, *Later Corresp. KG III*, Vol. 1, p. 318. PW to KG III, 19 August 1787.

7 Ibid., 9 October 1787.

8 Nicolas, Vol. 1, p. 250. Nelson to PW, 27 July 1787.

9 *Naval Miscellany*, Nelson and Lieutenant Schomberg, p. 289. PW to Nelson, 3 December 1787.

10 PW's Letter Book, NMM. LBK 33. Stilling fleet to PW, 21 October 1787.

11 Ibid., Church to PW, 28 October 1787.

12 Dyott's Diary, pp. 36–45.

13 Keats Papers 1, NMM.

14 Dyott's Diary, pp. 36–45.

15 Aspinall, *Corresp. of P of W*, Vol. 1, p. 324 PW to P of W, 8 October 1787.

16 Dyott's Diary, pp. 45–6.

17 *Naval Miscellany*, Nelson and Lieutenant Schomberg, p. 290. PW to Hood, 26 December 1787.

18 Aspinall, *Corresp. of P of W*, Vol. 1, p. 330. PW to P of W, 27 December 1787.

19 *Naval Miscellany*, Nelson and Lieutenant Schomberg, p. 291. Hood to PW, 1 January 1788.

20 Ibid., p. 292. PW to Hood, 5 January 1788.

21 Ibid., p. 293. Hood to PW, 8 January 1788.

22 Aspinall, *Corresp. of P of W*, Vol. 1, p. 330. PW to P of W, 27 December 1787.

23 Winne's 'Memorandums' book.

24 Nicolas, Vol. 1, p. 266. Nelson to Locker, 27 January 1788.

25 Winne.

26 Aspinall, *Corresp. of P of W*, Vol. 1, p. 338. PW to P of W, 8 March 1788.

27 PW to P of W, 7 April 1788. RA 44831.

28 PW to John Rolle, 29 June 1788. Chatham Papers 173, PRO.

29 Fidge, 18 February 1788. RA 44818–9.

30 Aspinall, *Corresp. of P of W*, Vol. 1, p. 336. PW to P of W, 16 February 1788.
31 Ibid., p. 339. PW to P of W, 27 December 1787.
32 Ibid., p. 336. PW to P of W, 16 February 1788.
33 Winne.
34 Hamilton, Vol. 1, pp. 119–21.
35 Winne.
36 Winne Papers. Princess Augusta to PW, 1788.
37 Ibid., Princess Elizabeth to PW, 1788.
38 Hamilton, Vol. 1, p. 123.
39 Ibid.
40 Aspinall, *Corresp. of P of W*, Vol. 1, p. 340. PW to P of W, 14 June 1788.
41 Winne.
42 Nicolas, Vol. 1, p. 275. Nelson to PW, 2 June 1788.
43 Winne.

8 A Time of Dissipation

1 Aspinall, of *Corresp. P of W*, Vol. 1, p. 343. PW to P of W, 20 July 1788.
2 Winne.
3 Aspinall, *Later Corresp. KG III*, Vol. 1, pp. 388–90. PW to KG, 20 August 1788.
4 Winne.
5 PW to Keats, 13 September 1788. Keats papers, KEA 1/1, NMM.
6 Hamilton, Vol. 1, pp. 124–5.
7 Nicolas, Vol. 1, p. 156. Nelson to Locker, 5 March 1786.
8 Hamilton, Vol. 1, p. 125.
9 Dyott's Diary, p. 41.
10 Ibid., pp. 53–4.
11 Log of HMS *Andromeda*. ADM 51/43, PRO.
12 Dyott's Diary, p. 54.

13 Hamilton, Vol. 1, pp. 125–6.
14 Dyott's Diary, pp. 53–60.
15 PW to P of W, 26 October 1788. RA 44850.
16 Aspinall, *Corresp. of P of W*, Vol. 1, p. 359. PW to P of W, 26 October 1788.
17 Log of HMS *Andromeda*. ADM 51/43, PRO.
18 Ida Macalpine and Richard Hunter, *George III and the Mad Business*, p. 42.
19 Christopher Hibbert, *George IV: Prince of Wales*, p. 82.
20 Aspinall, *Corresp. of P of W*, Vol. 1, pp. 453–4. PW to P of W, 24 January 1789.
21 Hamilton, Vol. 1, p. 133.
22 *Memoirs of Sir N. Wraxall*, Vol. 5, p. 171.
23 Digby to PW, 25 May 1789. RA 44859–60.
24 Aspinall, *Later Corresp. KG III*, Vol. 1, p. 417. PW to KG III, 28 May 1789.
25 Ibid., pp. 419–21, 1 June 1789.
26 Ibid., p. 433. The Queen to Prince Augustus, 15 July 1789.
27 D'Arblay, op. cit. Vol. 5, p. 11.
28 *The Times*, 21 February 1789.
29 Horace Walpole to Mary Berry. Walpole, *Letters*, 23 August 1791.
30 Ibid., 4 September 1789.
31 *The Oracle*, August 1789.
32 Walpole to Lady Ossory. Walpole, 9 October 1789.
33 *St. James's Chronicle*, 23 December 1790.
34 Selwyn to Lady Carlisle. Hist. Mss. Comm. Carlisle Mss.
35 Brian Fothergill, *Mrs Jordan*, p. 316.
36 William Hazlitt, *Dramatic Essays*, p. 69.
37 Leigh Hunt, *Autobiography*, Vol. 1, p. 244.

9 *What Girl But Loves the Merry Tar*

1 Nelson's Memoir, Clarke and M'Arthur, op. cit.
2 Nicolas, Vol. 1, p. 294, fn.

3 Ibid., p. 293. Nelson to Duke of Clarence, 3 November 1792.

4 Ibid., p. 288. Nelson to DC, 24 June 1790.

5 Ibid., p. 289. Nelson to DC, 21 August 1790.

6 Winne.

7 Aspinall, *Corresp. of P of W*, Vol. 2, pp. 71–2. DC to P of W, 15 May 1790.

8 DC to P of W, 15 May 1790. RA 44865.

9 Aspinall, *Corresp. of P of W*, Vol. 2, p. 73. DC to P of W, 27 May 1790.

10 Ibid., 25 July 1790.

11 Ibid., p. 76, 22 June 1790.

12 Ibid., 12 July 1790.

13 Aspinall, *Later Corresp. KG III*, Vol. 1, p. 490. DC to KG III, 25 July 1790.

14 Hibbert, *George IV*, p. 12.

15 Aspinall, *Corresp. of P of W*, Vol. 2, p. 81. Cumberland to P of W, 28 July 1790.

16 Ibid., p. 76. DC to P of W, 12 July 1790.

17 Winne.

18 Aspinall, *Corresp. of P of W*, Vol. 2, pp. 88–9. DC to P of W, 17 August 1790.

19 Ibid., p. 90, 5 September 1790.

20 Winne.

21 Aspinall, *Corresp. of P of W*, Vol. 2, pp. 94–5. DC to P of W, 20 September 1790.

22 Hamilton, Vol. 1, p. 133.

23 Fothergill, p. 129.

24 Ziegler, p. 78, *Morning Post*, July 1791.

25 Huish, pp. 327–8.

26 Aspinall, *Mrs Jordan and Her Family*, pp. 5–7.

27 Nicolas, Vol. 1, p. 292, fn. DC to Nelson, 12 September 1792.

28 Ibid., pp. 292–3. Nelson to DC, 3 November 1792.

29 Ibid., p. 249. DC to Nelson, 6 December 1792.

30 Ibid., pp. 294–7. Nelson to DC, 10 December 1792.

31 Watkins, p. 229.

32 Ibid., pp. 226–7.

33 Aspinall, *Later Corresp. KG III*, Vol. 1, p. 642. KG III to Chatham, 6 January 1793.

34 Nicolas, Vol. 1, p. 297. Nelson to Fanny Nelson, 7 January 1793.

35 Log of HMS *Agamemnon*. PRO, ADM 51/1104.

10 A Matter of Scandal and Discomfort

 1 Aspinall, *Corresp. of P of W*, Vol. 1, p. 645. DC to KG III, 19 January 1793.

 2 Ibid., KG III to P of W, 19 January 1793.

 3 Hamilton, Vol. 1, pp. 132–3.

 4 Lord Glenbervie, *Diaries*, Vol. 1, p. 59.

 5 *Parliamentary History of England*, Vol. 30, col. 659.

 6 Aspinall, *Corresp. of P of W*, Vol. 2, p. 349. P of W to Duke of York, 14 April 1793.

 7 Ibid., pp. 389–90. Lord Moira to P of W, 18 September 1793.

 8 Naish, p. 96. Nelson to Fanny Nelson, 1 December 1793.

 9 Nicolas, Vol. 1, pp. 311–15. Nelson to DC, 18 July 1793.

10 Naish, p. 24. Nelson to Fanny Nelson, 3 March 1786.

11 Nicolas, Vol. 1, pp. 343–4. Nelson to DC, 27 December 1793.

12 Ibid., p. 297. Nelson to Fanny Nelson, 7 January 1793.

13 Fitzgerald, Vol. 1, pp. 92–3.

14 Ibid., pp. 93–4.

15 Ibid., pp. 94–5. DC to KG III, 24 March 1794.

16 Nicolas, Vol. 1, p. 480. Nelson to DC, 6–10 August 1794.

17 Ibid., p. 500, 7 November 1794.

18 Ibid., Vol. 2, p. 52, 15 July 1795.

19 Aspinall, *Later Corresp. KG III*, Vol. 2, pp. 621–2. KG III to William Pitt, 13 September 1797.

20 Nicolas, Vol. 2, p. 369. Nelson to DC, 2 April 1797.

21 Ibid., pp. 387–8, fn. DC to Nelson, 30 April 1797.

22 Watkins, p. 282. DC to Nelson, 4 July 1797.

23 Ibid., p. 289.

24 Nicolas, Vol. 2, p. 441. Nelson to DC, 7 September 1797.

25 Watkins, p. 282.

26 Oliver Warner, *A Portrait of Lord Nelson*, p. 133.

27 Watkins, pp. 290–2.

28 Ibid., p. 293.

29 Nicolas, Vol. 3, p. 83. DC to Nelson, undated.

30 Clarke and M'Arthur, op. cit., Chapter 7.

31 Nicolas, Vol. 3, p. 168. Nelson to DC, c. 10 November 1798.

32 Ibid., p. 253, 11 April 1799.

33 Ibid., p. 324, 11 April 1799.

34 Ibid., p. 410–11. c. 13 July 1799.

35 Ibid., Vol. 4, p. 95, 9 November 1799.

36 *Parliamentary History of England*, Vol. 29, col. 1349.

37 Ibid., Vol. 36, cols. 1092–1105.

38 DC to Keats, 25 April 1800. Keats papers 1/32, NMM.

39 Huish, pp. 612–13.

40 *Parliamentary History*, Vol. 36, cols. 161–2. 3 November 1801.

41 Nicolas, Vol. 4, p. 520. Nelson to Captain Sutton, 31 October 1801.

42 Huish, p. 442.

43 *Parl. Hist.*, Vol. 36, cols. 936–8, 23 November 1802.

44 Tom Pocock, *Horatio Nelson*, p. 311. Nelson to William Haslewood, August 1805.

45 *Parl. Hist.*, Vol. 36, col. 1502, 23 May 1803.

46 DC to Keats, 1 December 1802. Keats Papers 1/50, NMM.

47 *European Magazine*, 1803, p. 326.

48 Fitzgerald, Vol. 1, p. 117. DC to Captain Wright, 15 December 1803.

49 Nicolas, Vol. 5, p. 77. Nelson to DC, 3 June 1803.

50 Ibid., Vol. 6, p. 156, 15 August 1804.

51 Ibid., Vol. 6, p. 455. Nelson to DC, 12 June 1805.

52 DC to Keats, 22 August 1805. Keats Papers 3/64.

53 M. Eyre Matcham, *The Nelsons of Burnham Thorpe*, p. 230.

54 Creevey Papers, Vol. 1, p. 73, 5 December 1805.

55 Fitzgerald, Vol. 1, p. 120. DC to Captain Hargood, undated.

56 Eyre Matcham, op. cit., pp. 245–7.

57 Fitzgerald, Vol. 1, p. 121. DC to Captain Berry, 2 April 1806.

11 Admiral Tarry Breeks

1 Nicolas, Vol. 7, p. 388. Lady Hamilton's Will.

2 Aspinall, *Mrs Jordan and Her Family*, p. 123.

3 Dorothy Jordan to DC. Munster Papers 133.

4 Farington Diary, Vol. 3, p. 237. May, 1806.

5 Glenbervie, op. cit., Vol. 1, p. 71.

6 Aspinall, *Mrs Jordan and Her Family*, pp. 70–1. DC to Thomas Coutts, 5 November 1808.

7 31 July 1809. RA Add. 39/20.

8 Aspinall, *Mrs Jordan and Her Family*, p. 205. Jordan to DC, 1 October 1811.

9 Ibid.

10 James Boaden, *Life of Mrs Jordan*, Vol. 2, p. 207.

11 Aspinall, *Mrs Jordan*, p. 178.

12 Aspinall, *Letters of Princess Charlotte*, p. 208.

13 Aspinall, *Mrs Jordan*, p. 211, October 1811.

14 Ziegler, p. 108.

15 Fitzgerald, Vol. 1, p. 112. DC to Lady Collingwood, undated.

16 Aspinall, *Letters of Princess Charlotte*, p. 103. Princess Charlotte to Miss Mercer, 11 January 1814.

17 DC to Earl of Mayo, January, 1814. RA Add. 4/43.

18 Watkins, p. 439.

19 Fitzgerald, Vol. 1, pp. 123–4.

20 DC, 12 February 1814. RA 45020.

21 Ibid., 14 February 1814. RA 45023–4.
22 Aspinall, *Letters of King George IV*, Vol. 1, pp. 415–17. DC to Colonel McMahon, 23–6 March 1814.
23 Cornelia Knight, *Autobiography*, Vol. 1, p. 282.
24 Lord Melville to DC, 26 May 1814. RA 45092–5.
25 *Gentleman's Magazine*, July 1814.
26 Hamilton, Vol. 1, p. 18.
27 W. G. Gates, *Naval History of Portsmouth*, p. 206.
28 *Gentleman's Magazine*, July 1814.
29 Hamilton, Vol. 1, p. 16.
30 DC to George FitzClarence, RA Add. 39/190.
31 DC to Colonel McMahon, 9 June 1814. RA 45114–5.
32 Melville to DC, 10 June 1814. RA 45119–22.
33 DC to George FitzClarence, 26 April 1818. RA Add. 39/302.
34 Ibid., 5 March, 1818. RA Add. 298
35 Canning to House of Lords, 16 April 1818.
36 DC to George FitzClarence, 21 March 1818. RA Add. 39/300.
37 Lady Williams Wynn, *Correspondence*, p. 211.

12 The Eloquence of Our Guns

1 Benjamin Haydon, *Diary*, p. 339.
2 Lady Lyttelton, *Correspondence*, p. 241.
3 Charles Abbot, *Diary*, Vol. 3, p. 142.
4 H. W. Dickinson, *Robert Fulton*, p. 194.
5 DC to KG IV, 13 February 1827. RA Add. 45182.
6 Princess Lieven to Prince Matternich, *Private Letters*, p. 372.
7 Henry Moses, p. 5.
8 Abbot, *Diary*, Vol. 3, p. 495. DC to Hope, 6 May 1827.
9 Sir John Briggs, pp. 10–12.
10 Add. Mss. 41368 f116.
11 Fitzgerald, Vol. 1, p. 167.
12 Huish, p. 637.

13 Sir John Barrow, *Autobiographical Memoir*, pp. 339–47.
14 Moses, pp. 14–17.
15 Barrow, p. 349.
16 Lady Bouchier, *Memoirs of the Life of Admiral Codrington*, Vol. 1, pp. 97–8.
17 Ibid., pp. 370–1. Codrington to DC, 9 June 1827.
18 DC to Codrington, 24 July 1827.
19 C. M. Woodhouse, p. 53.
20 Bouchier, Vol. 1, p. 395. Codrington, 28 July 1827.
21 Ibid., p. 425. DC to Codrington, 3 October 1827.
22 Woodhouse, p. 42.
23 William James, *Naval History of Great Britain*, Vol. 7, p. 722.
24 DC to Lord Mayo, 12 November 1827. RA Add. 4.
25 Fitzgerald, Vol. 1, p. 171.
26 KG IV, 11 November 1827. RA Add. 4/81.
27 Woodhouse, p. 152.
28 Bouchier, Vol. 2, p. 115.
29 Ibid., p. 118.
30 Woodhouse, p. 171.
31 *Parliamentary Proceedings*, 20 January 1828.
32 Fitzgerald, Vol. 1, p. 176.
33 DC to Sir William Knighton, 15 January 1828. RA 45191.
34 Hoste Papers, NMM.
35 Ibid.
36 Ibid.
37 *Gentleman's Magazine*, September 1836.
38 Johnstone to Melville, 1815. ADM 1/4783, Letter J/206, PRO.
39 Sidmouth to Johnstone, 15 October 1813. Ibid., PRO.
40 Walter Greaves to William Marchant, author's collection.
41 Admiralty Minutes, 19 April 1828. ADM 3/216, PRO.
42 Ibid.
43 ADM 12/255.
44 Hoste Papers, NMM.

45 Barrow, pp. 358–9. DC's memorandum, 10 July 1828.

46 *Wellington Despatches*, Vol. 4, p. 517. DC to Admiralty, 10 July 1828.

47 Ibid., pp. 517–18. Cockburn to DC, 10 July 1828.

48 Ibid., p. 518. DC to Cockburn, 10 July 1828.

49 Ibid., p. 520. DC to Wellington, 11 July 1828.

50 Ibid., p. 520. Wellington to KG IV, 11 July 1828.

51 Ibid., p. 528. DC to Wellington, 13 July 1828.

52 Ibid., p. 524. Wellington to DC, 12 July 1828.

53 Barrow, p. 362.

54 *Wellington's Despatches*, Vol. 4, p. 531. KG IV to DC, 15 July 1828.

55 Ibid., p. 535. DC to KG IV, 17 July 1828.

56 Barrow, p. 363.

57 *Wellington's Despatches*, Vol. 4, p. 539. DC to KG IV, 18 July 1828.

58 Barrow, p. 366.

59 DC to Admiral Smith, 27 July 1828. RA 45194.

60 Lord High Admiral's order, 1 July 1828. ADM 3/217, PRO.

61 *Wellington's Despatches*, Vol. 4, p. 579. Wellington to DC, 8 August 1828.

62 Ibid., p. 595. KG IV to Wellington, 11 August 1828.

63 Barrow, p. 367.

64 *Wellington's Despatches*, Vol. 4, p. 601. DC to KG IV, 14 August 1828.

65 Ibid., p. 602. Croker to Wellington, 14 August 1828.

66 Croker Papers, Vol. 1, p. 429.

67 Barrow, p. 369.

68 *Wellington's Despatches*, Vol. 4, pp. 620–1. Croker to Wellington, 16 August 1828.

69 Ibid., p. 621, 16 August 1828.

70 Briggs, p. 13.

71 C. J. Bartlett, p. 202.

72 Lord High Admiral's memorandum, 11 December 1827. RA Add. 39/429.
73 Lord Ellenborough's *Diary*, p. 193. 8/8/2.

13 Happy as a King

1 Queen Adelaide's Diary. RA Add. 21/7a.
2 Waller Papers, CR 341/202.
3 Queen's Diary.
4 Lord Broughton, *Recollections of a Long Life*, Vol. 4, p. 33.
5 Fitzgerald, Vol. 1, p. 216.
6 *Greville Memoirs*, Vol. 2, p. 9.
7 Ibid., Vol. 1, p. 3.
8 Abbot, op. cit., Vol. 3, p. 495.
9 Duke of Buckingham and Chandos, *Private Diary*, Vol. 1, p. 5.
10 Barrow, p. 340.
11 Mary Frampton, *Journal*, p. 366.
12 Princess Lieven, *Letters*, p. 230.
13 Doran, *Queens of England of the House of Hanover*, Vol. 2, p. 434.
14 Fulford, *Hanover to Windsor*, pp. 38–9.
15 Ziegler, p. 152.
16 Greville, op. cit., Vol. 2, p. 197.
17 Ibid., p. 13.
18 Fitzgerald, Vol. 1, p. 221, fn.
19 Earl of Munster to KW IV, November 1830. RA 39/493.
20 Fitzgerald, Vol. 1, p. 232.
21 Ibid., fn.
22 Munster to KW IV, July 1831. RA 39/523.
23 Earl Grey, *Correspondence with KG IV*, Vol. 1, p. 331.
24 Greville, op. cit., Vol. 2, p. 150.
25 Anne Somerset, p. 121.
26 Fitzgerald, Vol. 1, p. 237.

27 Fulford, *Hanover to Windsor*, p. 34.

28 Wharncliffe, *The First Lady and her Family*, Vol. 2, p. 99.

29 Fulford, *Hanover to Windsor*, p. 35.

30 Ellenborough, op. cit., p. 357.

31 Fulford, *Hanover to Windsor*, p. 37.

32 Huish, p. 672.

33 Barrow, pp. 373–4.

34 Christopher Lloyd, *Captain Marryat and the Old Navy*, pp. 187–8.

35 KW IV to Palmerston, 1 June 1833. Broadlands Mss. RC/A/247.

36 Barrow, pp. 373–4.

37 Queen Adelaide's Diary, 10–11 October 1831. RA Add. 21/7a.

38 Greville, Vol. 3, pp. 309–10.

39 Walpole, op. cit., Vol. 1, p. 269. Melbourne to Russell, 26 November 1836.

40 Reid, *Durham*, Vol. 2, p. 103.

41 Somerset, p. 217.

42 Melbourne Mss., RA, 20 June, 1837.

43 Rev. J. Wood, 'Last Days of KW IV.' RA Add. 4/11.

44 Disraeli, *Correspondence with His Sister*, p. 66.

45 Wood.

46 Huish, pp. 672–3.

47 Fitzgerald, p. 371.

48 *The Times*, 15 July 1830.

49 Ibid., 20 June 1830.

Short Bibliography

Aspinall, A. (ed.), *The Letters of George IV*, (Vols. 1–3), Cambridge 1938.

— *Mrs Jordan and Her Family*, London 1951.

— *The Later Correspondence of King George III*, (Vols. 1–3), Cambridge 1962–7.

— *The Correspondence of George, Prince of Wales*, (Vols. 1–5), London 1963–70.

Barrow, Sir John, *An Autobiographical Memoir of Sir John Barrow*, London 1847.

Bartlett, C. J., *Great Britain and Sea Power*, 1815–53, London 1963.

Bouchier, Lady (ed.), *Memoir of the Life of Admiral Sir Edward Codrington*, (2 Vols.), London 1873.

Briggs, Sir John, *Naval Administrations*, 1827–92, London 1897.

Dillon, Vice-Admiral Sir William, *Narrative of My Professional Adventures* (1790–1839), London 1956.

Fitzgerald, Percy, *The Life and Times of William IV*, (2 Vols.), London 1884.

Fothergill, Brian, *Mrs Jordan*, London 1965.

Fulford, Roger, *Royal Dukes*, London 1933.

— *Hanover to Windsor*, London 1960.

Hamilton, Sir Richard (ed.), *The Letters and Papers of Admiral of the Fleet Sir Thomas Byam Martin*, (3 Vols.), London 1898–1903.

Hibbert, Christopher, *George IV* (2 Vols.), London 1972–3.

Hopkirk, Mary, *Queen Adelaide*, London 1946.

Huish, Robert, *The History of the Life and Reign of William IV*, London 1837.

Jennings, Louis J. (ed.), *The Correspondence and Diaries of John Wilson Croker*, (2 Vols.), London 1884.

Lieven, Princess, *Unpublished Diary and Political Sketches*, London 1925.

Lloyd, Christopher, *Mr Barrow of the Admiralty*, London 1970.

Maxwell, Sir H. (ed.), *Creevey Papers*, London 1904.

Moses, Henry, *The Visit of William IV when Duke of Clarence as Lord High Admiral in the Year 1827*, London 1840.

Naish, George P. B. (ed.), *Nelson's Letters to His Wife and Other Documents*, London 1958.

Nicolas, Sir Harris (ed.), *The Dispatches and Letters of Vice-Admiral Lord Viscount Nelson*, London 1844–6.

Pocock, Tom, *Horatio Nelson*, London 1987.

Robertson, Gillian. *The Royal Race*, London, 1977.

Somerset, Anne, *The Life and Times of William IV*, London 1980.

Walpole, Horace, *Letters*, Yale University, 1941–70.

Watkins, John, *The Life and Times of William IV*, London 1831.

Wellington, Duke of, *The Despatches, Correspondence and Memoranda of Field Marshal Arthur, Duke of Wellington* (Vols. 4, 7 and 8), London 1871–80.

Woodhouse, C. M. *The Battle of Navarino*, London 1965.

Woodward, E. L., *The Age of Reform*, London 1938.

Wright, G. N., *The Life and Reign of William the Fourth* (2 Vols.), London 1837.

Ziegler, Philip, *King William IV*, London 1971.

About the Author

Tom Pocock is the author of 18 books (and editor of two more), mostly biographies but including two about his experiences as a newspaper war correspondent.

Born in London in 1925 - the son of the novelist and educationist Guy Pocock - he was educated at Westminster School and Cheltenham College, joining the Royal Navy in 1943. He was at sea during the invasion of Normandy and, having suffered from ill-health, returned to civilian life and in 1945 became a war correspondent at the age of 19,the youngest of the Second World War.

After four years wth the Hulton Press current affairs magazine group, he moved to the Daily Mail as feature-writer and then Naval Correspondent, becoming Naval Correspondent of The Times in 1952. In 1956, he was a foreign corresponent and special writer for the Daily Express and from 1959 was on the staff of the Evening Standard, as feature writer, Defence Correspondent and war correspondent. For the last decade of his time on the Standard he was Travel Editor.

He wrote his first book, NELSON AND HIS WORLD in 1967 on his return from reporting the violence in Aden and his interest in Nelson has continued. Indeed, eight of his books are about the admiral and his contemporaries; his HORATIO NELSON was runner-up for the Whitbread Biography Award of 1987.

Tom Pocock has contributed to many magazines and appeared on television documentaries about Nelson and the subject of another of his biographies, the novelist and imperialist Sir Rider Haggard.